HISTORY AND LEGACY OF ISOTYPE

History and Legacy of Isotype

Christopher Burke · Günther Sandner

BLOOMSBURY VISUAL ARTS
LONDON · NEW YORK · OXFORD · NEW DELHI · SYDNEY

BLOOMSBURY VISUAL ARTS
Bloomsbury Publishing Plc
50 Bedford Square, London, WC1B 3DP, UK
1385 Broadway, New York, NY 10018, USA
29 Earlsfort Terrace, Dublin 2, Ireland

BLOOMSBURY, BLOOMSBURY VISUAL ARTS and the Diana logo
are trademarks of Bloomsbury Publishing Plc

First published in Great Britain 2024

Copyright © Christopher Burke and Günther Sandner, 2024

For legal purposes the Acknowledgements on p. 6 constitute
an extension of this copyright page.

Cover image: 'Ancient American Cultures Around 1500',
chart 13 from *Gesellschaft und Wirtschaft*, 1930.

This work is published open access subject to a Creative Commons Attribution-NonCommercial 4.0 International licence (CC BY-NC 4.0, https://creativecommons.org/licenses/by-nc/4.0/). You may re-use, distribute, reproduce, and adapt this work in any medium for non-commercial purposes, provided you give attribution to the copyright holder and the publishers, provide a link to the Creative Commons licence, and indicate if changes have been made.

Bloomsbury Publishing Plc does not have any control over, or responsibility for, any third-party websites referred to or in this book. All internet addresses given in this book were correct at the time of going to press. The author and publisher regret any inconvenience caused if addresses have changed or sites have ceased to exist, but can accept no responsibility for any such changes.

A catalogue record for this book is available from the British Library.

A catalog record for this book is available from the Library of Congress.

ISBN: Hardback: 978-1-3503-5907-9
Paperback: 978-1-3503-5906-2
ePDF: 978-1-3503-5909-3
eBook: 978-1-3503-5908-6

Designed and typeset by Christopher Burke
Printed and bound in India

To find out more about Bloomsbury authors and books,
visit www.bloomsbury.com, and sign up for our newsletters.

Contents

	Prologue	7
1	The Vienna Method in school	11
2	Branching out	33
3	Pictorial statistics in times of dictatorship	61
4	Isotype in exile	75
5	The Austrian Social and Economic Museum after 1945	105
6	Following Otto Neurath: Marie Neurath and Gerd Arntz on separate paths	127
7	Rudolf Modley in America	151
	Epilogue	171
	Reference notes	177
	Select bibliography	191
	Archive sources (Abbreviations)	197
	Image sources	197
	Index	199

Acknowledgements

The authors are grateful for advice and assistance from the following colleagues: Ingrid Bauer, Benjamin Benus, Alborz Dianat, Jason Forrest, Gerhard Halusa, Yvonne Heigl, Steven Heller, Robert Hoffmann, Wim Jansen, Jan de Jong, Eric Kindel, Robin Kinross, Sabine Koch, Lise Koning, Chang Chi Lan-Ying, Sabine Lichtenberger, Emma Minns, Josef Mitterer, Peter Modley, Guido Müller, Elisabeth Nemeth, Olaf Osten, Dietlinde Peters, Robert Pfundner, Georg Spitaler, Friedrich Stadler, Eva Stina Lyon, Erika Thurner, Ádám Tamás Tuboly, Michael Twyman, Gernot Waldner, Nora Walch, Sue Walker, Zarah Weiss, Heidrun-Ulrike Wenzel, Florian Wenninger and Sarah Zublasing.

Research for this book was supported by the Austrian Science Fund FWF project P 31500 *Der Wissenschaftsfonds.*
'Isotype: Entstehung, Entwicklung und Erbe'

Production of the book was supported by the **RD Foundation Vienna**
Research | Development | Human Rights
Gemeinnützige Privatstiftung

Prologue

The work in visual education known as Isotype was originally called the Wiener Methode der Bildstatistik (Vienna Method of Pictorial Statistics). This reflected the context of its initial development at the Gesellschafts- und Wirtschaftsmuseum (Social and Economic Museum) of Vienna, established in 1925. This institution was supported by the socialist municipal government of Vienna, capital of the newly independent Austrian state that emerged from the First World War. The founding director of the Museum, and the initiator of Isotype, was the economist, sociologist and philosopher of science, Otto Neurath.

Neurath, who had been intrigued by visual communication since his youth, proposed to 'cultivate and propagate consistent, pictorial representations' at the Museum and – in one of his first published essays on its work – he cautiously accepted the description 'Vienna Method', which had been applied to it by friendly critics. Yet he denied that it was entirely new: 'some of it is ancient and can already be found among the Egyptians, but the team that has been working together in this Museum for a long time is determined to create a system of pictorial representation that has been worked out in detail – a *method* that can be learned.'[1]

The raw material for the Vienna Method and Isotype consisted of scientific data and facts. Making pictorial statistics with this method – for exhibitions, for teaching or for publications – was based on interdisciplinary cooperation. Geographers, economists, social scientists, statisticians and art historians all consulted with the designers of pictorial charts. The central person in this process was the 'transformer', who mediated between consulting experts and graphic artists, deciding what should be shown and how. This role was a prototype of today's information designer, given that the profession of graphic design hardly existed in the 1920s. Marie Reidemeister (later Marie Neurath) was the key figure who occupied this role during its defining years. Her transformation sketches were executed in finished form by graphic artists, among whom Gerd Arntz was the most important figure. Despite its scientific and artistic elements, however, Isotype was neither science nor art – above all, it was about education. Its aim was to use visualization to reach a broad audience, but especially younger age groups and social classes who were disadvantaged by the prevailing system. The Isotype 'transformer' was referred to by Otto and Marie Neurath as the 'trustee of the public'.[2]

Isotype is underpinned by some theoretical ideas that relate to Otto Neurath's involvement in the Vienna Circle, a philosophical group that discussed the use of language to accurately describe the physical world. A basic principle of Isotype is that an increase in quantity should not be indicated by increasing the size of a picture, but instead by repeating pictogram units in greater numbers, at the same size; and, within any given example, the value represented by a pictogram should remain constant. For Neurath, this was a logical depiction of mass or quantity.

Yet, despite Neurath's initial proposal that Isotype should be a learnable method, it was never fully codified as such. The working process did not give rise to simply sequential steps that could then have been repeated by other people in other places. Rather, it was based on experience, teamwork and openness to new challenges. From the beginning, there was a principal focus on the pictorial representation of social and economic contexts through 'quantity pictures' (*Mengenbilder*). These were based on statistics, although they were not intended to convey exact numbers but instead to enable understanding of social and economic relationships by comparing orders of magnitude. However, not all early examples of Isotype were statistical: accident prevention and health education were also important and recurrent themes.

Due to Otto Neurath's desire to maintain flexibility in Isotype design, and not to be bound strictly by a pre-defined set of rules, he was determined to control the production process as closely as possible. This was to play an important role in the discussions and debates about further developments, adaptations and attempts to imitate Isotype. One consequence of this reflexive approach was that Neurath placed high demands on his team, but also on all others who were active in visual education and who referred to Isotype in some way. When visual representations did not meet Neurath's standards, there were harsh judgements.

Some chapters in the history of Isotype have been researched quite thoroughly, but others less so. This book attempts to fill in some gaps, especially concerning work done by rivals or successors to the original creators of Isotype. On the other hand, we have also endeavoured to explore lesser-known aspects of well-known periods: for example, the use of the Vienna Method in schools is a rather neglected part of the history of educational work in inter-war Vienna; it is presented in detail in chapter 1. Chapter 2 examines the spread of the

Vienna Method through its branches and international outposts, including a museum venue in Berlin. One controversial episode is the Vienna team's collaboration with Izostat, an institute for pictorial statistics in the Soviet Union, which produced propaganda for the Five-Year Plans.

The role of pictorial statistics in the two dictatorships in Austria (1934–8 and 1938–45) is little known, at least in English-speaking countries, and is dealt with in chapter 3. In doing so, an attempt is made to identify breaks with the formative period of Isotype, but also some continuities. Chapter 4, on the other hand, examines the work of the protagonists – especially Otto Neurath, Marie Reidemeister (Neurath) and Gerd Arntz – in Dutch, and later in English exile. After the end of the Second World War, attempts were made in Vienna to reconnect with Otto Neurath's legacy and the Vienna Method of Pictorial Statistics. Chapter 5 examines the reformed Austrian Social and Economic Museum, which still exists today. Otto Neurath died suddenly soon after the war, and chapter 6 follows the diverging paths of Gerd Arntz in the Netherlands and Marie Neurath in England after 1945. Chapter 7, on the other hand, deals with the story of Rudolf Modley, who started at the Vienna Museum but went to the USA in 1930 and reconfigured pictorial statistics in an American context. His later project to resolve a standard set of information symbols reflects international efforts in this area during the 1950s and 1960s, and sheds light on their relationship to Isotype.

We can now look back on around a hundred years in the history of Isotype. Such a length of time makes it possible to discuss some important questions based on archival evidence. In particular, the application of picture-statistical graphics in different political contexts sharpens the view of where the boundaries lie between democratic education and empowerment on the one hand, and propaganda and manipulation on the other. But it also becomes apparent that these boundaries cannot always be clearly drawn. Social-Democratic 'Red Vienna', fascist dictatorships, the Stalinist Soviet Union, British wartime and post-war society, the USA of the New Deal and afterwards: in these and other contexts, Isotype was adapted and sometimes distorted by imitators or usurpers.

To what extent did the pioneering work of Otto Neurath's team offer the certainty that such visual educational work is fundamentally in the service of democratic enlightenment? After the death of all the founding figures and the consequent break of direct continuities, is there such a thing as a legacy of Isotype in the twenty-first century?

1   The Vienna Method in school

This chapter borrows its title from the first lengthy account of the method later known as Isotype, written by its initiator – Otto Neurath's book *Bildstatistik nach Wiener Methode in der Schule* (Pictorial Statistics by the Vienna Method in School, 1933). That text refers not only to the formative period of Isotype but also to the fact that experiments with the new method in schools formed part of its testing ground, along with its uses in adult education. These were just two examples of the rich background to Isotype in so-called 'Red Vienna' of the First Austrian Republic. Education was a major priority of the Social Democratic municipal government of Vienna, in which Otto Neurath was well connected. He was able to secure generous funding and support from the municipality for the Gesellschafts- und Wirtschaftsmuseum (Social and Economic Museum) that he conceived, and which he envisioned as the centre for developing a method of visual education. It grew out of the Museum für Siedlung und Städtebau (Museum for Settlement and Town Planning), which had consolidated material from exhibitions of the Austrian Settlement and Allotment Garden Association, directed by Neurath. As his influence on the social housing programme of Vienna waned, he sought to re-establish the museum with a wider educational scope. Integral to his plans was his partnership with Marie Reidemeister, a young German with a scientific background, but who was also skilled in technical drawing – an ideal combination for the kind of pictorial charts that Neurath had in mind for the new museum. Some experiments in producing such material had been made at the Museum for Settlement and Town Planning (and to some extent at the Museum of War Economy, Leipzig, directed by Neurath from 1917 to 1919), but a pictorial method of education would become the central focus of the Social and Economic Museum in Vienna, which opened on 1 January 1925.

In proposing the Museum to influential figures in the Social Democratic Party, such as Julius Deutsch, Neurath emphasized that it could have a 'tremendous importance for our workers' movement and the Vienna Municipality in general', but he also hoped that it would be the 'necessary teaching resource centre for social education', serving primary and secondary schools as well as institutes for workers' education. Indeed, he suggested to Deutsch that the Museum could serve to remedy the gaps in current school education, and asked him to engage the interest of Otto Glöckel, chairman of the Viennese Stadtschulrat (School Board), who oversaw school reform in Vienna between the wars.[1] In a memorandum addressed to Anton Weber, city councillor for housing, Neurath stated: 'The modern museum should be a teaching museum, a means of education, a schoolbook on a grand scale.'[2] He rejected the conventional view of a museum as a repository of rare and precious objects: 'Unique exhibition pieces of a reliquary character' played no part in the 'social museum', he asserted.[3] Instead, his intention was to originate educational material that was reproducible with modern techniques. Although the Museum had a principal exhibition in an iconic building – Vienna's Neues Rathaus (New Town Hall) – from December 1927, material was produced centrally for showing in decentralized locations. The concept of this Museum was not tied to a particular venue. It also produced travelling exhibitions and made displays for larger exhibitions, such as 'Wien und die Wiener' (Vienna and the Viennese, 1927), 'Frau und Kind' (Woman and Child, 1928; both in Vienna), and 'Pressa' (Cologne, 1928). Indeed, it is questionable that 'museum' was the right term for the institution conceived by Otto Neurath in 1925. Marie Neurath later described it as a 'visual centre', taking into account the service it offered to teachers in lending out lantern slides of Isotype charts.[4]

The collaboration of the Social and Economic Museum with schools in Vienna was of equal importance to workers' education in the development of the Vienna Method; and, in some ways, it more closely prefigured the longer term ambition of Isotype for universal, educational validity. It is telling, perhaps, that the first major publication conceived and designed at the Museum was the book *Die bunte Welt* (The Vivid World, 1929; fig.1.1), subtitled 'quantity-pictures for youth'. It made extensive use of colour, which had more than just a decorative purpose, as Marie Reidemeister explained: 'So we must bring into the schoolroom a reduced, schematic and judiciously arranged picture of the world, but a picture that always recalls the living world outside and leaves behind very colourful images in children's memory.'[5] Yet, shortly after the book's publication, in an article sharing its title, she asserted the prime relevance of pictorial statistics to the workers' movement. (Admittedly, her article was published in a trade-union journal).[6] These two audiences were always in mind at the Museum, which often aimed to produce material that was appropriate for both simultaneously. When pointing out that the Vienna Method went 'against bourgeois ideology', Neurath remarked also that it 'incidentally has become part of the Vienna school reform, in to the structure of which it fits perfectly.'[7]

1.1 Cover and pages of *Die bunte Welt* (The Vivid World), 1929. 144 × 210 mm.

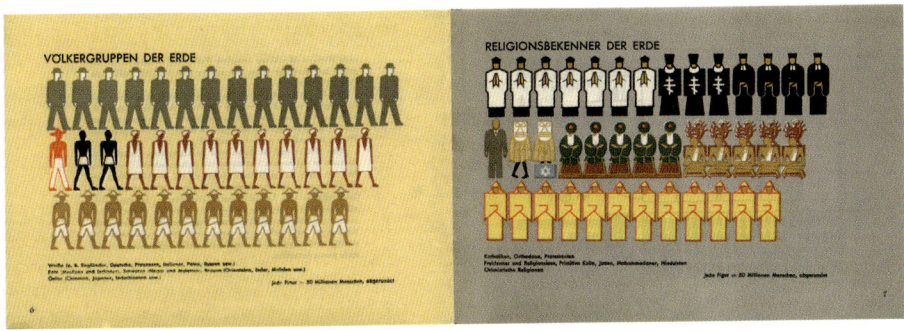

The Vienna School Board recommended that school classes visit the Social and Economic Museum. When its exhibition space at the New Town Hall opened, the Museum stated that its 'central position will favour a close contact with the public, not least with schools, which the Museum seeks to serve'. It was open for schools at any time, but it was recommended that teachers visit first by themselves to assess which sections of the Museum would be most relevant to the subjects they taught. To enable teachers (as well as other working people) to make such visits, the Museum was open beyond normal working hours.[8]

Otto Neurath held weekly meetings with teachers at the Museum to discuss possible applications of the Vienna Method in schools. From the end of 1928, these teacher discussions were superseded by a seminar given by Neurath every Tuesday evening at the Pedagogical Institute of Vienna. This department of Vienna University was directed by Charlotte and Karl Bühler, who conducted pioneering research into child psychology. In his seminar, Neurath showed examples of pictorial material used in teaching practice, and reports were given by individual teachers on such experience in their specialist subjects.[9]

Efforts were made at the Museum to assess the pictorial material it produced, as Otto Neurath explained: 'Judgements are collected from grown-ups and children about the effectiveness of Museum charts, also from psychological investigations, which stimulate their design. The observations made up till now have shown, for example, that 4 to 5 year-old children can already grasp simple picture statistics.'[10] Later, he recalled: 'Some of our observations were made by students of psychology, who made notes and sometimes asked questions to learn about the visitors' reactions. The experience collected in this way was used afterwards in preparing new visual material.'[11] This was a very early attempt to build an element of evaluation into developing a technique of graphic design. It followed the empirical principle that Otto Neurath recommended in general.

Much later, in England, Neurath received some anecdotal evidence of the impression left on schoolchildren who visited the Museum. A colleague told him that two friends of hers grew up in Vienna 'and say that, as schoolchildren, it was your Museum which first aroused their interest in social and civic problems and they feel they owe you a debt of gratitude'. Neurath replied that even the 'unreliable memories of children are most interesting', quoting a sentence by feminist educational reformer Ellen Key: 'Culture – that is what remains after having forgotten what you have learned.'[12]

The Museum's supplement to educational journal *Das Bild*

The process of testing and evaluating the Vienna Method in its formative stage was partly documented in a monthly supplement that the Museum edited for an educational journal, *Das Bild* (The Image). This was an offshoot of *Die Quelle* (The Source), a journal of pedagogical reform. The contributions to the Museum's supplement are generally uncredited but seem to be written mainly by Otto Neurath or Marie Reidemeister, or perhaps both together.[13] Otto Neurath wrote numerous essays at this time about the new method, many with an emphasis on socialist education, but the texts in *Das Bild* concentrated on practical applications, as well as technical and pragmatic matters of design.

The first issue of the supplement, in March 1927, published a programmatic essay 'The Social and Economic Museum and School':

> The Museum shows how social structures determine life conditions, and it makes everyone conscious of how they fit experientially and actively into this complex system [*Getriebe*]; it instructs, but also functions educationally. It addresses grown-ups and those who are still growing. Here we come into contact with school. The material treated by the Museum coincides to some extent with that which appears in school curricula. But both are also related in method; what proves itself in one context can also be adapted for the other. ... Like schools, the Museum will endeavour to ascertain what sticks in the memory.[14]

The Museum proposed that its material could be used directly in schools, and it began to have handbills of its charts printed for this purpose. This initiative increased in scale, with series of printed leaflets on various themes (such as 'World economy' and 'Economic history'), which could be collected in a 'Vienna Method' folder.[15] It was also suggested that a stylistic aspect of early charts in the Vienna Method, in which some pictograms were apparently cut with scissors, lent itself to application in school exercises:

> For the sake of clarity and simplicity the Museum uses scissor cutting, which is familiar to all schoolchildren under the reform of schools. In this way, the possibility is created to unite teaching of manual dexterity closely with other subjects! Figures of the greatest possible distinctiveness should be cut out from coloured papers, which can then be combined in groups, in order to reproduce statistical quantities. ... In this way, children become accustomed to accord greater importance to things in the world that are quantifiable, and so come closer to a true scientific approach, even at a primitive level.[16]

Here, in the last sentence, is the ideology behind the application of the Vienna Method in schools, corresponding to Otto Neurath's contemporary role in the Vienna Circle group of philosophers. Reform of school and education was listed in the Vienna Circle manifesto as part of its 'Scientific World-Conception'.[17] Neurath sought to challenge metaphysics and obscurantism in all areas of life, and no doubt he considered the Vienna Method as a non-metaphysical, descriptive tool that could help to curb the traditional influence of the Catholic Church in Austrian schools, which lingered despite a decree by education minister Otto Glöckel in 1919 to minimize it. Hence the emphasis above on 'things in the world that are quantifiable' and a 'scientific approach'. Children could engage with pictorial material as the basis for a 'question and answer game ... which remains throughout in the realm of the visible'.[18] This aligns broadly with the approach called 'physicalism' developed by Neurath and Rudolf Carnap in the Vienna Circle. In an essay on 'Unified Science and Psychology', Neurath asked: 'Must everyone in turn go through metaphysics as through a childhood disease – perhaps the earlier he gets it, the less dangerous it is – to be led back to unified science? No. *Every child can in principle learn to apply the language of physicalism correctly from the outset*, first in a crude form, then in a more refined and precise way.'[19]

In June 1927, *Das Bild* reported 'A school visit to the Social and Economic Museum', documenting schoolchildren's reactions compiled from responses to a questionnaire, which had been published in the previous issue of the journal (fig. 1.2). The report began with a plea for teachers to send more responses, 'as it is of great importance for the Museum to know how the exhibitions work, what is understood and what is not'. Among the questions asked were: 'Which charts did you like best, and which least? Why?' and 'What would you like to

1.2 Questionnaire circulated to visitors at the Social and Economic Museum, 1927.

see added or changed in the interests of clarity? (content, form, colours, explanations, etc.)' One child responded: 'When we arrived, my first impression was that the things were strange and must be laborious to make. Then I got more and more interested in what they showed … it obviously takes great education and time to study matters in such detail.' The most frequent response to what could be changed was that the Museum should be bigger.[20] (The visit was made to the initial, small exhibition rooms at Parkring, Vienna.)

The following month, the supplement published a teacher's report of an experiment in making pictorial statistics with very young pupils. The children themselves determined the task of depicting a comparison of those with light eyes and those with dark eyes in the class. They mostly chose to depict the varying numbers of children in each category by drawing heads of different sizes. This contradicted a fundamental rule of the Vienna Method, which always depicted an increase in quantity by repetition of pictograms at the same size. Indeed, an editorial note was added to this report suggesting that the children chose this method of representation under the influence of examples that they had seen, but commenting that it compromised the clarity and vividness

(*Anschaulichkeit*) of the comparison. The Museum consequently avoided this technique but nevertheless stated that 'it would be very valuable to obtain further information from teachers on this point'.[21]

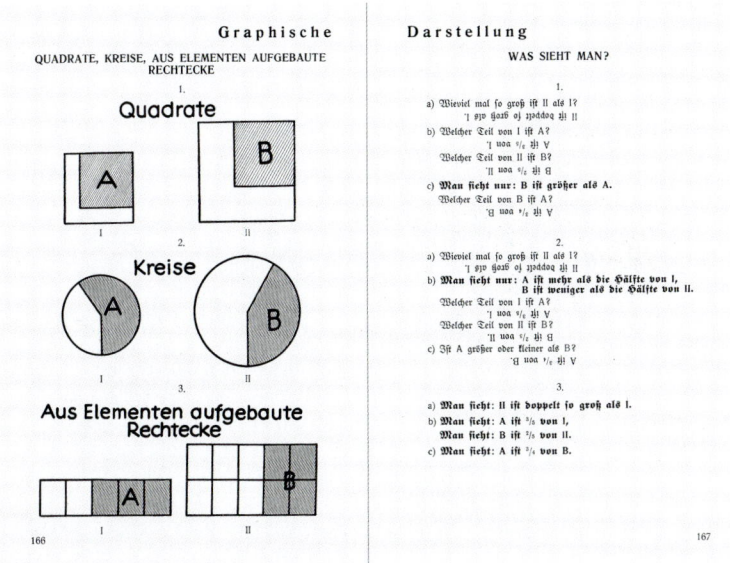

1.3 Quiz on 'Graphic representation' from *Das Bild* (September 1927). 229 × 154 mm.

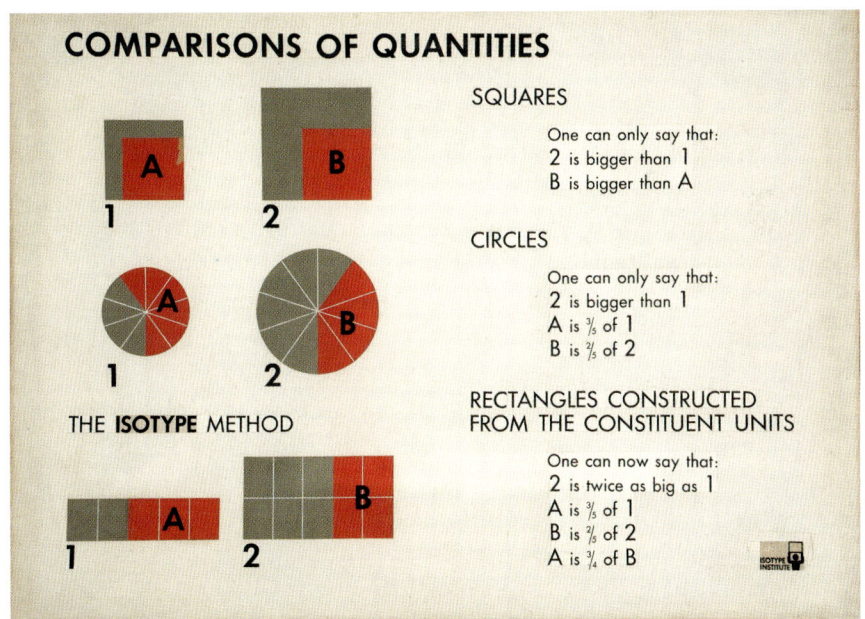

1.4 Exhibition chart explaining the principles of the Vienna Method/Isotype, 1933. 63 × 84 cm. It is based on the example in fig. 1.3. In the 1940s, 'Vienna' was pasted over with 'Isotype' and the Isotype Institute logo replaced the original credit 'Mundaneum Wien'.

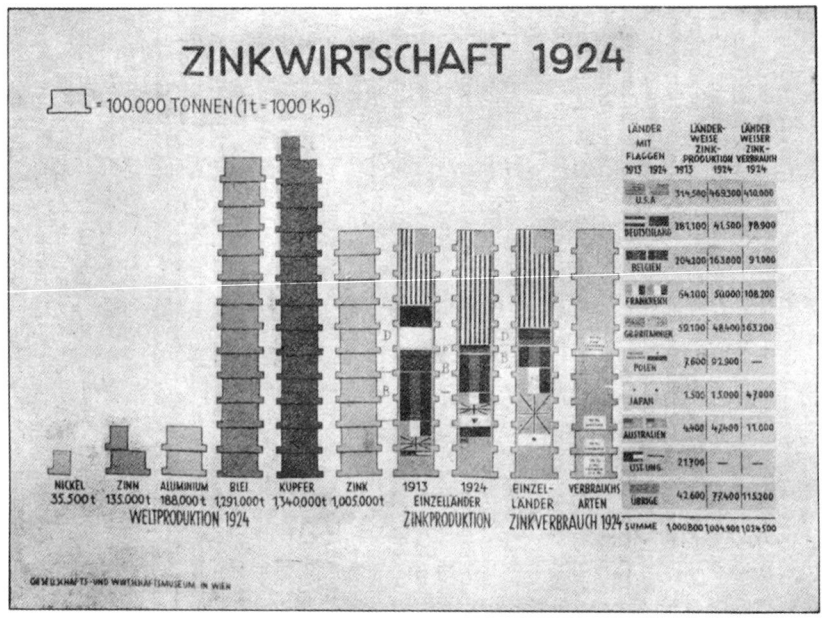

1.5 'Zinc economy 1924', from *Das Bild* (October 1927).

This experience may have prompted the Museum to publish several key articles about the principles of its graphic method in *Das Bild*. The first examined the disadvantages of using circles (pie charts) to indicate different quantities, and instead put forward the Museum's central principle of repeatable, modular units (figs 1.3 & 1.4).[22] An article entitled 'Orienting diagram and eloquent, mnemonic picture' asserted that 'any vivid representation, even if it is defective, attracts more attention and sticks in the memory better than a table of figures'. The problem with groups of numerals, which may differ greatly in value, is that they have similar visual lengths; a 'memorable picture' combining numerical values with a representation of objects was more effective for schoolchildren, according to the Museum. In a spirit of trial and error and experimental enquiry, this essay offered an enlightening self-critique of the Museum's own early chart about zinc production and why it failed (fig. 1.5). Apart from it being unclear that there are two parts to the chart – a comparison of world production of different metals, followed by national production of zinc – the superimposition of national flags on the towers of ingots (each representing 100,000 tonnes) complicates the chart and 'disturbs the clarity' of the statistical image. (Indeed, the practice of using flags in this way was soon abandoned, and all the visual clutter entailed by including numerical values to back up the images also disappeared). In what appears to be the voice of Neurath and/or Reidemeister, the article stated:

> These are no longer questions of *logic*, rather of *pedagogical tact*. There are many logically justifiable solutions, but they are not all of equal psychological suitability. In deciding on one, psychological factors must be considered, colours and forms assessed for their conspicuity, the viewer's capabilities for perception must be taken into account; one must simplify, omit, underline, and point out connections, not with words, but by the design of the whole, through choice of colours etc.²³

This is a rare, candid reflection on the graphic design process, which has usually remained tacit, as a kind of craft supported by secret expertise. Otto Neurath's guiding principle was a scientific attitude of argumentation and discussion, hence the examination of mistakes here in the interest of improvement. The motive of the team at the Vienna Museum was to produce educational material, not 'commercial art' (as graphic design was commonly known at that time – *Gebrauchsgraphik* in German). Yet, ironically, the very pragmatism reflected in the citation above hints that the Vienna Method could not be fully codified; it had to compete visually in the landscape of modern entertainment: 'Next to the cinema, the illustrated magazine, pictorial advertising, emerges something new, and no less necessary, the mnemonic picture [*Merkbild*].'²⁴ The data sources for such images should be as scientific as possible, but it soon became clear that the process of making them was not, in itself, scientific. The Museum admitted: 'There are no universally valid rules; decisions must be left to pedagogical tact, which may only be directed by rules that are kept very loose. Therein lies their danger and their weakness.'²⁵ The pitfalls of the process meant that the creators of the Vienna Method became increasingly protective of their skills, especially when re-establishing it as Isotype after leaving Vienna.

Neurath once declared that 'the "Vienna Method" is, unlike the usual graphic methods, not a machine into which one throws sequences of figures in order to get quantitative pictures. The "Vienna Method" presupposes *creative pedagogical work*.'²⁶ One of the 'usual graphic methods' referred to here was the line graph, which was subjected to criticism by Marie Reidemeister in the Museum's supplement to *Das Bild*. In particular, she asserted that the parts of a curve drawn between data points are meaningless interpolation, and that pictorial statistics offered a better alternative:

> If one switches to illustrating statistical quantities with quantities of pictograms, then one is freed from the strict rules of coordinate representation, without losing anything in correctness or visibility. … Curves are subject to much stronger demands for precision than pictorial representation. And so it is all the more embarrassing when they do not fulfil these demands. A method of statistics that works with countable elements, as pictorial

statistics does, hardly gives any occasion for error. Its advantages are not only educational but also logical.[27]

In April 1928, after a year of the Vienna Museum's supplements to *Das Bild*, it published another summative article, entitled 'Pictorial statistics for children'. It noted the enthusiasm for pictorial charts among schoolchildren during class visits to the Museum, but remarked further that:

> Also on days of general opening – Sunday visits often bring more than 900 people – young people come on their own to the Museum and often stand for a long time in front of one chart, enjoying the little pictures and studying the content. Many sketch what they see, or note down figures. Those growing up today are immensely open-minded to all that concerns quantities. By the detour through *quantity-pictures* they arrive at a strong understanding of social and economic life. What remains more or less undefined and variable in words is communicated more realistically by *quantity-pictures* and *organizational pictures*. Of course, these can only provide starting points for very complex economic and social connections, not definitive insight. But every teacher knows how difficult it often is to find such starting points.[28]

Quantity-pictures could assist less gifted pupils, who may be daunted by the difficulties of study: 'In short, "relative mass" is apparently graspable at an early stage, whereas its arithmetical treatment presupposes long preparation. … From such purely observational operations one can progress to counting.' At the end of this article, the Museum repeated its request for feedback from teachers about visits of their classes to its exhibitions and, in particular, about examples that had proven effective when applied to teaching.

In February 1929, *Das Bild* published a report by a teacher at a further education college (*Fortbildungsschule*) about using pictorial statistics to teach 16-year-olds. The results were very satisfying in the teacher's view, but the questions asked to elicit responses to the material were not adequately neutral. The teacher asked the pupils: 'What advantages do pictorial statistics have?' and 'What do you particularly like about them?' These were bound to skew responses towards the positive. Unsurprisingly, there were few negative comments from around 200 pupils questioned. The teacher also explained this by the tendency of students at such schools to be 'visual types', and concluded, rather prematurely, that the pictorial material of the Social and Economic Museum 'corresponded completely to the youth psyche'.[29]

The example used in the survey was a leaflet published by the Museum about 'the development of agriculture and trade in Germany'.[30] One chart in particular provoked interesting responses from the students: it compares rural and urban populations by using pictograms of an ungainly peasant and

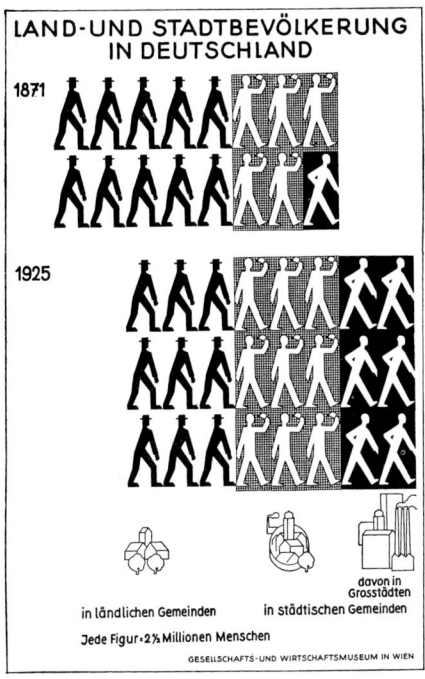
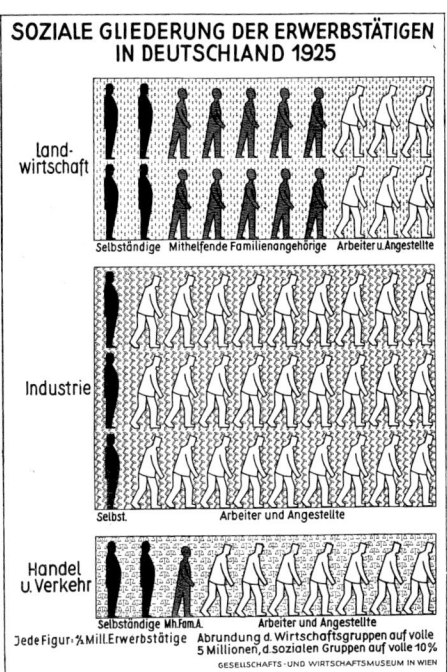

1.6 'Rural and city population in Germany' from *Entwicklung von Landwirtschaft und Gewerbe in Deutschland* (Development of Agriculture and Trade in Germany), 1928.

1.7 'Social division of gainfully employed in Germany 1925' from the same publication as fig. 1.6.

a chirpy city dweller (fig. 1.6). The teacher cited the following feedback from different students:

> … the artist indicates by the demeanour of the man which stratum of population he stems from … You can compare the lolloping [*schleppenden*] steps of the peasant with the light steps of the city dweller, which suggests that the city dweller is more disposed to intellectual development.[31]

This characterization was undoubtedly intended by the artist who executed the chart, but these published responses would have given the Museum team pause for thought. This example contradicts an intention to avoid bias in the design of pictograms that was expressed by Neurath two years earlier: 'Nothing is more dangerous than a symbol that says more to many visitors than what one really wants to express.'[32] The data contained in this chart relates solely to population and should not have implied anything about the character or intelligence of the people depicted. A chart on a similar theme in the same leaflet (perhaps drawn by a different artist; fig. 1.7) is less biased but still tends

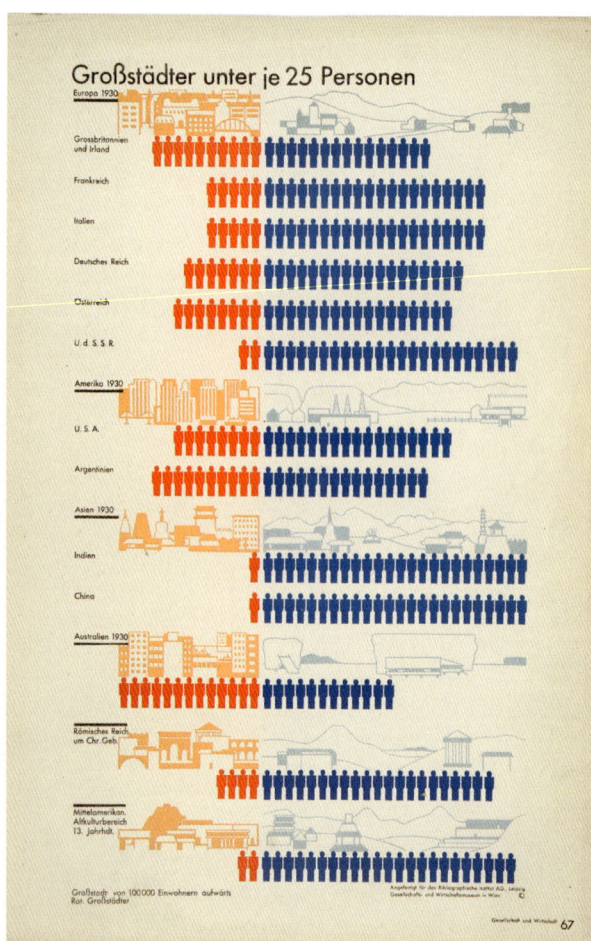

1.8 Chart 67 from *Gesellschaft und Wirtschaft*: 'Big city living per 25 persons', 1930. The underlined categories are:

Europe 1930
America 1930
Asia 1930
Australia 1930
Roman Empire around time of Christ's birth
Region of ancient Central American cultures 13th century

Big cities, depicted by orange 'guide-picture', are defined as containing 100,000 inhabitants or more.
Red = big city dwellers.

towards a depiction of human character. These examples show the inconsistencies in the early years of the Vienna Method, before the full involvement of Gerd Arntz, a German artist who specialized in woodcut prints. He moved to Vienna in 1929 to work full-time at the Social and Economic Museum, and he determined the lasting, more objective style of the pictograms. An internal guideline written at the Museum around 1930, headed 'Character', stated the following: 'the pictogram may not denote more than is necessary to the statement of facts for which it is chosen.'[33]

For comparison, one could examine chart 67 from the atlas of 100 charts, *Gesellschaft und Wirtschaft* (1930), a highpoint in the history of Isotype, with which the Vienna Method reached maturity (fig. 1.8). This shows the number of big-city dwellers, per 25 persons, in various countries, and in two historical places/periods for comparison. Here, a person is depicted by the same simplified pictogram whether a city dweller or not. Colour is an added resource here, to distinguish big cities (the colour usually allocated to 'rural' – green – is not used for the rest, which presumably includes inhabitants of both smaller towns and villages). There is still 'character' in the chart, conveyed by the so-called 'guide pictures', which are different for each region and for the historical periods. So many elements have been artfully squeezed in that there is barely a millimetre of space spare on the vertical dimension. But the subdued colours of the guide-pictures mean that the rows of human pictograms are still prominent.

The progress in design that is visible here, in the space of just two years, was no doubt due to the major contribution of Arntz, and of his colleagues Peter Alma and Augustin Tschinkel, two further artists employed to work on *Gesellschaft und Wirtschaft*; but this progress must also have been informed by the feedback received from schoolteachers and students, as well as visitors to the Museum.

Trials of the Vienna Method in school teaching

The Vienna Method was taken up by some enthusiastic teachers in its early years, and also received support from the Vienna School Board and individual school inspectors.[34] Trials in Montessori schools seem to have been of decisive importance, as Neurath explained: 'The assumption, cherished from the beginning, that understanding of quantity-pictures begins at a very early stage, has proved itself comprehensively with the first trials made at the Montessori kindergarten and school in Vienna.'[35] The ideas of Maria Montessori to encourage independent learning exercised a general influence on Viennese school reform: this was reflected in Otto Glöckel's ambition to 'replace rote learning with independent study and self-discovery' and to 'supplement intellectual with manual learning'.[36] There was certainly a kinship of Montessori methods with school applications of the Vienna Method, which sometimes used practical tasks as a vehicle. Both methods sought to challenge the tyranny of 'book-learning'.

Neurath reported that very small children (5 to 9 year-olds) had made quantity-pictures in school 'with success on every level':

> They draw rows of signs, make them by potato printing, or cut them out and stick them next to each other. 'Statistical' matters do not always come to the fore. If the children who spent Sunday in the country are to be contrasted with those who spent the day in the city, then a child full of fantasy may well draw the group of children in the country in correct numerical terms as tree climbers between branches. In these early phases the symbolic achievements are often remarkable.[37]

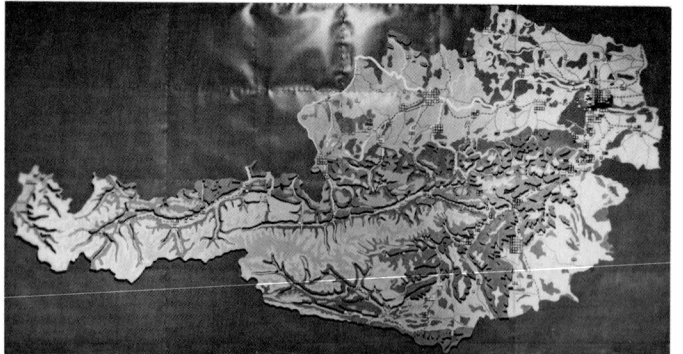
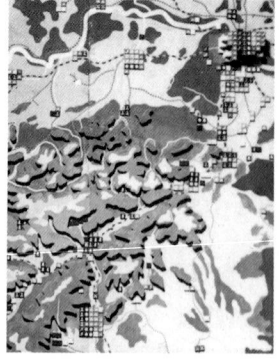

1.9 Magnetic map of Austria (with detail), 1927 (IC T87a). An iron sheet with the mountainous areas overlaid in wood; the magnetic symbols (of approximately 2 cm length) were attached only to the areas under 1000 m. The specialist consultant for the map was Otto Lehmann of Vienna University: in the Museum's supplement to *Das Bild* (January 1928), he insisted that it was not a map but a '3-d cartogram'.

Experience showed that pictures drawn by older children tended to be more naturalistic and 'overloaded with details', making them less suitable for the Vienna Method. Neurath recommended that secondary school pupils should 'put together quantity-pictures in an orderly way from *prefabricated elements*'.[38] The Museum provided prints of its pictograms to schools for this purpose, and also allowed school classes visiting the Museum to take over its small printing press to make fresh prints from linocuts. Allowing pupils to draw their own pictograms was especially inadvisable for representing large quantities, 'the production of which would take a disproportionate amount of time, and gives rise to the danger that the children's carrying out of the task would be restricted by the inadequacy of their own figure drawing'.[39]

'The active work of the learners', according to Neurath, 'consists primarily in *analysing* the quantity pictures'. The creation of such pictures by schoolchildren themselves took second place. The production of teaching material to stimulate activity, and 'above all serve self-teaching' (which he recognized as a commonality with Montessori methods) was of such importance, in Neurath's view, that its producers carry a great responsibility.[40] For the pictorial method to be effective, it required a certain degree of rigour. This reflected an ever-present tension in Isotype between creative freedom and adherence to rules.

One technical innovation that the Museum developed for schools were magnetic maps, modelled on a prototype made for the exhibition 'Wien und die Wiener'. These could have magnetic symbols placed on them and moved around, encouraging practical, active learning. Such a map of Austria was installed in the entrance hall of the Museum's main exhibition (fig. 1.9), with movable symbols of industry. The Museum also proposed a blank magnet board for schools, which could have a paper map held in place by magnets in the corners, and then have magnetic symbols placed on it. These tools had great potential in the teaching of arithmetic, having the advantage of building groups to indicate quantity. One could even assign values of ten or a hundred to one sign. But the Museum warned:

> One must take care that always only *one sign with a specific meaning* occurs on a single chart, so that a quantity can only be represented in one way, namely by lining up the signs of the same-size and significance that are to hand. In this way, the magnetic charts educate simultaneously, and unnoticeably, towards logical methods of visualizing statistical facts, and make possible the enlivening of statistics as they occur in geography and history teaching.

This technique could also be used to show 'schematic order and movement' in anything from the postal service to money circulation – and even atomic physics.[41]

Initial trials of the Vienna Method in Montessori kindergartens and schools were followed by close collaboration with teachers trained in the Vienna school reform. Between 1930 and 1932, the Vienna School Board gave permission to test pictorial material at a municipal school for children of 10 to 14 years of age. It was applied to as many subjects as possible in this *Hauptschule* (the new unified kind of secondary school) at Schweglerstrasse in Vienna's fourteenth district. At the Museum, meetings were held in which Neurath briefed the teachers and demonstrated the material. The curriculum of this school included 'the development of functional thinking, especially by graphic representations of correlations', which is the essence of the Vienna Method and Isotype. In this respect, the schoolchildren responded not only to ready-made charts produced by the Museum, but also discussed in groups how to make their own charts based on given statistics. Designs were made at the school and were executed by pupils gifted in drawing during their leisure time. Even so, it seems that the lesson learned from the exercise of making pictorial charts was to better appreciate the 'official' material, as compared to the 'home-made' efforts.

Reports of the experiment by several teachers were published in the pedagogical journal *Die Quelle*, and they all agreed that pictorial statistics made lessons more vivid and lively. The school's headmaster concluded that they were best applied to geography, history and the sciences.[42]

Trials were also made in many other schools, and lectures to explain the Vienna Method were given to parents' associations, not only in Austria but in Germany, too. Pre-printed pictograms were distributed to Montessori schools in Berlin, and material from the Social and Economic Museum was applied extensively in the early 1930s at Berlin's Karl Marx School, one of the leading reform schools in Germany. The Berlin School Board supported these efforts with special lectures to propagate the method. School classes could visit the exhibitions at the German branch of the Vienna Museum, established in 1931 at the Gesundheitshaus am Urban, Berlin-Kreuzberg (see chapter 2). In Mannheim, the further education college made an exhibition of pictorial statistics that Neurath considered to be exemplary. Trap bars were set up along corridors to hold interchangeable charts, in a way that emulated the Museum's own exhibitions in Vienna.[43]

A decade later, Neurath reflected on the experiences with the Vienna Method in schools up to 1933:

> … we had an opportunity of keeping in touch with the teachers from various types of schools who applied our technique to some extent. The meetings with these teachers were particularly instructive, because they told us of experiences we could get in no other way at that time. They told us, for example, how backward children who hardly reacted towards normal teaching because of their shyness became active when looking at Isotype charts, even expressing themselves spontaneously in loud voices when confronted with these simple pictures and not with people of whom they were afraid in some way or another.
>
> These reactions were so overwhelmingly positive that we did not hesitate to attempt to evolve the Isotype technique more and more. It may be used only in addition to the usual educational technique, but there is also a possibility of putting the Isotype technique in the centre and building up the educational process around this backbone, without giving the visual material too much space. It is to be feared that supporters of visual education will overstep the limits of this new technique, which would discredit it from the beginning.[44]

The book *Bildstatistik nach Wiener Methode in der Schule* (1933)

The title of Otto Neurath's book – 'Pictorial Statistics by the Vienna Method in School' – demonstrated the importance of school experiments to the development of Isotype. 'This should, above all, be a book for teachers', stated Neurath in the foreword. Until then, he had consciously held back from publishing a full summary of the Method because, for at least five years after founding the Social and Economic Museum, he was making statements to say that it was still under development. In this book, he ventured to say that 'it is probably only a question of time until it will be taught as a *closed system*'. This was uncharacteristic of Neurath, who disliked pretensions to definitive knowledge; and indeed Isotype remained an open-ended 'system', always adapting.

1.10 Cover of Otto Neurath's book, *Bildstatistik nach Wiener Methode in der Schule* (Pictorial Statistics by the Vienna Method in School), 1933. 230 × 158 mm.

The book was announced in the Vienna Circle manifesto of 1929, with an optimistic publication date of that same year (it was described then as being 'in preparation', and finally published in 1933). Neurath described it as follows:

> Contains pointers to the affinity between the Scientific World-Conception and the transformation of the present; the connection between statistics as numerical description, their pictorial representation, and the pursuit of a systematic 'grid' [*Raster*] by means of the Scientific World-Conception.

This is rather obscure, but it implies that the Vienna Method of Pictorial Statistics was a practical manifestation of the Scientific World-Conception. In a substantial article of 1931 (published in the educational journal *Die Volksschule*) that seems to rehearse some of the material for the book, Neurath clearly aligned usage of the Vienna Method in school to the Vienna Circle philosophy of Logical Empiricism. Outlining the advantages of exploiting children's 'early optical maturity', he wrote:

> This means of course a retreat to some extent from the predominant scholastic tradition based on words and concepts, which often works against an empirical attitude, while pictorial education favours empiricism. Pictorial statistics operate from the outset with *spatio-temporal patterns*, while in verbal language the possibility exists of using *senseless links*, which often can only be eliminated with difficulty.[45]

The political dimension of the Vienna Circle's Scientific World-Conception was evidently not excluded from Neurath's ambitions for the Vienna Method:

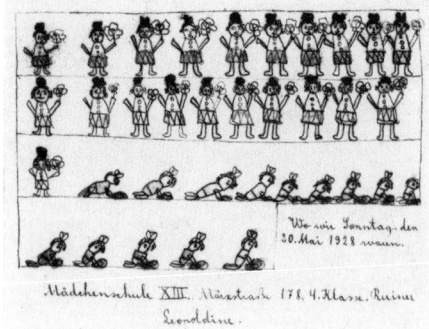 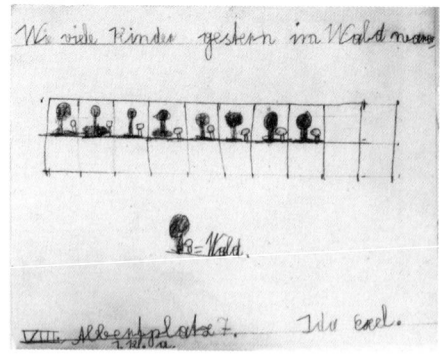

1.11 & 1.12 Examples of pictorial statistics drawn by schoolchildren aged 6–7. (Left) 'Where we were on Sunday 20 May 1928', and (right) 'How many children were in the forest yesterday' (IC N544 and N546).

Neurath was particularly impressed with the symbolism in the example above: the child explained that a tree alone was not enough to signify a forest, hence the accompanying mushroom.

> Pictorial statistics press towards making schoolchildren familiar in growing measure with social and economic facts, towards reflecting public life and making it understandable, and where that is made difficult by political conflict, it aspires at least to provide assistance for independent self-orientation later on.[46]

Neurath stressed the importance of making 'fact-pictures scientifically correct and generally understandable at the same time'. He perceived scientific illustration of his time as alternating between specialist diagrams and naturalistic images that served the vanity of the artist more than the non-specialist viewer. Isotype should navigate a middle way: it eschewed perspective and favoured 'clear outlines and simple shapes' with 'no place for shading, and wishy-washy, nervous lines'.

A much-quoted dictum by Neurath about Isotype is that a chart should communicate all that is necessary in three levels of looking, each revealing new layers of detail.[47] In *Bildstatistik nach Wiener Methode in der Schule*, he stated something similar: a first glance should result in a 'usable impression', followed by the perception of details under 'more precise examination'. 'This graduated structure of fact-pictures', he explained, 'is intended to make what one wants to set out in a logical sequence optically discernible in a sequence.'[48] The Vienna Method sought to produce 'memorable pictures' (*Merkbilder*), attracting the attention visually while carrying scientific information, and making a lasting impression.

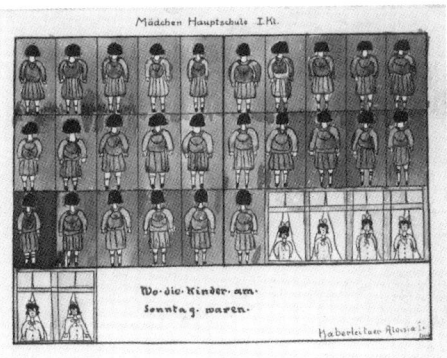

1.13 A further example of pictorial statistics drawn by a schoolchild, c.1928. This was made by a 10-year-old girl. Otto Neurath felt that older children tended to fill the pictograms with extraneous detail (IC N540).

In Neurath's view, pictorial statistics were part of a modern trend to 'reduce the absolute domination of the written and spoken word'. 'As we discovered, the whole essence of school was scholastic and Talmudic – that is, free of pictures and fundamentally founded on the word.' He suggested that children could make sense of pictures earlier than words:

> School trials have really shown that from certain graphic representations of compound interest calculation and prime number grouping (sieve of Eratosthenes) executed on the basis of the Vienna Method, a way can be found to more difficult graphic methods of reckoning already at an early stage of teaching.[49]

Neurath compared attempts by children of different ages in making their own pictorial charts based on the question, 'How many children of the class were at home last Sunday and how many outdoors?' In a class of very young children (ages 6–7) in a working-class area, Neurath found it very revealing that one girl depicted the children outdoors with flowers in their hands, but those at home were shown kneeling down and scrubbing the floor (fig. 1.11). In another case, a child depicted 'Sunday in the open air' with a pictogram combining a tree with a mushroom. When asked why, the pupil replied that a tree alone could be a park, but that the accompanying mushroom made it clear that it was a forest (fig. 1.12). This reasoning was 'in accordance with the best pictorial education', commented Neurath. By contrast, a class of 10–14 year-olds filled their pictures with details of dresses, hats and curtains in the windows from which the children at home looked out (fig. 1.13). 'It is therefore increasingly recommendable', concluded Neurath, to use 'pre-printed pictograms, little stamps or other tools, through which the creative design can be concentrated on purposeful, statistical layout [*Anordnung*], which remains the enduring task of picture-statistical work in education'.[50] The design of pictograms was never the whole point of Isotype.

For these exercises, Neurath exhorted teachers to prevent placement of precise figures next to pictures, so as not to detract from them: 'Pictorial statistics should provide *rough*, memorable images, which reliably imprint themselves on the memory. A store of *precise figures* should be acquired in another way.' 'Pictorial statistics force us', he continued, 'to make hard, clear statements in all school subjects, controllable by statements about quantities that confront us in pictures'.[51] This reflects Neurath's empiricist principle identified by Thomas Uebel as 'controllable rationality' or 'intersubjective accountability'.[52]

In *Bildstatistik nach Wiener Methode in der Schule*, Neurath summarized the principles and process of the Vienna Method. Regarding the design of pictograms, he stated: 'The individual signs should be easily understandable, quickly recognized and strongly differentiated from each other.' In terms of form, there is an enormous variety of memorable possibilities, but the situation is different with colour: there are only a few that stick well in the memory. Experience showed that it was best to restrict the palette to a small range (black, grey, white, red, green, blue, brown, yellow). For this reason, it was not entirely possible to reserve certain colours for particular groups of objects, although it was important that a certain colour had only one significance within any particular chart. In the atlas *Gesellschaft und Wirtschaft*, green was used to denote 'agrarian', red for 'modern production and modes of life', and blue for intermediary stages. 'Clearly', remarked Neurath, 'such a threefold division compels much simplification, which has many educational advantages'.[53]

The book included an informative example of how Isotype charts were conceived and designed:

> The transformer receives from the scientist material grouped according to certain viewpoints. Not every series of numbers is equally suitable to representing a certain thing that one wants to show. The transformer will therefore consider, if the crisis in the field of iron production is to be shown, for example, what will provide the most optically effective pictures – the number of blast furnaces, their efficiency, the production of pig iron, the production of crude steel, or something else, e.g. the number of workers employed. Sometimes this decision can only be made after the graphic artist has already made some sketches.
>
> But this selection is not enough. As already mentioned, it would be tedious to replace boring rows of numbers by boring rows of pictures. Where possible, only the figures for a few years should denote the facts. Three, four, or five rows are clearly discernible. Three rows are enough to distinguish *descent*, *ascent* and *fluctuation* from each other. But to express any *periodicity*, at least five rows are needed. The transformer must consider, in close consultation with the scientific staff, whether series with equal year intervals can be used, which is particularly desirable, or whether maxima and minima should be selected. It must be taken into account that there

will be charts intended for comparison that should, when possible, depict the same years. Quantity-pictures in the Vienna Method should enable comparison to each other. That is why the preferred publication format is single sheets, which can be connected in the most various ways.[54]

Neurath was unabashed about the necessity to simplify pictorial statistics in ways that might be perceived as verging on distortion. He openly explained that sometimes, when transforming statistical data into pictures, figures had to be 'incorrectly rounded off' to 'bring out the decisive proportions':

> But these are difficulties which have to be overcome by every pedagogy that seeks to familiarize the developing person with difficult problems in a simple way. ... It is no surprise that the specialist statistician takes offense at such methods of rounding off. We derive their justification from the fact that many people are not helped by transmitting masses of correct, numerical statistics, because they can do little with the fragments that remain in their memory, especially since they are often not aware of the main proportions. Quantity-pictures according to the Vienna Method, on the other hand, stick well in memory and so remain forever at the disposal of somebody who has once seen them.

Neurath concluded this point with his oft-repeated catchphrase about the Vienna Method (which was letterspaced in his original text for emphasis): *'To remember simplified pictures is better than to forget accurate figures.'*[55]

2 Branching out

Locations in Vienna

The objective of the Social and Economic Museum of Vienna was to educate a broad public about social and economic connections by means of an innovative, visual technique. Schoolchildren and workers were particular target groups of this project of education for active citizenship. To achieve this objective, the Museum was continually expanded with new locations in Vienna, and there were four exhibition venues by 1933.

When established in 1925, the Social and Economic Museum took over the office from which Neurath had directed its precursor, the Museum for Settlement and Town Planning. The exhibition space of that museum, on the Ring around Vienna's city centre, now became the Social and Economic Museum. In 1926, the Museum office moved to the administration building of Vienna's third district, where there was more room for collaborators to work on exhibitions, including the Austrian section for 'GeSoLei' in Düsseldorf. ('GeSoLei', a German abbreviation for 'Health Care, Social Welfare and Physical Exercise', was the largest exhibition of the Weimar Republic, visited by 7.5 million people in 1926.) Around May 1927, the office moved to two floors in the building of the Central Savings Bank (in an outlying district), where the Museum had about a dozen rooms at its disposal. These contained workshops for the design and production of exhibition charts and publications, model-making, and an in-house printing press. Up to fifty staff worked there in the busiest periods.[1]

The central, permanent exhibition of the Museum was opened in the Volkshalle (People's Hall) of Vienna's New Town Hall on 7 December 1927. The location in this neo-Gothic edifice also had a representative significance, for the New Town Hall had been the seat of municipal government by the Social Democratic Workers' Party (SDAP) since the founding of the Austrian Republic. The People's Hall was transformed from a former meeting place into a museum and lecture venue, provided rent-free to the Social and Economic Museum. Otto Neurath explained that this central exhibition should function

partly as an account to the public of how their taxes were spent in the extensive municipal construction and welfare programme.² Otto Leichter wrote in the Social Democrats' newspaper *Arbeiter-Zeitung* that 'one can hardly think of a method by which the great social work of the municipality of Vienna could be brought before one's eyes more clearly and memorably than the pictures of the Social and Economic Museum'. Leichter also emphatically pointed out the advantages of the Vienna Method for the educational work of the SDAP, and lamented that it was still used far too little. Finding the 'method that best demonstrates social and societal development' was 'the undoubted merit of Otto Neurath', he remarked.³

The permanent exhibition in the New Town Hall contained sections on 'mankind', 'Germany and Austria', 'the world economy', 'population' and 'the labour movement', as well as charts about municipal achievements in housing and transport, welfare, education and public spaces (fig. 2.1).⁴ With red carpet runners and a framework for charts in light oak, to which lamps were fixed, architect Josef Frank succeeded in leaving the Gothic vault of the hall in darkness and directing the visitors' gaze to the exhibition display, as Marie Neurath recalled.⁵ At either end of the People's Hall were an entrance room and a lecture room. In the entrance area, there was a large map of Austria with topographical colour distinctions. It was an innovative magnetic map made for the Social and Economic Museum, on which movable, magnetic pictograms

2.1 (opposite) View of the principal exhibition of the Social and Economic Museum in Vienna's New Town Hall, c.1933 (IC N1570).

2.2 (left) The exhibition on 'World Economy' at the branch of the Museum in the municipal apartment building Am Fuchsenfeld, Vienna, 1930 (IC N957).

showed the distribution of industries and the number of workers (fig. 1.9). The lecture room contained a projection apparatus for photographs and for films of animated pictorial statistics that the Museum produced. The New Town Hall exhibition was open until 7 pm during the week and on Sunday mornings, always free of charge.

After the opening of this principal exhibition space, the initial venue of the Museum became its section on 'Settlement and town-planning'. A further permanent venue also opened in 1927, housing its exhibition on 'Social hygiene and social insurance' in rooms at one of the new municipal apartment buildings, Am Fuchsenfeld (fig. 2.2). In addition to apartments, this large complex also contained shops, laundries, baths, a kindergarten, a clinic and function rooms. Most importantly, it was located in the Viennese district of Meidling, a working-class area: so the workers did not have to go to the centre of Vienna to visit the Museum; instead it came to them. In October 1930, a new exhibition on 'World Economy' was added at this location, showing the original charts reproduced in the atlas *Gesellschaft und Wirtschaft*, which was presented at the opening of the exhibition (figs 2.3 & 2.4). The *Wiener Zeitung* reported that 'colourful picture panels' were on display, providing a broad historical framework and clearly showing the progressive concentration of economic and political power in just a few areas of the world.[6]

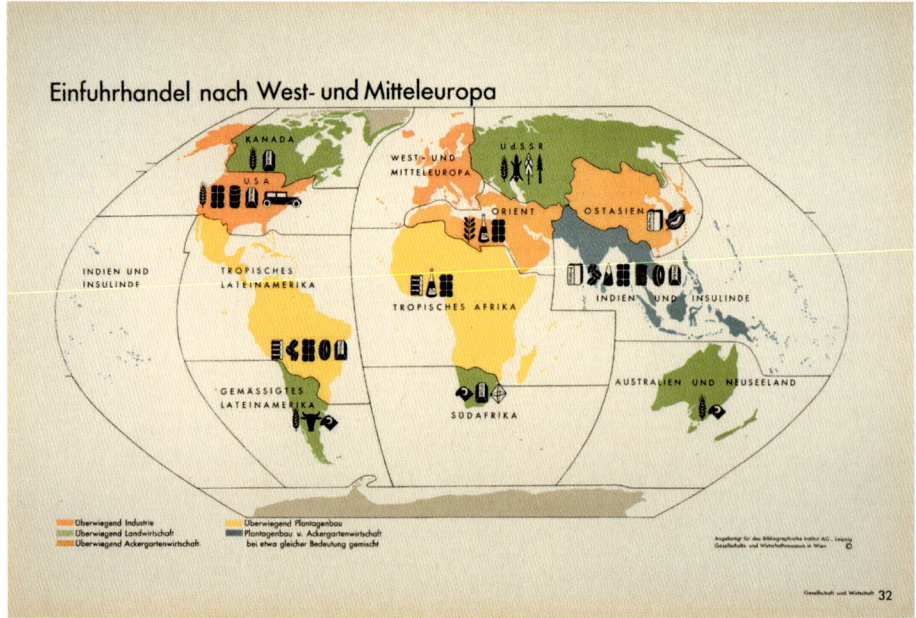

2.3 Chart 32 from *Gesellschaft und Wirtschaft*: 'Import trade to Western and Central Europe', 1930. It shows the twelve 'greater economic areas' (*Großwirtschaftsräume*) employed in the atlas (thirteen including the Antarctic, but this was neglected because it played no important role economically).

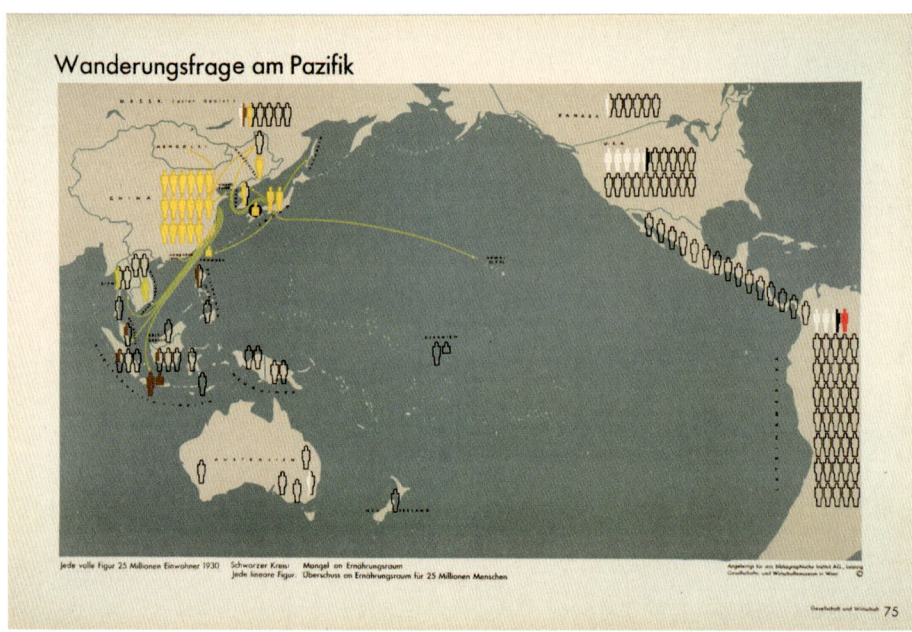

2.4 Chart 75 from *Gesellschaft und Wirtschaft*: 'Migration in the Pacific', 1930.
Each full figure = 25 million inhabitants in 1930.
Black circle = lack of space for nutrition.
Each outlined figure = surplus of space for nutrition for 25 million people.

2.5 The 'Zeitschau' branch of the Social and Economic Museum, located at the head office of the Municipal Insurance Service, Tuchlauben, Vienna, 1933 (IC N1752).

Finally, in 1933, a fourth permanent exhibition was opened at the headquarters of the municipal insurance company in the heart of Vienna's old city. Named 'Zeitschau' (Topical Show), it differed from the other exhibitions by showing photographs and charts about current events and dealing with topics such as the world economic crisis, disarmament, population development and vocational guidance. It also contained 'psycho-technical' apparatuses for testing skills and intelligence, designed and built with advice from career-counselling expert Gustav Ichheiser.[7] In rooms accessible from the street, passers-by could take occupational aptitude and skill tests, and check for themselves to what extent they could solve certain tasks (fig. 2.5). The newspapers reported on the large crowds at the new exhibition, especially at the testing apparatus – although, admittedly, it was also noted that there were hardly any women among the visitors.[8] According to Neurath, the 'Zeitschau' alone received 2,000 visitors per day.[9]

At all four exhibition sites of the Social and Economic Museum, lectures were held regularly until the beginning of 1934. In autumn of 1933, for example, Gustav Ichheiser and Louis Pointer gave talks in the 'Zeitschau',[10] and Marie Jahoda spoke at the municipal building Am Fuchsenfeld.[11] Ichheiser was scheduled to talk on 'Actors and Spectators in Social Life' at the People's Hall as late as 11 February 1934 – one day before the beginning of the brief civil war between the labour movement and government forces, which spelled the end of the Social and Economic Museum.[12]

The Berlin branch

Cooperation with Germany was not only possible because of the geographical proximity; there was also a traditionally close relationship between the Austrian and German workers' movements – although in Germany the movement had a stronger communist wing than in Austria. The intellectual and cultural climate of a 'Red Berlin' emerged despite a long-term liberal mayor.[13] Numerous political, cultural and scientific interactions also existed between the cities of Vienna and Berlin. During the Weimar Republic, Berlin – with over four million inhabitants, by far the largest city in Germany – presented itself as the most progressive metropolis in the world.[14]

Otto Neurath himself had many experiences of Germany: his studies in Berlin (1903–06), his time as director of the Museum of War Economy in Leipzig (1917–19) and as president of the Central Economic Office in Munich after the Bavarian Revolution (1919) were important cornerstones of his life. His conviction for high treason in connection with this last episode, and the consequent ban on re-entering Germany, led to an interruption of several years in his previously continuous travels and contacts there. However, through the contribution of the Social and Economic Museum to the major exhibition 'GeSoLei' (Düsseldorf, 1926), he was able to continue his work there again.[15]

Additionally, the philosophy of the Vienna Circle, in which Neurath played a leading role, developed partly through a fruitful intellectual and personal exchange between the Ernst Mach Association of Vienna and the Berlin Society for Empirical Philosophy. In connection with this cooperation, Neurath repeatedly travelled to Berlin for lectures.[16]

Travelling exhibitions prepared by the Social and Economic Museum were shown in German cities (Nuremberg, Hamburg, Stuttgart) in 1927 and, in that same year, it designed the exhibition 'Das junge Deutschland' (Young Germany) for showing in Berlin. Following this, discussions began for a more permanent outpost at the Gesundheitshaus (Health House) am Urban in Berlin's Kreuzberg district. This was one of many such social healthcare centres opened during the Weimar Republic. Its spacious building (destroyed during the Second World War) contained several counselling centres and outpatient clinics, but also a lecture/reading room as well as space for a permanent exhibition.

In June 1928, plans took concrete shape to add a branch of the Social and Economic Museum to the Kreuzberg Health House, with the district council explicitly referring to the good impressions that the work of the Vienna Museum had left on the Düsseldorf 'GeSoLei'. The institution in Kreuzberg should therefore follow this example, but primarily to depict Berlin life. The planned topics were housing, social affairs, transport and hygiene.[17] Otto Neurath maintained close contact with the SPD politician Carl Herz, who was elected district mayor of Kreuzberg in 1926. According to Marie Neurath, Herz

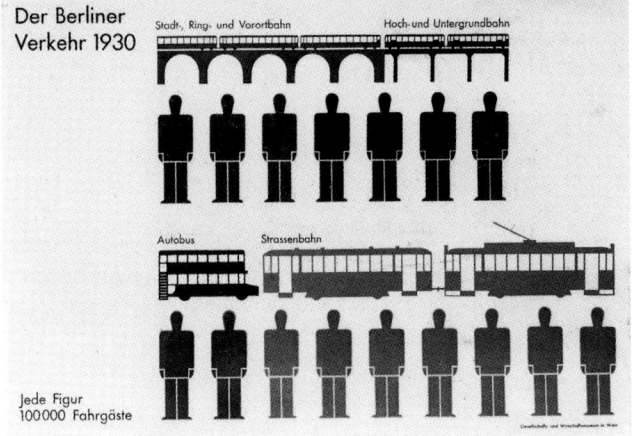

2.6 Charts exhibited at the Berlin branch of the Social and Economic Museum:

'Berlin transport 1930', 1931. Each figure = 100,000 travellers (IC T97b).

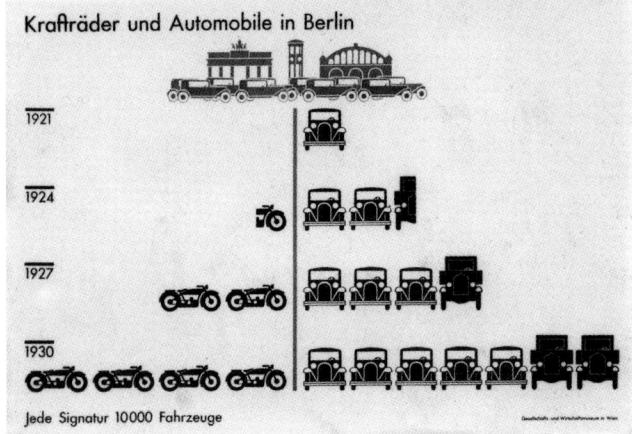

'Motorcycles and cars in Berlin', 1931. Each pictogram = 10,000 vehicles (IC T98b).

had visited the exhibition at the People's Hall in Vienna and subsequently 'ordered' a museum for Berlin-Kreuzberg: 'Lively contacts and something like a satellite branch for us (until 1933)', is how she described it later.[18]

The cooperation quickly materialized: from 9 to 31 March 1929, the exhibition 'Wien im Bild' (Vienna in Pictures) was shown in the Health House. Among the organizers of this 'special show' – in addition to the Kreuzberg district office and the Vienna Museum – was the Österreichisch-Deutscher Volksbund (Austro-German People's League). This is perhaps surprising at first glance, because that League was a non-party organization openly advocating the abandonment of Austria's independent statehood in favour of integration into the German state. However, until the National Socialists came to power in Germany in January 1933, this was also the position held by Austrian Social Democrats. The SDAP wanted to realize socialism by uniting with the German working class. Consequently, in addition to German nationalists, Social Democrat functionaries were also active in the Austro-German People's League.

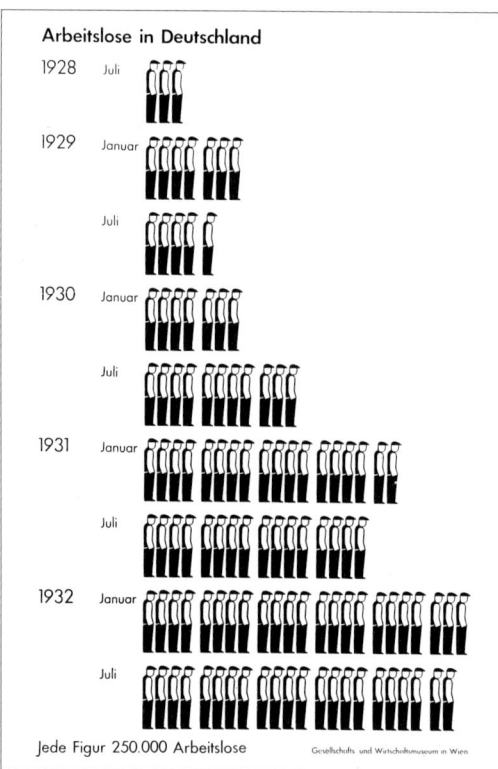

2.7 Chart exhibited at the Berlin branch of the Social and Economic Museum: 'Unemployed in Germany', 1932. Each pictogram = 25,000 unemployed (IC T788).

The founder of the organization was the later Viennese (Nazi) mayor Hermann Neubacher, whom Neurath knew from their time together in the settlers' movement.[19]

At the opening of 'Vienna in Pictures' on 8 March 1929, speeches were given by numerous politicians: Kreuzberg mayor Carl Herz, Reichstag President Paul Löbe (chairman of the Austro-German People's League), Vienna city councillor Paul Speiser (chairman of the Social and Economic Museum) and the mayor of Berlin Gustav Böß; the event was also broadcast on Berlin radio.[20] 'All speakers emphasized the togetherness of the two peoples and Lord Mayor Böß particularly underlined the strong social spirit that was so wonderfully alive in Vienna,' reported the Austrian *Arbeiter-Zeitung*.[21] Following the opening speeches, Otto Neurath gave a guided tour of the exhibition.

Carl Herz actively promoted the exhibition and explained in an article why it was generally important to impart knowledge of other countries and cultures. Herz also wanted the exhibition to counter misconceptions that 'Vienna is the fun-loving city of cheerful hedonism, where the serene charm of Schubertian melodies does not permit a gloomy atmosphere to arise. It is often overlooked that Vienna is, like Berlin, a city of serious work, economic hardship and profound social and political tensions.'[22] He emphasized the internationally

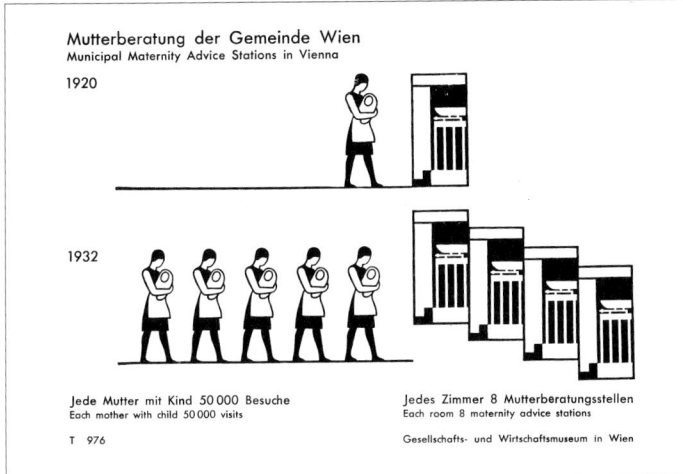

2.8 Chart exhibited at the Berlin branch of the Social and Economic Museum: 'Municipal Maternity Advice Stations in Vienna', c. 1932.

recognized achievements of the Viennese municipal administration as one reason why an even closer relationship should be built between the two cities.

The main room of the exhibition contained picture-statistical charts showing, for example, the increase in maternity counselling in Vienna since 1919, and welfare initiatives for apprentices (fig. 2.8). Germany and Austria were contrasted pictorially and compared according to size, number of inhabitants, production, age structure and social breakdown. Pictorial charts on Germany and Berlin, and on the world economy, were intended for subsequent use in the permanent exhibition (figs 2.6 & 2.7). In a departure from Neurath's concept of the 'social museum', an Arts & Crafts section was included with Baroque and contemporary objects displayed in glass cabinets. This was supplemented by two rooms representing interior decoration of the Baroque era and the present day. Examples of historical information graphics from the Vienna Museum's Archive of Pictorial Education were also displayed.[23]

According to a report in a daily newspaper, around 1000 visitors were counted daily during the first week. The exhibition was also visited by school classes – from secondary and vocational schools, but also middle and primary schools – and Otto Neurath gave lectures on the subject to teachers in Berlin.[24] Neurath repeatedly tried to anchor the Vienna Method of Pictorial Statistics more firmly in Berlin, to create a stable institutional background. For example, he wrote to the German Minister of Culture and National Education, Adolf Grimme (SPD), and was also invited by him, in autumn 1930, to give a lecture on visual education to directors of pedagogical academies and heads of the Prussian national education system. In this lecture, Neurath presented the Vienna Method and explained its possible applications to adult education and to school teaching.[25]

The permanent exhibition that remained in Berlin was covered by an article in the newspaper *Vorwärts*, which also profiled the Vienna Method of Pictorial Statistics and Otto Neurath. Journalist Richard Junge mentioned the newly published atlas *Gesellschaft und Wirtschaft* as an outstanding example, and emphasized that 'picture pedagogy is not a gimmick but a serious educational matter'.[26]

In October 1933, the Kreuzberg district office invited the press to the Health House for a preview of a further exhibition designed in collaboration with the Vienna Museum, entitled 'Germany's Economic Situation'.[27] However, there are no more mentions of this exhibition in later newspaper editions, and it can be assumed that it was no longer open to the public a short time later in the wake of the National Socialist takeover. In fact, Otto Neurath wrote to Josef Frank that 'the Nazis liquidated the exhibition, but executing German orderliness returned all Vienna property to us, with a label on SS STURM with a signature etc'.[28]

The Berlin episode ended brutally. The Jewish Social Democrat Carl Herz was hounded out of office in March 1933, publicly abused by National Socialists and imprisoned.[29] Only by a stroke of luck was he released. In 1939, he managed to escape to England, where he was interned as an 'enemy alien' like Otto Neurath and Marie Reidemeister. In English emigration, Neurath and Herz remained in contact and, despite some political and philosophical differences, Neurath in particular was still optimistic about joint projects in visual education: 'I can already see the time coming when we will open branches in The Hague, Kreuzberg and Vienna,' he wrote to Herz in November 1944.[30]

International offices

Otto Neurath explored further possibilities for foreign branches or offices under the umbrella of an affiliated institute named Mundaneum, which was announced as 'a special organization that has taken over the international agenda of the Social and Economic Museum of Vienna'.[31] The name Mundaneum was borrowed with permission from Paul Otlet of the Palais Mondial (Brussels), a kind of technical museum established in 1910. Otlet had far grander plans to construct a World City on the shores of Lake Geneva as a forum for intercultural exchange. Leading modernist architect Le Corbusier provided designs for this unrealized project, and together they published a book about it titled *Mundaneum* (1928). So, by adopting this term, Neurath also became associated with the theories of Le Corbusier, whom he encountered at the congress of the international architectural association CIAM in 1933. Despite a certain personal antipathy between them, there were some similarities in their ideas.

On the other hand, Neurath and Otlet found extensive common ground for cooperation. At the Congress of the World Federation of Educational Associations (July–August 1929, Geneva), where charts made with the Vienna Method were exhibited, Neurath and Otlet announced a plan to collaborate on a wide range of publishing and exhibition projects. They agreed a protocol for an 'Atlas of World Culture' – the 'Novus Orbis Pictus' – and a 'World Museum ("Mundaneum") copied in as many regional museums as possible'.[32] The design of these initiatives would be unified according to the Vienna Method of Pictorial Statistics. The name of the planned atlas emulates Comenius's *Orbis sensualium pictus* (1658), a pictorial encyclopedia that continued to be published in numerous languages for more than a century, and was a recurrent touchstone for Neurath. His plan for a great encyclopedia began around 1920 and became more ambitious in subsequent decades, forming a kind of ideal aim for Isotype – although economic conditions never favoured it, especially during the global financial crisis of around 1930. In that year, Neurath proposed that the two parts of his and Otlet's grand plan be separated somewhat, and the Vienna Museum began to use the name Mundaneum, applying it to the 'World Economy' exhibition that opened in October 1930 at its Am Fuchsenfeld branch.[33] This coincided with the publication of *Gesellschaft und Wirtschaft*, which Neurath announced as the first instalment of the 'international atlas of civilization' planned together with the Mundaneum in Brussels (figs 2.3, 2.4, 2.9 & 2.10).[34]

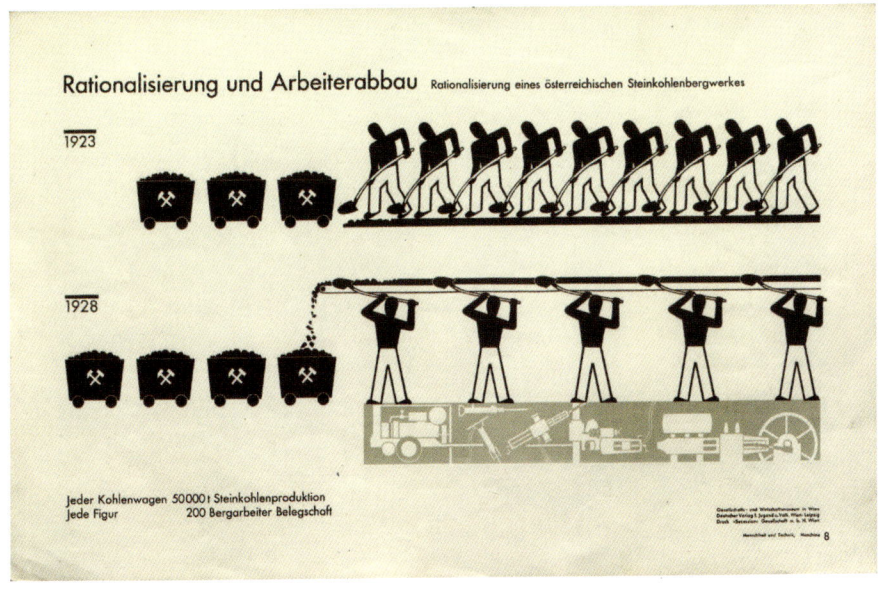

2.9 Chart from *Technik und Menschheit* (Technology and Humanity): 'Rationalization and labour arrangements', 1932. This was the second (shorter) atlas produced by the Social and Economic Museum of Vienna.

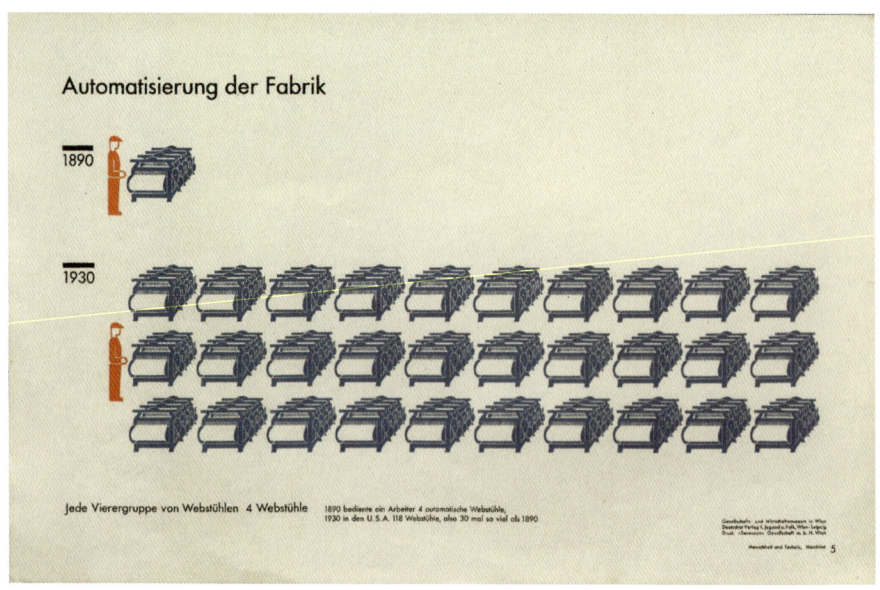

2.10 Chart from *Technik und Menschheit*: 'Automatization of the factory', 1932.

The Mundaneum Wien was officially established as an institute in April 1932, with Neurath as its director. Semi-permanent exhibitions outside Austria, with material produced by the Vienna Museum, were considered international branches of the Mundaneum. The first of these was established in Amsterdam, building on strong contacts in the Netherlands that had been developing for several years. In 1929, the Social and Economic Museum contributed to an exhibition at the International Peace Palace (The Hague); this was seen by Peter and Anneke De Kanter, who ran Het Vredeshuis (Peace House) in the same city, and they commissioned charts to be displayed there. Further groundwork for a Dutch branch was laid by Neurath's illustrated lecture at the World Social Economic Congress (Amsterdam, August 1931; fig. 2.11). It was organized by the International Industrial Relations Institute (IRI), directed by Mary Fleddérus, who became an important supporter of Neurath and his team. Following the congress, the Mundaneum was offered permanent exhibition space in Amsterdam at the Economisch-Historische Bibliotheek (Economic-Historical Library), founded by Nicolaas Posthumus in 1932. Marie Reidemeister travelled there to help install the charts made in Vienna. More exhibition space was then found at the Museum van den Arbeid (Museum of Labour), also in Amsterdam.

Nader Vossoughian has remarked that the collaboration with Otlet led to Otto Neurath treating the Vienna Method less 'as an instrument of empowering

2.11 Chart from Otto Neurath's lecture and subsequently published essay for the World Social Economic Congress (Amsterdam, 1931). Titled 'Humanity and production', it compares average population and annual production of bread flour, sugar, cotton, coal and ships. In black are figures for 1870–9 (set to a value of 1); in red are the decades after the First World War.

the working class' and 'more as a tool for promoting international understanding'.[35] A more pragmatic motive for establishing Mundaneum offices outside Austria and Germany was to secure avenues for possible emigration, in order to continue the work begun in Vienna elsewhere. To Neurath, this seemed ever more likely due to the creeping tide of fascism. 'I never saw him so depressed as in 1932' – recalled Marie Neurath late in her life – 'things could not carry on much longer in Austria, hemmed in between Mussolini and the threat of Hitler; but where to go? We had friends already in Holland.'[36]

Indeed, the existing Dutch connections proved valuable in setting up offices in Britain and the USA. A former colleague of Mary Fleddérus at the IRI, Brenda Voysey, became the secretary of the Mundaneum in London, which had a correspondence address at the World Association for Adult Education from early 1933.[37] On the advisory committee of the British office was Richard S. Lambert, founding editor of the BBC magazine, *The Listener*, which published an article by Neurath in September 1933, titled 'Pictorial statistics – an international problem'. A series of charts in English were made for exhibition in London (fig. 2.12), and collections of printed examples were also distributed.

Neurath engaged two representatives in Britain: Wolfgang Schumann, a colleague of Neurath's from socialization projects after the First World War, who was a foreign correspondent in London at that time, and Philip Morton Shand, an architectural journalist, whom Neurath had met during the CIAM congress in summer 1933. Shand attempted to form committees for a planned 'British Institute for the Promotion of Visual Education'. Neurath made a lecture tour of Britain in November 1933 to further build connections. He explained to

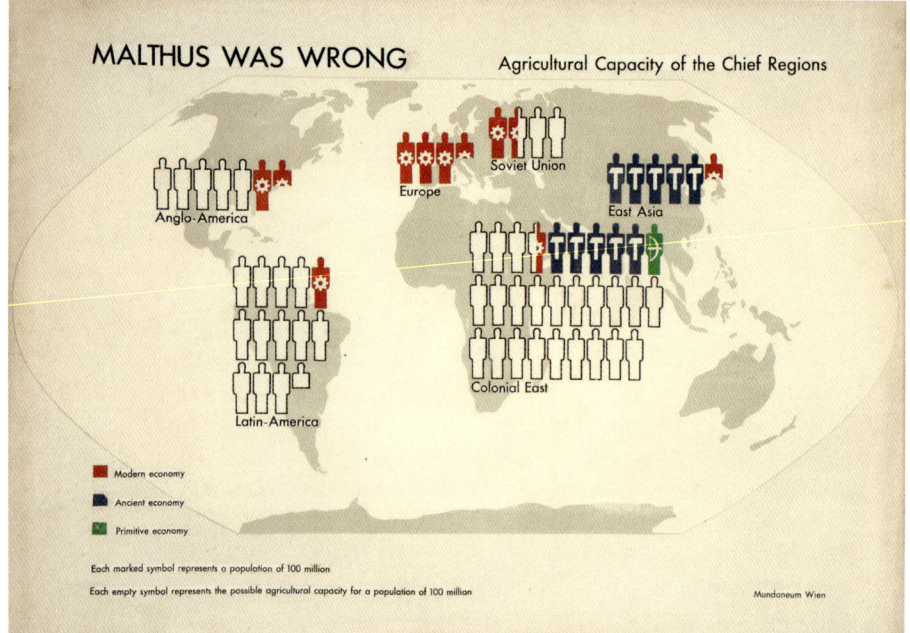

2.12 Original exhibition chart made for the London office of the Mundaneum, 1933. It was unusual for an Isotype chart to have such a tendentious title, not allowing the viewer to draw their own conclusion, but instead dictating the interpretation that agricultural capacity outstrips population, contrary to Malthus's famous theory.

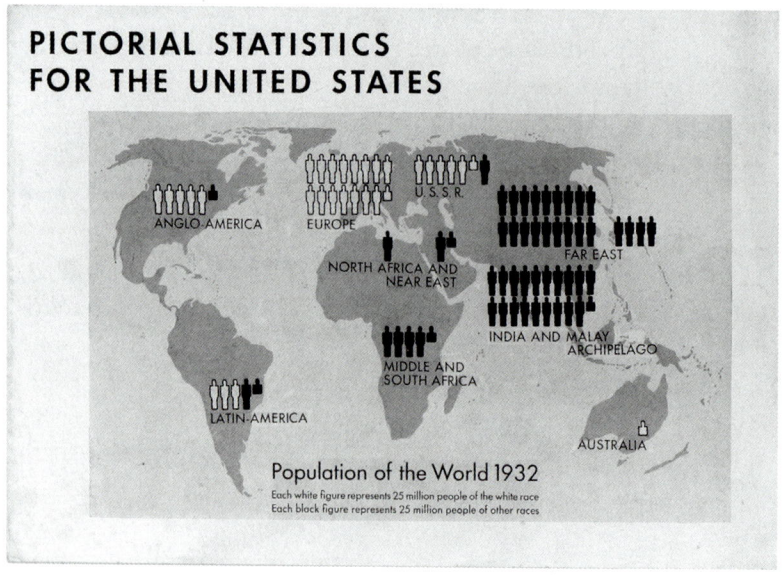

2.13 Leaflet published by the Organizing Committee for the Institute for Visual Education, New York, 1933. 177 × 255 mm.

Shand the principle behind the international expansion of the Mundaneum: 'Service to humanity, taking into account all national ties. Adaptation to these seems natural to us. ... We are used to adaptation in Austria.' But after the Isotype team were forced to leave Vienna a few months later, it was financially necessary to 'liquidate' the promotional activity in Britain.[38]

Mary van Kleeck, associate director of the IRI and director of the Russell Sage Foundation (New York), was active in promoting the interests of the Mundaneum in America from 1932, together with Otto Neurath's cousin, *New York Times* journalist Waldemar Kaempffert, and Ann Brenner, who was associated with the journal *Survey Graphic* (and had met Neurath in Vienna). Neurath travelled to the USA in January 1933 to cultivate these connections, and this encouraged the formation of an 'Organizing Committee for the Institute for Visual Education', to be based in New York (fig. 2.13). A complex of different factors meant that this was never established (see chapter 7).

A sign board of the Mundaneum Vienna, probably designed for display in London, lists 'corresponding centres' in London and New York, but also branches in Amsterdam, Berlin and Prague. This implies that Neurath came to consider the Berlin branch as such; but the inclusion of Prague was premature: Neurath discussed it with Czech government officials during 1933, but it became clear to him that Czechoslovakia could fall prey to Nazism, and the Prague branch remained wishful thinking.

Izostat

Between 1931 and 1934, the Vienna team were involved in producing pictorial statistics for official Soviet purposes, but this experience did not take the form of work commissioned from the Mundaneum, nor was there a Russian branch of the Social and Economic Museum: instead they trained and advised staff of a Soviet institute, Izostat (its full title was All-Union Institute of Pictorial Statistics of Soviet Construction and Economy).[39]

An Austrian society for 'the promotion of intellectual and economic relations with the USSR' was established in 1925, and Otto Neurath was active in it, along with other members of the Vienna Circle. He proposed ideas for exhibitions, sparking the interest of officials from the Soviet Embassy in Vienna, who came to visit the Museum. Negotiations began for a concerted introduction of the Vienna Method to the USSR, and Neurath agreed to be director of the new institute, which opened in November 1931. It was contractually agreed that Neurath would spend sixty days per year in Moscow, and that at least five members of the Vienna Museum staff would always be present at Izostat for instruction and guidance. Arntz recalled later that there were 'misgivings' in Moscow about the 'political climate' in which the Vienna Method originated:

 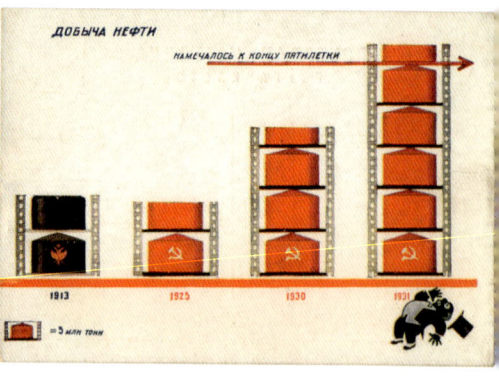

2.14 Postcards from the series *Dognat' i peregnat' v tekhniko-ekonomicheskom otnoshenii peredovye kapitalisticheskie strany v 10 let* (To catch up with and overtake the leading capitalist countries in technical and economic relations in ten years), 1931. A6.

(Left) 'The Soviet sugar industry': each sugar loaf = 2 million centners (200,000 tons) produced.

(Right) 'Oil output in USSR': each oil tank = 5 million tons.

In each case, the red arrow shows the target for the end of the Five-Year Plan.

'Vienna was administered by their deadly enemies, the Social Democrats, which meant a kind of reformism.'[40] Stalin had labelled social democracy as a moderate form of fascism, and Neurath referred ironically to this view when describing his own experience in the USSR: 'As a social fascist, one is of course ideologically completely isolated in Moscow, but as a specialist one can loyally sympathise in the concrete construction.'[41]

Lenin himself had emphasized the importance of statistics, and popular communication of them became Soviet policy in order to inform citizens (many newly literate) about the radical plans afoot. Moreover, pictorial statistics had potential as a lingua franca in the multi-ethnic Soviet empire with its various, officially recognized languages. Shortly before the Izostat Institute opened, the Council of People's Commissars passed a decree stating that 'all public and cooperative organizations, unions and schools are obliged to apply pictorial statistics according to the method of Dr Neurath'.[42] Thus, with this authoritarian edict, Isotype came closest to being imposed as an orthodoxy, although the capricious politics of the USSR prevented a consistent enforcement of it; otherwise the protagonists of the Vienna Method were disinclined to attempt such domination, and lacked the power to do so in any case.

Izostat built on a Russian tradition of pictorial statistics in illustrated atlases that bore similarities to those published in the Austro-Hungarian Empire. For example, the pocket atlas by the Austrian Hickmann was published in several Russian editions (1900–15). Hickmann's work had served as a kind of counter-example for Isotype, with its enlargement of images to indicate quantity – a

2.15 Front cover of Ivan Petrovich Ivanitskii's booklet, *Izobrazitel'naia statistika i venskii metod* (Pictorial statistics and the Vienna Method), 1932. 180 × 258 mm.

common feature also of many examples from Russia, with its strong illustrative tradition. Yet there was an awareness in Russia of precedents that informed Isotype, too, such as Willard Brinton's book *Graphic Methods for Presenting Facts* (published in Russian translation in 1927).[43]

Influence from the Vienna Method began to appear in work published by the State Publishing House of Fine Arts (Izogiz), established in July 1930. In the spirit of 'agitprop', Izogiz sought to spread information celebrating Soviet achievements. The populist potential of pictorial statistics was naturally suited to this task, especially in disseminating propaganda for the Five-Year Plans. Although Izogiz was based in Moscow, its Leningrad office initially distinguished itself with such work. Lenizogiz, as it was known, housed a Department of Pictorial Statistics, which was the direct predecessor of Izostat. It produced material combining statistics with illustrative backgrounds. A prime example was a series of seventy-two postcards, the title of which translates as 'To catch up with and overtake the leading capitalist countries in technical and economic relations in ten years' (1931).[44] It was overseen by Ivan Petrovich Ivanitskii, who then moved to work at the Izostat Institute in Moscow. The postcards combine elements of the Vienna Method with a technique that Ivanitskii championed – an illustrated 'filmstrip' of which each frame could be divided into ten parts (marked by sprocket holes on the edge) and which, in his view, could present data with greater accuracy than Vienna Method pictograms (fig. 2.14).[45] Ivanitskii went on to write a booklet about applying the Vienna Method in the USSR, expressing the importance of the Viennese contribution, especially with regard to the design of pictograms (fig. 2.15).[46] Marie Neurath described him as a 'scientific collaborator' who 'had made pictorial statistics in the USSR before we arrived, but then had to acknowledge that ours were better, and he worked with us quite happily'.[47]

Some encouragement for the Viennese team to become involved in Izostat may have been provided by Neurath and Reidemeister's friendly relationship with designer El Lissitzky and his wife, art historian Sophie Lissitzky-Küppers. Lissitzky had been an important figure in international constructivism while living in Germany and Switzerland, and had supervised the design of the Soviet Pavilion at the International Press Exhibition 'Pressa' in Cologne (1928). The Social and Economic Museum contributed to its Austrian section, and the two couples became acquainted there. Lissitzky-Küppers implied later that this connection led directly to the arrival of Neurath and colleagues in Moscow, although Lissitzky did not collaborate with Izostat during the period of their residential consultancy.[48]

The initial cohort to travel by train from Vienna to Moscow in winter 1931 consisted of Arntz, Reidemeister and technician Josef Scheer. Reidemeister visited only twice, but succeeded in teaching the skills of transformation to an able Russian colleague, Maria Orlova. The other transformer from the Vienna Museum, Friedrich Bauermeister, spent far more time in Moscow, being almost permanently based there between 1932 and 1934. (While there, he divorced his German wife in order to marry Orlova, and he remained in the USSR after the end of the Viennese contract with Izostat.) Arntz went several times, including a stay of nine months with his family during 1933. Edith Matzalik (chief linocutter in Vienna) also spent much time in the USSR, supervising several groups of technicians (she too remained at Izostat after 1934). Matzalik worked partly at a branch of Izostat in Kharkiv (present-day Ukraine), which seems to have operated somewhat independently of the Moscow institute. Dutch artist Peter Alma was also mainly based at the Kharkiv branch. Alma had no permanent position at the Vienna Museum, having been employed especially for the intensive work on *Gesellschaft und Wirtschaft*, but he seemed to have been re-engaged after a short break, to participate as a Viennese envoy to Izostat. Although both he and Arntz expressed strong left-wing tendencies in their artworks, Alma had closer previous links to the USSR: he joined the Dutch Communist Party in 1918 and attended the congress of the Third International in Moscow (1921). He had personal connections with many leading Soviet artists, such as Lissitzky, Malevich and Tatlin. After the Viennese contract with Izostat ended, Alma returned to Amsterdam and set up his own office for designing pictorial statistics.[49]

Izostat had an additional 'red director', a role occupied by a series of Communist Party officials during its short history. None of them lasted long in the post, some falling foul of Stalin's purges.[50] The number of co-workers in Moscow grew to around seventy-five. Among them was Ivy Litvinova (née Low), the English wife of the Soviet Minister of Foreign Affairs, Maxim Litvinov. She taught English at Izostat and, as an enthusiast for Charles Kay

Ogden's Basic English, she sparked Otto Neurath's interest in this simplified form of the language.⁵¹ The Litvinovs' daughter Tat'iana became an apprentice artist at Izostat in 1934. There were around thirty people working in the drawing and printing department, including the artist Nikolai Kurganov, who took a leading in role in some later Izostat publications.

Neurath's hopes for the development of pictorial statistics in the USSR are clearly expressed in an article he wrote for the German-language Soviet newspaper *Moskauer Rundschau* in June 1932:

> The Institute of Pictorial Statistics, newly founded at the end of 1931, which is to make the whole of the Soviet Union aware of the new method from its base in Moscow, is training a team of Soviet specialists, who are to devise pictorial statistics for newspapers, schools, business operations and many other purposes. Special games, teaching aids and other tools of enlightenment will be developed. Exemplary museums and touring exhibitions are planned according to the Vienna Method, and the construction of a large museum in Moscow is already being considered, along with the establishment of an Institute building with all the necessary test facilities.⁵²

A central Moscow location was earmarked for the museum, opposite the Bolshoi Theatre on what is now Teatral'naia Square, although it was never established.⁵³ Perhaps the closest thing to a touring exhibition was the boxed set of twenty charts *15 let Oktiabria* (15 Years Since the October Revolution, 1932), which contained instructions for how to display them (fig. 2.16).

2.16 Charts from *15 let Oktiabria* (15 years since the October Revolution), 1932. 284 × 582 mm.

'Production of tractors in the USSR': each tractor = 10,000 tractors.

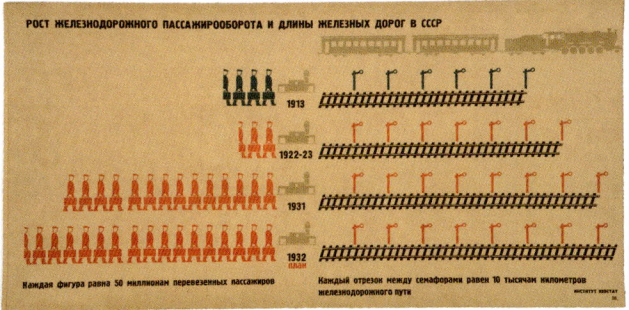

'Growth in the number of railway passengers and the length of railway lines in the USSR': each figure = 50 million transported passengers.

The intended venues may have been schoolrooms or workers' clubs. These charts show a dominant influence of the Vienna Method, both in conception and style. Arntz later recalled:

> When I was in Moscow every artist's work went through my hands so a style resulted that was much simpler than ever in Vienna, where left-overs had to be contended with. ... As far as the visual form is concerned, or the main pictograms – these were dictated by the Viennese: Arntz, Bernath and Matzalik.[54]

Some charts in *15 let Oktiabria* are colour versions of small charts that appeared in a regular column for the national newspaper *Izvestia*. In the use of colour developed at the Vienna Museum, red was deployed to connote urban modernity and progress; the traditional association of red with socialism had probably fed into this. Internal guidelines of the Social and Economic Museum put it bluntly: 'black is always used for the worse thing, red always for the better.'[55] This usage lent itself naturally to Soviet purposes: in Izostat charts, pre-revolutionary statistics were black or dark blue, and figures from 1917 onwards were red.

1932 was a busy year for Izostat: a folder of loose-leaf charts about the first Five-Year Plan was published in both Russian and English editions, making clear the intention to publicize its achievements beyond the USSR (fig. 2.17). There are some examples of Ivanitskii's filmstrip method in these editions and, intriguingly, a few charts change from a more illustrative style in the Russian version to the schematized sobriety of the Vienna Method in the English.[56] A significant feature of these charts is their inclusion of speculative figures for 1932, given that official statistics were not available during their preparation. These were included as the last line of pictograms, always with increased value, qualified by the word 'Plan'. Use of estimated statistics was not unknown in

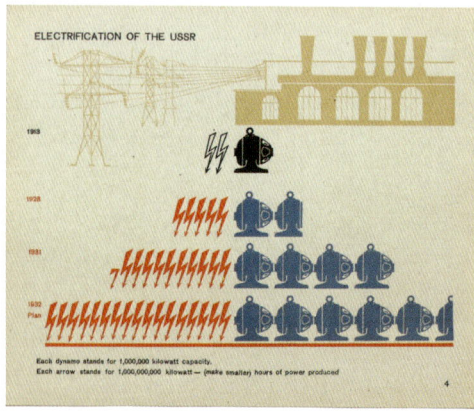 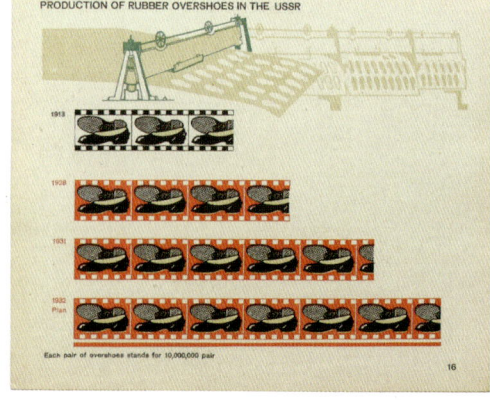

2.17 Charts from *The Struggle for Five Years in Four* (Moscow: Izostat, 1932). 183 × 227 mm.

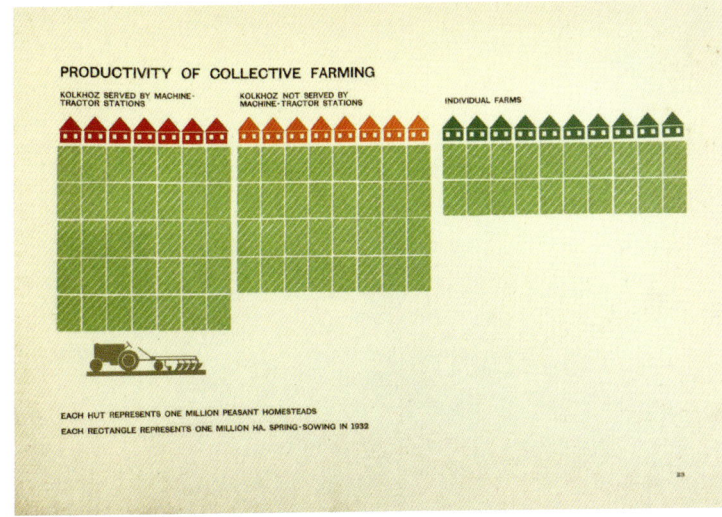

2.18 Chart from *Reconstruction of the Soviet Union Under the Five-Year-Plan* (Moscow: Izostat, 1933). 230 × 320 mm. The depiction of 'progress' in statistics masked the famine in large parts of the USSR at that time.

early work of the Vienna Museum: for example, some charts on world population featured an estimate for a future year. But an estimate of global population is less controversial than estimates provided by a government for its own activity and printed in pictorial charts published by that same government. Isotype work always depended on published statistics, in accordance with the empiricist principles behind it. Sourcing reliable data must always have been problematic, and especially so in the Soviet Union, where a conflict arose between official statisticians and ideological politicians. Three quarters of the staff in the Central Statistical Bureau were replaced, and one of its many short-term directors spoke about the 'death of statistics'.[57]

In reality, 1932 marked the height of the man-made famine largely caused by enforced collectivization of the grain-producing areas in the USSR. Accurate figures for the number of fatalities in this tragedy are still not known. Timothy Snyder, in his harrowing book *Bloodlands*, states that 'no fewer than 3.3 million Soviet citizens died in Soviet Ukraine of starvation and hunger-related disease'.[58] Contrarily, Izostat charts about collectivization presented a clinical impression of success and are clearly examples of political propaganda (figs 2.18 & 2.19).

Charts about social progress had been produced at the Vienna Museum for the municipal government, but Red Vienna's 'experiment in working-class culture' (as Helmut Gruber called it) has remained on the right side of history.[59] What we know today about the human suffering under Stalin's reign outweighs any communist ideals, so the colourful Izostat publications of the 1930s, with their depiction of economic success in rationalized graphic form, now arouse suspicions of duplicity.

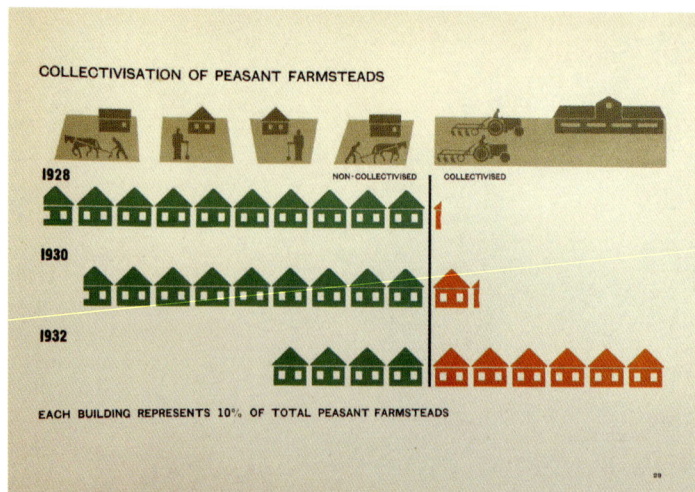

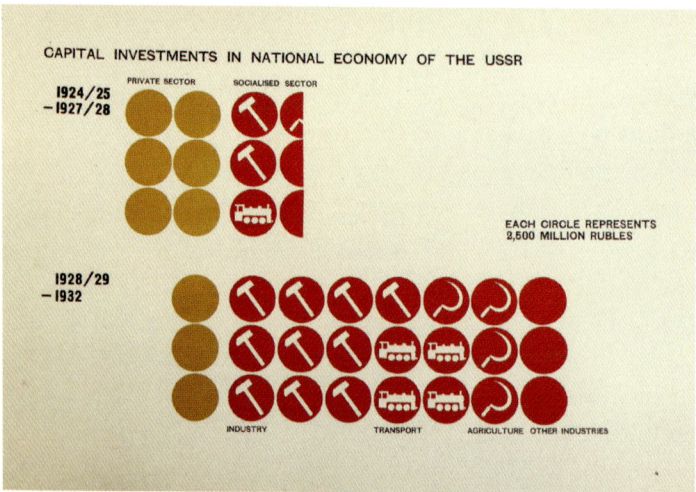

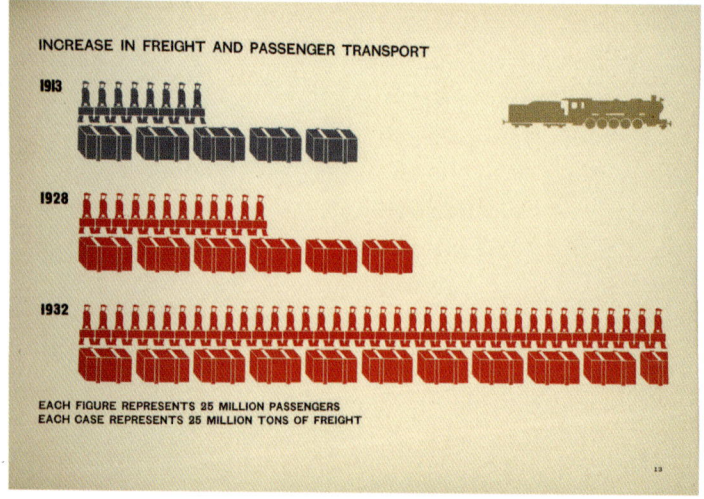

2.19 Further charts from *Reconstruction of the Soviet Union Under the Five-Year-Plan*, 1933.

Marie Neurath explained later:

> Otto Neurath had foreseen that certain things might be asked from us which were against our convictions; in the negotiations on the contract he had therefore insisted on a clause that we could not be forced to execute work which we thought to be against our principles; to counter-balance this, the Soviet institute would not publish or exhibit any of our work of which they did not approve.[60]

There may have been occasions that led to a refusal by one or other of the partners to publish something, but the frequent representation of projected data did not, apparently, lead to such a veto by the Viennese. Indeed, in practice, their objections or refusal to handle certain subjects may not have prevented publication of charts, which could have been prepared by other members of Izostat.

Otto Neurath gave details of one disagreement with Soviet officials in a letter he wrote (in faulty English) to Carl Herz:

> I remember that communists [were] very irritated, as in USSR, after they have told me of the decrease of illiteracy I said, of course you have an increase of suicide, but they explained, since the living conditions increased the suicides have to decrease (I do not know, whether this is Marxism or not), but by chance I know that the suicide figures increased up to 1927 and then – the government ceased to publish them, perhaps out of ideology [*Anschauung*].[61]

Questioning Stalinist manipulation of statistical data could lead to deadly consequences. In 1932, Ivan Kraval – then director of the Central Statistical Bureau – drew attention to the famine and the consequent decline in population, but he was accused of sabotage and was later murdered in the purges of 1937/8.[62]

An accusation of collusion in Soviet propaganda was made by Clive Chizlett against Otto Neurath, whom Chizlett described erroneously as a 'professional philosopher, political revolutionary, museum-director and descriptive statistician' – only museum-director is correct. More seriously, he assumed that Neurath was a Communist Party member (which he was not) and alleged that he had visited Moscow in 1930–1 to try to persuade Stalin to adopt his version of Logical Empiricism as 'the official form of scientific, materialist, analytical philosophy to be followed by all straight-thinking Marxists-Leninists'.[63] This is an outlandish assertion, with no basis in fact; Neurath would not have wanted to court Stalin (he was once offered the opportunity of meeting Trotsky, but declined).[64] These inaccuracies undermine Chizlett's argument, which centres on Neurath's personal culpability. It should be remembered that the Vienna Method and Isotype were the work of a team, and the number of workers at Izostat grew to exceed that of the Vienna Museum, with a maximum of only seven Viennese consultants. Marie Neurath recalled that several teams were trained at Izostat to carry out all stages of the work. The difficulties of translation must also have limited the power of the Viennese visitors to exert control over the production process. Although Otto Neurath was nominally the director, he was only in Moscow for a maximum of two months per year (presumably split across short visits), and there was also a co-director who was a Communist Party official and who reported directly to the Central Executive Committee.

Shortly before the cooperation with Izostat, Otto Neurath had expressed some positive views about the Soviet planned economy, seeming to imply that he accepted the official version (which, as we now know, was skewed by suppression and manipulation of statistics). In a lecture on 'The current growth in global productive capacity' of August 1931, he remarked that the USSR 'does not have unemployment and does not suffer an [economic] crisis'. Moreover, he asserted that these problems could not be overcome by market politics within a capitalist economy, but only by 'concrete planning and centralized organisation of the processes of production'.[65] Yet he was careful not to say that the USSR was exemplary in this respect; he did not believe that such planning had to be exercised by an authoritarian regime, and he was far from being a 'totalitarian ideologist', as Chizlett implied.[66] Neurath admitted that planning could be guided by oppressive policies, but he believed that it could also be used to positive ends. Similarly, the Vienna Method could potentially be abused to mislead and deceive, as it was to some extent at Izostat, but this does not negate the Method entirely, which could also be used responsibly as a tool for civic education – and that was the overriding intention of its creators.

In his reply to Chizlett's accusations, Robin Kinross pointed out: 'The best Isotype charts show a system, a logic, an honesty of thinking that is remarkable'.[67] Indeed, but this depended on the tight control over conception and execution by people with these principles. Much of Izostat work was guided by different principles stemming from the ruling Party. As historian Robert Conquest remarked, in the case of the man-made famine, 'deception was the crux of every move' made by Stalin's regime.[68]

Gerd Arntz personally witnessed signs of the so-called 'terror famine', Stalin's deliberate attempt to exterminate the peasantry in Ukraine and to wipe out nationalist tendencies there. In the summer of 1933, for his outstanding work at Izostat, Arntz and his family were offered a month's holiday at the Black Sea resort Sochi, in a luxury hotel normally reserved for *apparatchiks*. During the long train journey through Ukraine, Arntz saw:

> the homeless children travelling along under the wagons, the starving farmers, and again and again the throngs of begging children at the

stations. ... Much could be reported about sacrifice on all sides, caused by collectivization. The sight of the swathes of shelter-seeking exiles at the stations could in itself have provided material for such reports. One really had to close one's eyes and only read the 'victory announcements' in the newspapers in order to live in peace with this, even in Moscow.[69]

So, there was an awareness among Viennese consultants at Izostat of the disparity between the official version of Soviet life and the grim reality. By his own account, Arntz made a conscious effort to ignore this when working there. 'I have just done my work in Russia and kept my mouth shut', he revealed in an interview, late in life.[70] The Soviet authorities denied the existence of the famine, but it was reported in the press outside Russia, including in the Austrian Social Democrat newspaper *Arbeiter-Zeitung*.[71] Otto Neurath admitted to putting ideological differences aside in order to work in Moscow: 'Over there I'm a technical specialist and abstain from all arguments which only seem to lead to differences. ... But I accept the consequences of this ideological abstinence and concentrate on *the technical*.'[72] Neurath was dismayed that architect Margarete Schütte-Lihotzky (his friend and colleague from the Viennese settlers' movement) seemed to become a convinced communist while working in the USSR during the same period, and this led to the breakdown of their friendship.[73]

Statistics always exclude individual circumstances and the messy details of everyday life; pictorial statistics do also, but pictures of people and things, however schematized, encourage an expectation of their correspondence to reality. The folksier imagery that gained favour in the USSR of the mid-1930s – as opposed to the modernist style of the mature Vienna Method – provided an even more distorted picture, perhaps, with its heroic portrayals of muscular comrades. The name of this style, 'socialist realism', was evidently a misnomer. Arntz made his last visit to Moscow towards the end of 1934, when the tide was turning in this direction. He remembered that Izostat was inundated with work for the Second Five-Year Plan, including the English-language publication, *The Second Five-Year Plan in Construction* (1934). One chart in it, about the provision of crèches, featured a pictogram of an infant without facial features, as was customary in Isotype (fig. 2.20). This now ran counter to the officially approved style:

> We were asked why our figures had no faces. 'Facelessness' was an undesirable attitude with the Party. Also the 'western', constructivist, 'decadent' design [*Formgebung*] no longer toed the line of the now prescribed 'socialist realism'. There followed a discussion with the management, which allowed tests to be prepared with more 'Russian'-seeming figures.[74]

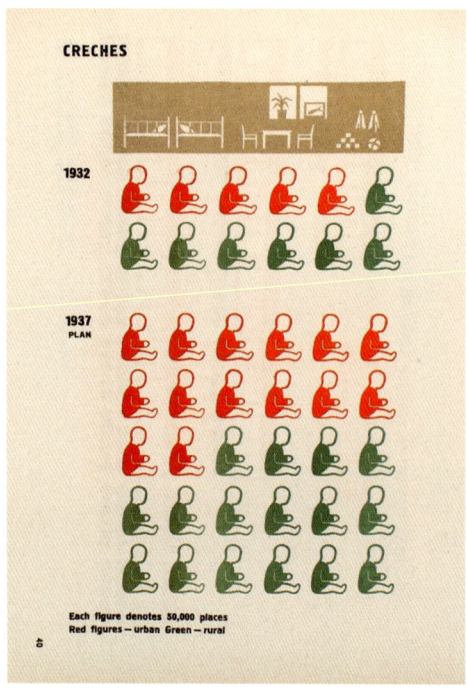

2.20 Chart from *The Second Five-Year Plan in Construction* (Moscow/Leningrad: Ogiz-Izogiz, 1934). 335 × 230 mm. The representation of 'faceless' figures would soon fall foul of the official trend towards 'socialist realism' in the USSR. The projected figures for 1937 are marked as 'plan'.

Some movement in this direction can be discerned in variant forms of a chart about literacy produced between 1933 and 1934, in which neutral, 'international' pictograms for workers were replaced with versions featuring Russian headwear (figs 2.21 & 2.22).

During 1932 and early 1933, in response to the looming threat of fascism, Otto Neurath was actively seeking a possible base outside Vienna for Isotype work. The USSR may initially have seemed like a possibility, although his experience working there no doubt disabused him of this notion. During his time at Izostat, Neurath also regularly met with delegates of the international architects' association CIAM, concerning its planned 1932 congress in Moscow. Negotiations for this broke down and the congress had to be postponed and held elsewhere.

The Netherlands presented more favourable prospects for relocating the Viennese operation, and existing Dutch connections enabled the establishment there of the International Foundation for Visual Education (IFVE). After the fascist takeover of Austria in early 1934, a core team from Vienna resettled in The Hague. Arntz made his final visit to Moscow after moving there. The first years of the IFVE were very difficult financially, exacerbated by the refusal of the Soviet authorities to pay the last instalment for their consultancy work. The Russians declared the contract invalid according to Soviet law, no doubt exploiting the fact that the Social and Economic Museum (the original contractual partner) had been usurped in the meantime by Austrian fascists.

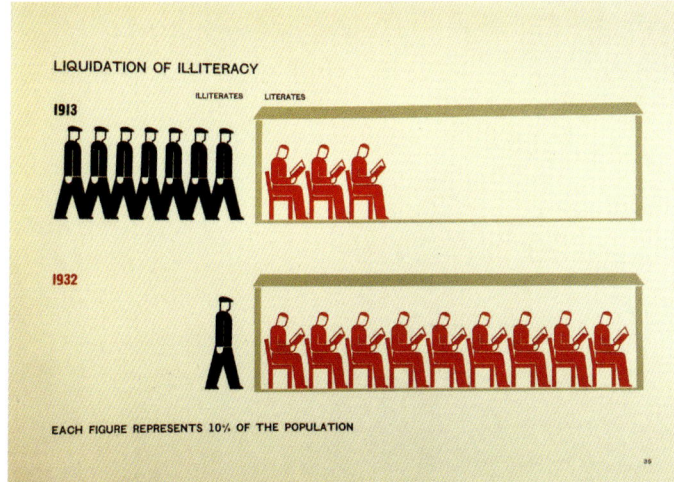

2.21 Chart from *Reconstruction of the Soviet Union Under the Five-Year-Plan*, 1933.

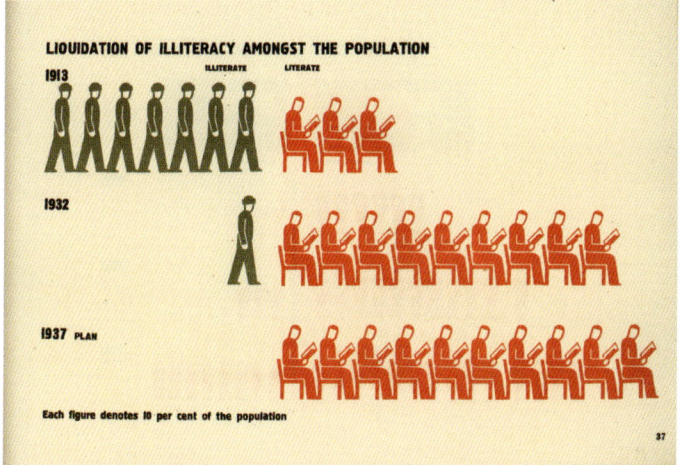

2.22 Chart from *The Second Five-Year Plan in Construction*, 1934. The headwear of the 'illiterates' changes from the worker's cap in the chart above to a more typically Russian hat.

3 Pictorial statistics in times of dictatorship

The Austrian Institute for Pictorial Statistics

It was clear to Otto Neurath that emancipatory educational work could not survive in a dictatorship. The Düsseldorf Economic Museum, which was founded soon after the Social and Economic Museum as a result of the major exhibition 'GeSoLei' (1926), was a case in point. Industrial interests, not workers' education, were the focus of the Düsseldorf institution, which was allowed to use the name Reichsmuseum für Gesellschafts- und Wirtschaftskunde (Imperial Museum for Social and Economic Studies) from the beginning of the 1930s. After the National Socialists took power in Germany in January 1933, Otto Neurath criticized the museum's self-image, stating that it took 'a pedagogically untenable standpoint'.[1] This criticism could also be made politically, since the Düsseldorf Museum had polemicized against peace treaties and reparations payments in exhibitions during the Weimar years, and was committed to racist propaganda under National Socialism.[2] The story in Vienna had been quite different.

In early 1933, the domestic political situation in Austria was also coming to a head. When, during the course of a controversial vote in March 1933, the three presidents of parliament resigned from office, the Christian Socialist Federal Chancellor Engelbert Dollfuß took advantage of the situation to eliminate parliamentarianism and to establish dictatorial rule. 'Austrofascism' established itself as an authoritarian system that was able to maintain independent statehood against National Socialist Germany for a few years. In 1934, an armed uprising of social-democratic workers' organizations was violently suppressed by the regime, which resulted in the final ban of the Social Democratic Workers' Party (SDAP). The chairman of the Social and Economic Museum, Paul Speiser (a Social Democrat councillor), received an official notice that the Museum was dissolved on 5 April 1934 at the 'special request of the mayor' – Christian Socialist Richard Schmitz.[3] The fact that the statutes of the Museum expressly stated that it was 'non-political' was of little use. The explicit reason given for the dissolution was its close connection with the now banned SDAP; indeed, an official letter to the Federal Chancellery stated that its known activity 'in the sense of this Party' meant that it ceased to be a legal entity.[4] The Museum's assets were immediately confiscated.

It soon became clear, however, that the dissolution of the Museum spelled the disappearance of an internationally renowned institution, which it could be in the interest of the new regime to continue. On 8 May 1934, the president of the Federal Statistical Office (conservative-nationalist politician Karl Drexel) wrote to the architect Rudolf Hellwig: 'As far as I know, the Social and Economic Museum has no equal anywhere in the world.' He therefore wished 'that the Museum be preserved in its essence and ability'.[5] Hellwig was a member of the Werkbund and had been regarded as a representative of progressive architecture: in 1932, he had contributed to the Werkbund housing exhibition in Vienna.[6] To facilitate the continuation of pictorial statistics under Austrofascism, he was appointed trustee administrator of the dissolved association that administered the Social and Economic Museum.

Hellwig wasted no time, organizing a meeting in mid-May of 1934 at the Vienna School Board, where representatives of various institutions discussed the matter. Drexel, who chaired the meeting, referred to the international reputation of the Vienna Method of Pictorial Statistics, and Hellwig emphasized that Otto Neurath, as former Museum director, had not only developed 'propaganda' in the sense of the Social Democratic 'municipal council majority', but had also understood how to 'achieve a commercial advantage'. The inventory of the Museum listed 700 images, 1,500 exhibition charts, over 1000 books, 150 printing blocks and 120 models; it also referred to impressive income from subsidies and proceeds, which would probably not continue, as the meeting recognized. Regarding the financial situation, an official document later stated that the association's assets were 'not directly over-indebted, but could be called illiquid'. At the meeting, all speakers present called for the preservation of the institution.[7]

The dissolution order was finally revoked on 27 November 1934. However, this revocation was accompanied by a note that the former functionaries of the association – i.e. Social Democrats such as Julius Deutsch, Paul Speiser and Julius Tandler – remained explicitly excluded from its management. Towards the end of 1934, the powers of the general assembly of the Museum were transferred to a newly appointed administrative committee, which was to coordinate further steps. Fritz Lahr, Karl Drexel and Richard Caminada were members of this committee.[8] On 4 December 1934, the confiscation of the Museum's assets was also lifted.[9]

Fritz Lahr was a leading figure of the right-wing, paramilitary Heimatschutz (Homeland protection). After the fall of the democratic Viennese city government, he had been appointed vice mayor. Lahr also had very good contacts within the National Socialists and was even mayor of Vienna for two days after the 'Anschluss' of Austria to Nazi Germany in March 1938.[10] Richard Caminada was also a Heimwehr functionary – as was Eduard Trautenegg, who was appointed head of the new Austrian Institute for Pictorial Statistics.[11]

Could enlightenment about social and economic contexts really be to the advantage of a dictatorship? The Institute presented itself to the public as early as April 1935 with the exhibition 'Wirtschaft und Aufbau' (Economy and Construction). The daily newspaper *Salzburger Volksblatt* stated that the new Institute was 'a continuation of the earlier Social and Economic Museum led by Dr. Neurath' and it could be of equal significance internationally, but its primary task was to adapt statistical representations 'to the forms of the new Austria'.[12] The leading daily newspaper *Neue Freie Presse* wrote: 'A political objective in opposition to the previous practice of the Institute remains out of the question. The new form of the Institute and its new staff have so far proved themselves in such a way that every objective assessor – fully recognizing everything created by Dr. Neurath and strictly rejecting plagiaristic tendencies – must admit that a conscious and successful development of the existing foundations has been achieved.' The same report pointed out, however, that the Institute would illustrate the constitution of the new state with the help of the picture-statistical method.[13] The *Arbeiter-Zeitung*, published in exile in Brno, had a different view of the 'plagiaristic tendencies' referred to: 'The Austrofascists steal better than the ravens. The ravens only steal physical property, Schmitz and Lahr also steal intellectual property.'[14]

Early work of the successor institute can be judged from a short-lived periodical that it helped to design, *Arbeitsschlacht* (Battle for Work, 1935). This was a propaganda magazine for the Austrofascist work creation programme, subtitled 'a monthly report in words and images' (figs 3.1 & 3.2). As such, it was dominated by artful photographs of healthy workers and construction projects that evoke the Soviet propaganda journal, *USSR in Construction*. The pictorial statistics featured in *Arbeitsschlacht* bear out the description given in some press reports: they reflect a certain continuity of style and design from the Vienna Method. While the pictograms were different, they were mostly still schematic and were repeated in modular fashion to indicate quantity, without adding numerical data on to the chart itself. Elements of traditional dress crept into some of the more illustrative depictions, but continuity was also assisted by employing the same Futura sans-serif typeface that had been used prior to 1934.[15] 'Arbeitsschlacht' was a term also used by the National Socialists for their work programme in Germany, which operated with threats and coercion, and was represented as an economic wonder by manipulating statistics.[16] It is likely that similar strategies lay behind the glowing reports in the Austrian journal.

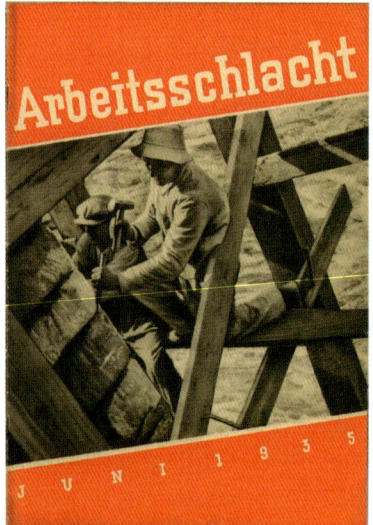
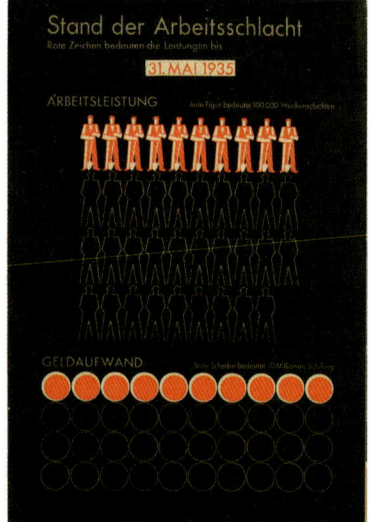

3.1 (above) Front and back covers of no. 1 and (right) back cover of no. 3 of *Arbeitsschlacht*, 1935. The back covers featured the same chart, successively updated to show progress in work creation and expenditure. Each figure = 100,000 weekly shifts; and each disc = 10 million Austrian shillings.

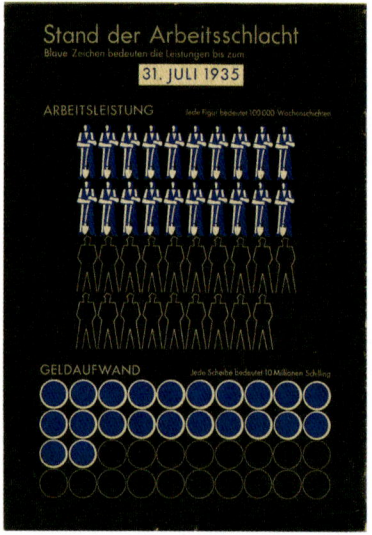

Although the statistical representations in *Arbeitsschlacht* were credited to the Österreichisches Institut für Bildstatistik (Austrian Institute for Pictorial Statistics), it was not until January 1937 that the former Social and Economic Museum was officially transformed into that institute by its administrative committee.[17] The proposal was made by Fritz Lahr, and one of the reasons he gave for this change of name was that museum activities no longer played a major role; in fact – as far as can be seen – there were no longer any major permanent exhibitions such as that formerly located at the People's Hall in Vienna.[18] Also at this meeting in 1937, Eduard Trautenegg was co-opted as a committee member.

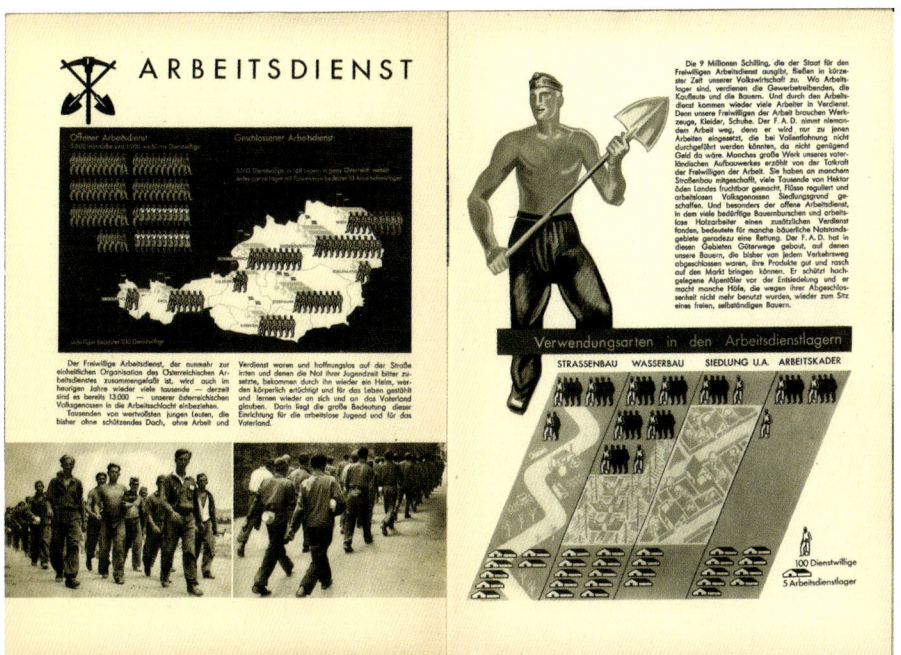

3.2 Pages from *Arbeitsschlacht* nos. 2 and 6, 1935. Statistical graphics by the Austrian Institute for Pictorial Statistics. This periodical ran for seven issues, from June to December 1935.

Although the Austrian Institute for Pictorial Statistics was far from being able to match the comprehensive and, above all, international activities of the Social and Economic Museum, it was at least active in a whole series of national exhibition projects. For example, it designed an exhibition for the Red Cross on the subject of health and hygiene, which started a tour of Austrian provincial capitals in Salzburg. In one of the exhibition rooms, the Mutterschutz der Vaterländischen Front (Maternity Protection of the Patriotic Front) drew attention to its beneficial work.[19] Pictorial statistics from the Institute were also shown at the 1937 Paris World's Fair, where it helped to design the Austrian pavilion.[20]

The most important project of the Austrian Institute for Pictorial Statistics was already shaped by the Nazi takeover in 1938: the publication *Industrie und Wohlstand* (Industry and Prosperity), commissioned by the Federation of Austrian Industrialists. The aim was to show how industry contributed to raising national prosperity. The individual sections were initially published in the course of 1937, in the journal *Die Industrie*. However, the two volumes were only published as a stand-alone edition around the time of the Anschluss. The main contributor to the design was a former employee of Otto Neurath's Museum, the economic statistician Alois Fischer, who also contributed a foreword to the first volume (dated March 1938) and the explanations to the individual chapters.[21] The second volume then dispensed with accompanying texts, but was already engaged in completely undisguised Nazi propaganda. According to the title page, the Austrian Institute for Pictorial Statistics was responsible for the scientific work, the artistic design and the overall execution of the publication.[22] In his introductory remarks, Fischer examined the connection between food production and population: statistics showed that the Earth's food production was sufficient for a population three times as large as the one currently living (a politically neutral fact that Neurath had also sought to convey; see figs 3.3 & 2.12).[23] However, in some passages of *Industrie und Wohlstand,* Fischer's loyalty to the Austrofascist dictatorship becomes clear, for example with regard to the development of social policy. He seemed to welcome the 'authoritarian systems of government' introduced in Italy and Germany (when Mussolini and Hitler came to power in 1922 and 1933 respectively) for having eliminated the 'class-struggle organisations' that had campaigned for workers' rights and welfare for the unemployed in the period after the First World War. In his view, this served to correct 'the power-political overreach of the left-wing parties', substituting new policies that corresponded to what he euphemistically called 'the changed content of the state'.[24]

Although some 'folksy' attributes entered the style of illustrative elements in this publication, the core of the Vienna Method remains in the quantitative handling of schematic pictograms (figs 3.3 & 3.4). In particular, depictions of

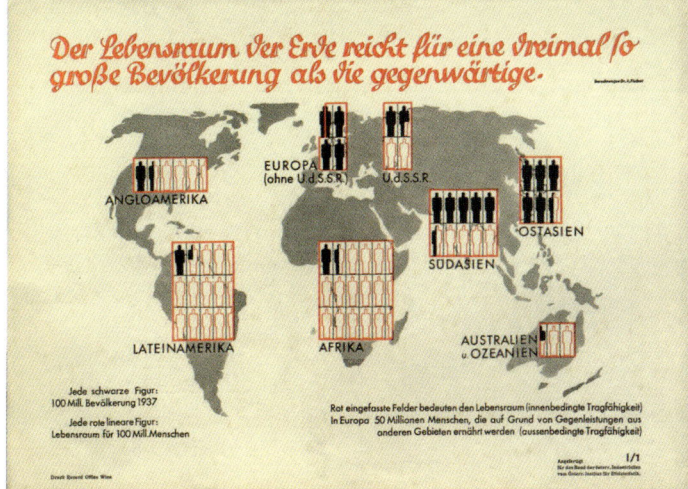

3.3 Sheets from *Industrie und Wohlstand: bildstatistisches Tafelwerk*, 1938. 200 × 280 mm:

'The room to live on the Earth is sufficient for a population three times as large as the present.' Each black figure = 100 million population 1937; each red outline figure = room to live for 100 million people.

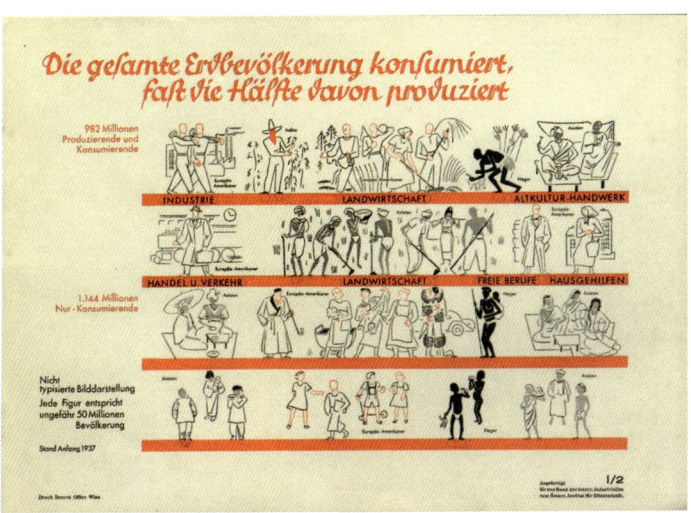

'The total world-population consumes almost half of what is produced.' A note tellingly explains: 'Not typified pictorial representation; each figure corresponds roughly to 50 million population.'

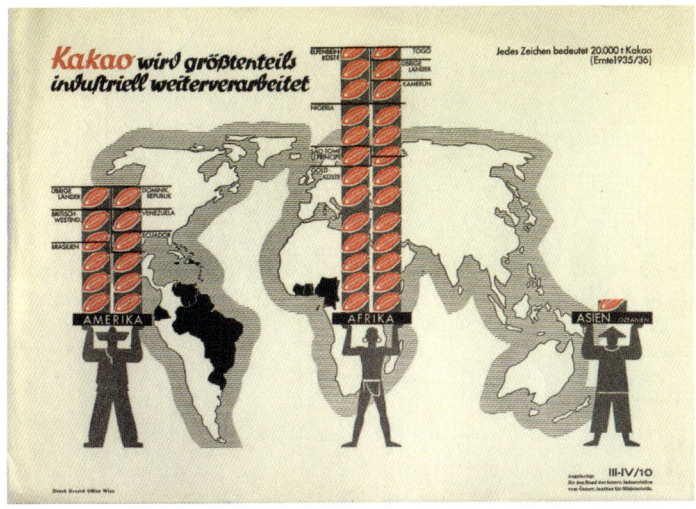

'Cocoa is mainly processed industrially.' Each sign = 20,000 tonnes cocoa.

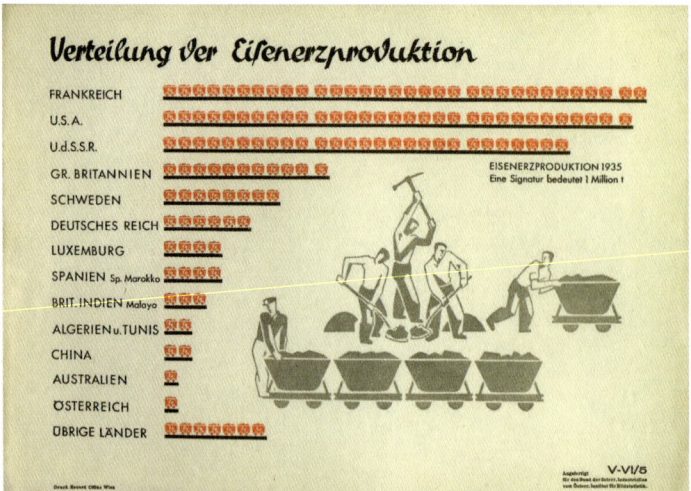

3.4 More sheets from *Industrie und Wohlstand*:

'Distribution of iron ore production.' Each pictogram = 1 million tonnes.

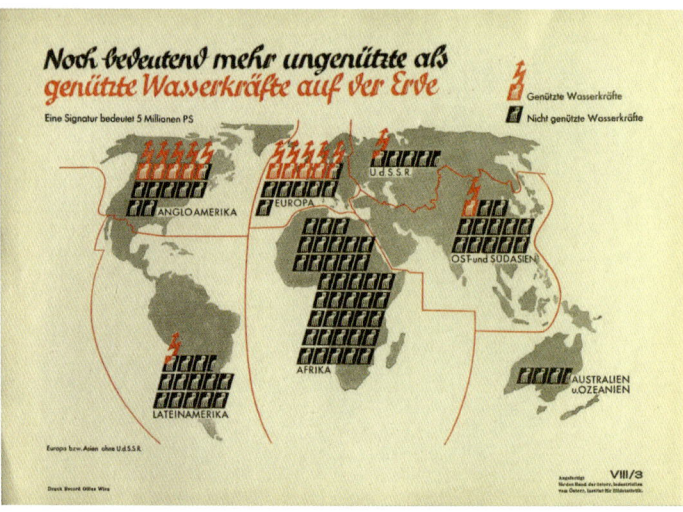

'Significantly more unexploited than exploited hydro-electric power on Earth.' Red pictograms = exploited power; black = unexploited.

'The level of social security contributions.' Each black disc = 1% of national income spent on social security, 1913; each red disc = 1% of national income spent on social security, 1935.

regional production on world maps reflect the guiding hand of Fischer, who had worked on many such examples for *Gesellschaft und Wirtschaft* (1930). The change in style is mostly visible in the use of a semi-Gothic script for titles and in the 'guide pictures' indicating the subject of charts, which tend towards a kind of 'National Socialist realism', instead of the previous modernist style that Arntz defined as 'figurative constructivism'. There is also a change in editorial stance: titles of charts, which were staunchly neutral at the Social and Economic Museum, were now written to inform viewers in advance what they should conclude, not letting them work it out for themselves. This was a subtle shift away from education and towards propaganda.

The fate of staff at the Social and Economic Museum was thus highly varied after its dissolution. Neurath, Reidemeister, Arntz and some others had to flee for political reasons and started a new life. Some employees of the Museum, although they were socialists, remained in Vienna for the time being, such as the economic statistician and draughtsman Friedrich Jahnel. He was arrested in a police raid at the Wirtschaftspsychologische Forschungsstelle (Economic Psychology Research Centre) in November 1936, together with numerous others (including its scientific director, social psychologist Marie Jahoda), and was sentenced to several months' detention.[25] In 1938, he too had to emigrate. Alois Fischer, however, continued his career in Austria through three regime changes. Not only did he work for the successor institutes of the Social and Economic Museum, but he also compiled publications such as the *Historisch-statistisches Handbüchlein* (Historical-statistical Handbook, 1935 & 1938) and the *Taschen-Atlas* (Pocket Atlas, 1937 & 1938).[26] These featured pictorial charts that continued the style of the Vienna Method to some extent, although usually with compromises (such as including numerical data alongside the pictograms and not letting them convey the values in themselves).

The Institute for Exhibition Technique and Pictorial Statistics

After Austria's 'Anschluss' to National Socialist Germany in 1938, the Austrian Institute for Pictorial Statistics was transformed into the Institut für Ausstellungstechnik und Bildstatistik (Institute for Exhibition Technique and Pictorial Statistics). After some administrative and personnel problems, the new name was also officially registered at the beginning of 1939. The renaming was carried out with some changes to the statutes, in particular the introduction of an Aryan paragraph and the Führer principle. The NSDAP's approval was required for the appointment of the association's leader. Numerous NSDAP functionaries, some of them well-known, became members of the association. In April 1939, Eduard Trautenegg was appointed 'Vereinsführer' (leader of the association), as the office was now called. Trautenegg was a former Imperial officer, and later Heimwehr official, who had married a Jewish woman in 1930, though he had the marriage annulled in good time for gaining favour with the Nazis.[27]

The Institute for Exhibition Technique worked closely with the Institute for German Cultural and Economic Propaganda, and it was involved in major exhibitions designed to give a hostile picture of the enemies of National Socialism. The technical implementation and design of these propaganda exhibitions was mostly carried out on behalf of the regional governor [*Reichsstatthalter*] or propaganda directorate. The painter and architect Otto Jahn (born in 1900), who had already worked at the Austrian Institute for Pictorial Statistics, became a key figure in this work. Like Trautenegg and Fischer, he embodied the continuity of pictorial statistics from Austrofascism to National Socialism. In 1938, the Institute was subordinated to the Reich Office for Statistics. 'The liaison man to Goebbels was a painter Jahn, who is still being sought today', Franz Rauscher wrote to Marie Neurath after the war.[28] Traces of Jahn were lost during the war: he was considered missing in 1945 and was declared dead in 1950.[29]

One of the Institute's first activities under National Socialism was its involvement in the exhibition 'Der ewige Jude' (The eternal Jew). This had been shown in Munich in November 1937 and came to Vienna in August 1938 in an expanded and adapted version. The Institute played a leading role in this, with a new section about Austria being added.[30] Under the direction of Eduard Trautenegg, Otto Jahn and Alois Fischer made particular contributions to the graphic material. The exhibition was seen by an enormous number of visitors, including all Viennese schoolchildren, for whom it was obligatory. Several exhibition projects in the territory of the former Austria followed, such as collaboration in the 'Reichsnährstandschau' (National Food Show, 1938) in Wels, and a propaganda exhibition in Vienna's Künstlerhaus on the referendum of 10 April 1938 (which resulted overwhelmingly in favour of German occupation of Austria).[31]

A number of exhibitions dealt with the representation of the former Austrian Republic as the 'Ostmark' of the German Reich. These included 'Berge und Menschen der Ostmark' (Mountains, People and Economy of the Ostmark), which was organized by the Vienna Künstlerhaus and shown in the Berlin Radio Tower from May to June 1939. The *Neue Wiener Tagblatt* wrote that the exhibition could be assessed 'as a festive inaugural visit with which the Ostmark now introduces itself to the Old Empire [*Altreich*]'. The article also praised the use of pictorial statistics and described the show as unprecedented in terms of the 'intellectual and indeed spatial extent' dedicated to a single country.[32]

If one follows newspaper reports about the 'Ostmark' in the first months after the Anschluss, one notices that pictorial statistics were regularly published to contrast the economic and social situation of Austria with that of the

3.5 Newspaper graphic titled 'The Jewification of Vienna before Reunification', published in the Viennese *Volks-Zeitung*, 1938.

Figures are given for the percentage of 'full Jews' (in black) in various trades, compared to 'Aryans' in white. The percentage diminishes from around 90% of bankers and lawyers to 0% of roofers. The pictograms are not standardized: those for Jews include various details of gesticualtion, conforming to a racial stereotype; the 'Aryans' are more subdued and apparently 'neutral'.

'Old Empire'. In April and May 1938, for example, the Viennese *Volks-Zeitung* brought out a whole series of pictorial statistics comparing the national income, the savings power or the unemployment of the two countries. Obviously, these comparisons always favoured Germany. The statistical pictures of this series, which continued until at least August 1938, were signed by the Austrian Institute for Pictorial Statistics, not yet adopting its new name of Institute for Exhibition Technique.

A central theme of these pictorial statistics was anti-Semitism. As early as 8 May 1938, the *Volks-Zeitung* published the charts 'Die Verjudung Wiens vor der Wiedervereinigung' (The Jewification of Vienna before Reunification; fig. 3.5), followed by 'Ziffern zur österreichischen Judenfrage' (Figures on the Austrian Jewish Question) in the *Kleine Volkszeitung* on 15 May 1938. The proportions of the Jewish population in various German cities were also vividly compared.[33] The Austrian Institute for Pictorial Statistics was again responsible for the anti-Semitic images, which – needless to say – would have been unthinkable at the Social and Economic Museum before 1934.

Pictorial statistics in the Austrian press after 1938 also dealt with neighbouring Czechoslovakia. Among other things, readers learned how many Jews and how many Czechs lived in the 'German settlement area' there. Additionally, thirteen European and sixteen overseas states were presented, all of which had fewer inhabitants than the Sudeten German area. Alois Fischer was responsible for this overview (again credited to the Austrian Institute for Pictorial Statistics).[34] The Munich Agreement, which forced Czechoslovakia to cede the Sudetenland to Germany, followed a few months later in October 1938.

The largest and most important project of the Institute for Exhibition Technology and Pictorial Statistics was the exhibition 'Das Sowjetparadies' (The Soviet Paradise, 1942), which it designed for the central Reich Propaganda Office. Otto Jahn was the 'artistic director' of the exhibition; among the contributors were Fischer and painter/sculptor Günter von Baszel.[35] After Nazi Germany's invasion of the Soviet Union on 22 June 1941, the subject was of great importance. Cynically picking up on the notion already circulating of the 'Soviet paradise', the exhibition focused on the depiction of unimaginable hardship, social misery and state violence. In an enormously large exhibition space, captured Soviet tanks and tractors, and even relocated buildings were displayed to reinforce the impression of an impoverished, subjugated land. The image of the 'Slavic subhuman' was constructed, and anti-Bolshevism and anti-Semitism reinforced each other. Catalogue images of the exhibition show painted displays and pictorial charts in a style which, ironically, was not too far from the 'socialist realism' that had displaced the modernist style of the Vienna Method in Izostat graphics around 1934. A popular appeal – literally 'folksy' [*völkisch*] – was evidently preferred by dictatorships of both political extremes (fig. 3.6).[36]

'Das Sowjetparadies' was on show in Vienna from December 1941 to February 1942, and in Berlin from May to June 1942. It was subsequently shown in many other cities. In seven weeks, around 470,000 people saw the exhibition in Vienna's Messepalast; in Berlin the number climbed to 1.2 million.[37] In his opening speech for the exhibition in Vienna, the head of the city's Reich Propaganda Office, Günter Kaufmann, described Trautenegg as one of the 'three most capable collaborators' on the project.[38] The exhibition ran with parallel programmes, such as film screenings, in many cities. The head of the Reich Ring for National Socialist Propaganda, Walter Tießler, described 'Das Sowjetparadies' as the 'most successful political exhibition ever'. According to National Socialist sources, it had reached a total of over three million people in seven cities by the end of October 1942. Moreover, as a travelling exhibition in multiple copies, it was shown in at least twenty-six further cities in Germany and occupied Europe.[39] Figures like these can only be explained against the background of extensive mobilization by the NSDAP and organizations close

3.6 Chart from the exhibition catalogue *Das Sowjetparadies* (The Soviet Paradise) (Zentralverlag der NSDAP, 1942). It is titled 'The Kolkhoz farmer explains'.

to the Party. The exhibition became a central element of Nazi propaganda. An attack was even carried out against it in Berlin by a communist resistance group. The members of the group were investigated and mostly executed. Hundreds of Jews from Berlin were subsequently deported to concentration camps and killed.[40]

In the few picture-statistical charts included in the exhibition catalogue (of which at least 800,000 copies were printed), the main principles of the Vienna Method again remain intact, with pictograms that are largely free of *völkisch* style. It is possible that some influence on this was exerted by a noteworthy study written in the 'winter of war 1940' and published in 1941, 'Zur Psychologie des volkstümlichen Zahlenbildes' (On the Psychology of the Popular, Statistical Picture). Its author, Hugo Keller, gave a decidedly positive account of the Vienna Method of Pictorial Statistics previously developed at the Social and Economic Museum.[41] Despite minor, mainly terminological criticism (for example, the term for 'statistical picture' *Mengenbild* should be replaced by *Zahlenbild*), the Vienna Method is cited as an outstanding approach to pictorial representation of quantitative comparisons, with some examples discussed in detail. The Viennese Museum was 'the only institution', wrote Keller, that had been striving since the mid-1920s for the 'systematic and consistent development of a strictly uniform (...) procedure' for the representation of pictorial statistics. In Keller's view, there was hardly any other institution that made so few mistakes in this area, or where even the most difficult tasks of representation were 'often solved with astonishing certainty'.[42] Concrete (positively evaluated) examples of work that are mentioned come almost exclusively from the time before 1934. The political persecution of the Social and Economic Museum's protagonists and the co-option of its reputation under Austrofascism were not mentioned, neither was the political instrumentalization of the Institute for Exhibition Technology and Pictorial Statistics by National Socialism.

4 Isotype in exile

The decisive foothold for Isotype outside of Vienna was set up in The Hague. The International Foundation for Visual Education (IFVE) was registered there as a Dutch organization in July 1933, with assistance from Mary Fleddérus, director of the IRI. Its statutes contained the telling clause that it was an 'unpolitical' organization, untethering the Vienna Method from its roots in Social-Democratic Vienna. Neurath recalled:

> Gesellschafts- und Wirtschaftsmuseum [Social and Economic Museum], supported by the Municipality, could not remain untouched by political changes in Austria. It was a Viennese and Austrian institute. The Mundaneum Institute, which made the international contacts for the Gesellschafts- und Wirtschaftsmuseum, could not survive much longer than the Museum. But the International Foundation for Visual Education could remain wholly untouched. We had an office in Vienna for months after the end of the Museum and the Mundaneum with the Dutch flag on our doorstep. The International Foundation was the legal successor of the Mundaneum Vienna, which was an Austrian institute, but the authorities accepted, as we suggested, that the International Foundation would automatically become the legal heir of the Mundaneum Vienna. In this way we got the international material out of Austria and some of our collaborators came with us.[1]

Shortly after the brief civil war of February 1934, which ended with the establishment of a right-wing regime in Austria, the political police came to search Neurath's office at the Museum in Vienna. He happened to be in Moscow at the time, and Reidemeister set in motion their emergency plans to leave, initially to Czechoslovakia. Neurath travelled directly there from Moscow, never to set foot in Austria again.

In April 1934, Neurath took a circuitous route via Poland and Denmark (avoiding Austria and Germany) to the Netherlands; Reidemeister took the shortest route through Germany: 'stupid,' she later recalled, 'because nowhere were one-way travellers to Holland treated with so much suspicion as at the border with Germany':

> They did not let me through; I was however allowed to telephone Miss Fleddérus in The Hague; Otto, who was already in The Hague, asked her to think who was the most influential person among her relatives; it was someone in the Home Office; then I was treated as an honoured guest by the officials on the Dutch side.[2]

They were soon joined by Neurath's then-wife, Olga. Initially, Fleddérus allowed them to work at her apartment in a large villa at Scheveningen, but when colleagues from Vienna – Gerd Arntz, Erwin Bernath, and Josef Scheer – joined them in autumn 1934, more working space was needed and two floors of a town house were rented for this purpose.

However, they now lacked the financial security that they had enjoyed at the Vienna Museum, and had to generate income to support the IFVE. This proved very difficult in their first years at The Hague, and they relied on gifts from friends and family. The situation was made worse by the Soviet authorities taking advantage of the political uncertainty in Austria and refusing to complete payment for the Vienna team's consultation work at Izostat. This was a significant loss – $6,000. 'After 1934', Neurath recalled, 'it was very difficult for us to exist at all', describing his first few years in the Netherlands as 'living like a better class of beggar'.[3] In July 1935, Neurath had to inform his colleagues at the IFVE that their salaries would be revised on a monthly basis, due to lack of work.[4]

The first few years in the Netherlands were occupied by a commission that reflected a new international orientation: to write two books about Isotype in Basic English for a series edited by C. K. Ogden. While not lucrative, this task was significant for the legacy of Isotype: the first of the books, *International Picture Language*, remains a key summary of the method. There was an obvious kinship between Basic English and Isotype, which were both intended to function as an auxiliary language – or a 'helping' language, as the reduced vocabulary of Basic termed it. The preface to the 1930 edition of *The Meaning of Meaning*, the classic book that Ogden co-wrote with I. A. Richards, claimed that Basic English had addressed 'the problem of a universal scientific language'; this was a dominating issue for Neurath during the 1930s, both in terms of visual education and his pursuit of 'unified science'.[5]

Work on these books gave the impetus to find a new name to replace 'Vienna Method of Pictorial Statistics', given that the ties with Vienna had now been severed. It was Reidemeister who came up with Isotype, an acronym of 'International System of Typographic Picture Education' analogous to Ogden's Basic (British American Scientific International Commercial). She described the rather tortuous process of finding the solution:

4.1 The back of a four-page leaflet announcing the new name of Isotype, c. 1935.

I followed the principle Ogden used in the construction of the acronym 'Basic', and so came upon 'Isotip' (International System of Teaching in Pictures); this was not acceptable as a name, though it led on to Isotype, for which the words that would make up the acronym then had to be found, after a fashion. Although it was not absolutely successful, the word was too good to lose.[6]

In fact, Isotype was never strictly 'typographic' in the sense of using metal or wood printing types for the pictograms (some early experiments in this were unsatisfactory), neither have the pictograms ever been made into fonts for subsequent technologies of photosetting or digital composition. The 'types' referred to in the name Isotype are the typified pictograms themselves, which remained as consistent as possible. Otto and Marie Neurath suggested a retrospective Greek derivation for the name – 'always using the same types'.[7]

A leaflet was issued to announce the name (fig. 4.1), and it was introduced in an article written by Neurath, 'Isotype en de grafiek' (Isotype and graphics). This overlaps with *International Picture Language* to some extent, but it usefully summarizes the new position:

> Isotype is a modern picture-language, which represents facts by the combination of certain symbols. It was created as a helping language for the dissemination of technical, social and economic knowledge. … This picture-language has a lexicon of around 2,000 signs as well as a grammar for them. While our written language is one-dimensional in construction, this picture-language uses two dimensions, as is also the case with statistical tables. … The development of picture-language is connected to the

development of the modern technology of communal life. Around the middle of the nineteenth century, at the time of the great world exhibitions, a great technical enlightenment was discernible, and at the beginning of the twentieth century a hygienic one; now, social progress gains ever more importance, both in general adult education and in school teaching. We live in the age of the eye and therefore we attempt to methodically apply the media of visualization in the field of social progress also. These efforts fortunately coincide with the efforts of some graphic artists who apply simplified human and object forms, mainly to depict social conditions [here Neurath refers to a woodcut by Gerd Arntz]. These graphic artists, who specialize in clear surface division and silhouette drawing – mostly in reproducible, firm lines – developed a figure composition that is always conducive to modification. Under the influence of this graphic direction, the pictograms of the new picture-script were developed, which increasingly take on the character of 'types'. For reasons of continuity, these types do not change too much over the course of time, just as our written characters remain more stable than the basic forms of graphic artists and painters.

Neurath reasserted the educational purpose of Isotype, but he seemed more inclined now to address the commercial sector; and, in this sense, he expressed a certain protective attitude against imitators:

In many respects this technique is related to advertising. But while each advertising poster speaks only for itself and must overpower neighbouring posters, the pictures prepared by the Isotype method form in a certain sense chapters of a great encyclopedia, which can be understood in all countries. *Words divide, pictures connect.* ... And so we encounter examples from this great Isotype-encyclopedia throughout the world, but unfortunately, in addition, all kinds of imitations that are alien to certain principles of the Isotype method and share no mutual coherence with it. To maintain the unity of Isotype work and to propagate its general use, the International Foundation of Visual Education has been founded. ...

The scientific and graphic workplace for Isotype is the Mundaneum Institute in The Hague. The experience of this work of many years will now be at the service of industry, trade and commerce through a specially established organization, Isotype Limited. We live in the era of the 'visible' [*aanschouwen*]. Those who want to make a quick and lasting impression make use of pictures. All our pictures from now on carry the trademark: Isotype, with the man holding up a chart.[8]

It seems that the new name and trademark were intended as a brand of quality for genuine Isotype work. The IFVE was essentially a 'scientific' body that promoted research in visual education, and the Mundaneum was the practical workshop. Yet it is revealing that a new incorporated company named 'Isotype'

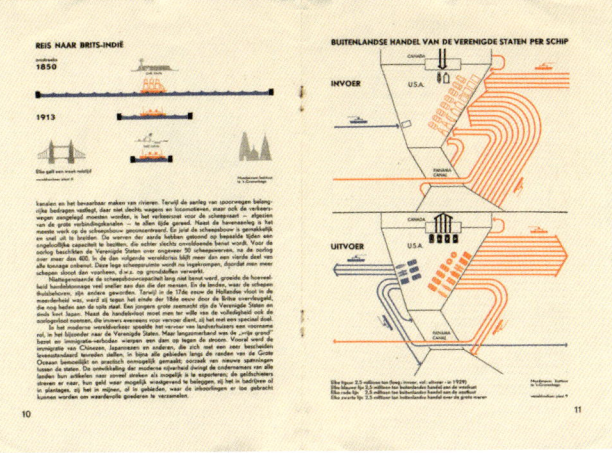

4.2 *Wereldverkeer* (World Transport). The first and only number in the 'Wide world series' issued by the Mundaneum in The Hague, 1935. 272 × 190 mm.

was announced here: no such entity had existed in Vienna, and it reflected the necessity to cultivate new business in the Netherlands – if not to make a profit then to at least cover the institutional costs.

The first publication designed by the Isotype team was the first (and only) number in a planned series named 'Wide World'. It was titled *Wereldverkeer* (World Transport, 1935), a theme often previously dealt with at the Vienna Museum, but also perhaps chosen here to appeal to commercial clients. Presumably the content was provided by the Isotype team collaboratively (fig. 4.2).[9]

International Picture Language and *Basic by Isotype*

Although Neurath was credited as the sole author of these two books in Basic English, Reidemeister co-wrote the texts and she discovered how difficult it was to write in Basic. Ogden's 'closest collaborator', Leonora Lockhart, came to The Hague for few days to assist.[10] In *International Picture Language*, it was suggested that 'the question of an international language' was important in supporting international developments to counteract the 'warring interests and broken connections' of that time. The book summarized the concept and main features of Isotype, but did not offer a set of rules for it. This was deliberate on Neurath's part, not only to avoid encouraging competition, but on the principle that 'long experience and special training is needed for the process of putting the material given by science into teaching-pictures. … Which details to put

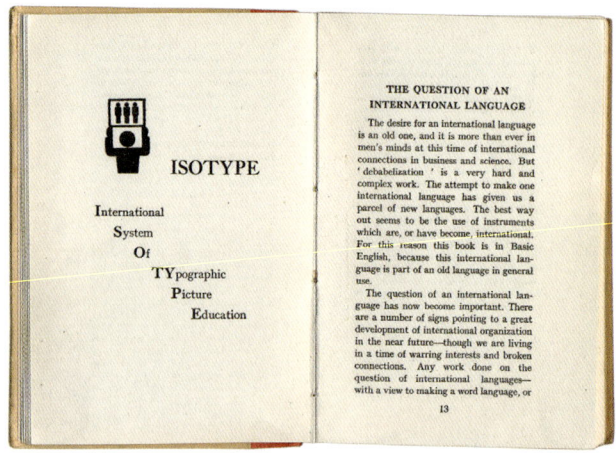

4.3 Cover and pages from *International Picture Language*, 1936. 150 × 104 mm.

in, which to keep out, is a hard question and one which is not to be answered generally but only in relation to special examples.'[11] Neurath always acknowledged the limitations of Isotype but felt that these could also be its strength:

> But the uses of a picture language are much more limited than those of normal languages. ... It is not in competition with the normal languages; it is a help inside its narrow limits. But in the same way as Basic English is an education in clear thought – because the use of statements without sense is forced upon us less by Basic than by the normal languages, which are full of words without sense (for science) – so the picture language is an education in clear thought – by reason of its limits.[12]

Nevertheless, *International Picture Language* hinted at new possibilities, such as the use of pictograms in signage and instructional material (fig. 4.4). Pictograms are ubiquitous today in signs that we encounter on our travels, but this development began only in the 1950s, and the particular forms of Isotype pictograms were never adopted for this purpose. Yet Neurath remarked: 'Most of the signs may be used not only in lines but as separate designs.' He suggested their use in hotels and airports, and even connected Isotype with the burgeoning standardization of road signs.[13] Only the antiquated pictogram for automobile dates the examples proposed in the book, but Neurath was fully aware that this would require revision in future: 'Certainly the Isotype signs are dependent on their times like all these old sign languages. Later times will see what their special qualities are and what the conditions were which made them.'[14]

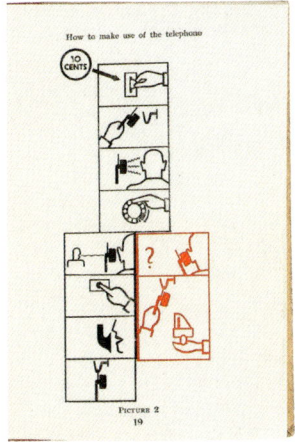
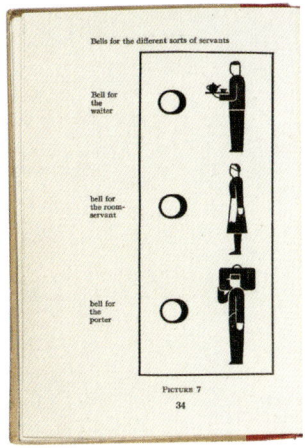

4.4 (above) More pages from *International Picture Language*, suggesting extended uses of Isotype for information graphics and signage.

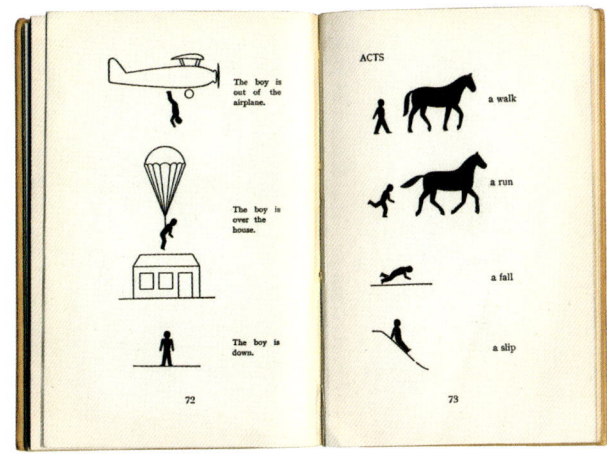

4.5 (right) Pages from *Basic by Isotype*, 1937. 150 × 98 mm.

The second book, *Basic by Isotype* (1937), is a delightful anomaly in the Isotype body of work – a pictorial primer of Basic English. It had been stated in *International Picture Language* that 'ISOTYPE picture language is not a sign-for-sign parallel of a word language. ... It has no qualities for the purpose of exchanging views, of giving signs of feeling, orders, etc.'[15] Ogden and Neurath were in agreement about separating 'the symbolic and the emotive' functions of language.[16] While *Basic by Isotype* avoids emotional phrases, it does attempt the equivalence of pictures with words, which usually have complementary functions in Isotype, rather than duplicating each other's meaning. Neurath had stated: 'Picture education is based on the principle: *what one can show in a picture should not be said with words.*'[17] But *Basic by Isotype* presents isolated pictograms for certain vocabulary (offering an informative snapshot of the Isotype 'lexicon' at that time) and depictions of given, descriptive phrases, which are not strictly pictographic but more diagrammatic, with narrative tendencies (fig. 4.5). As such, it provided an opportunity to stretch Isotype's capabilities.

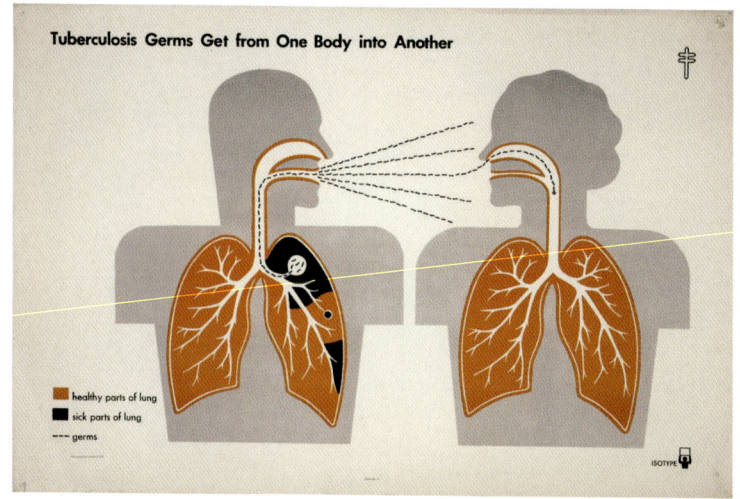
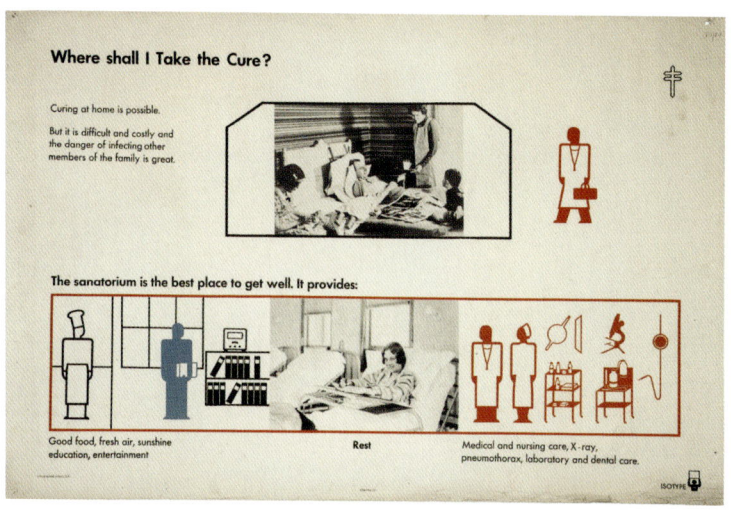
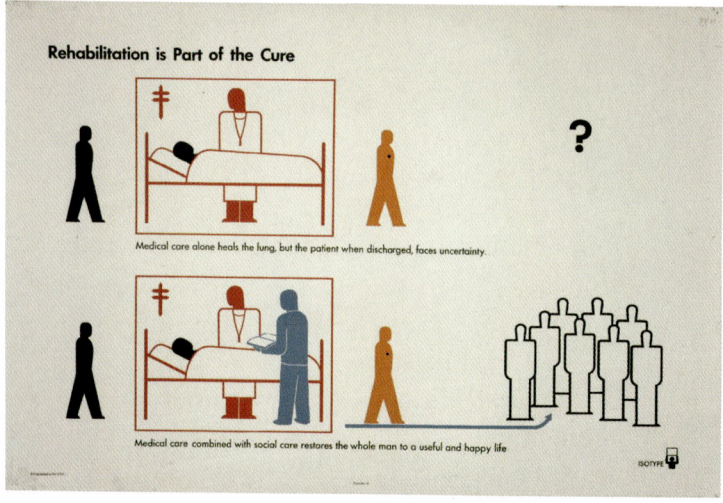

4.6 Posters from the series 'Fighting Tuberculosis', for the National Tuberculosis Association, 1938. 610 × 920 mm.

America summons

Given the lack of work for the IFVE originating in the Netherlands, Neurath set his sights on America as a source of commissions. Good prospects for this ensued from a visit to the IFVE in Spring 1935, by Harry Edwin Kleinschmidt, director of the Health Education Service at the National Tuberculosis Association (NTA), based in New York. He had travelled to Germany to visit museums and exhibitions, in particular the Berlin exhibition 'Das Wunder des Lebens' (The Wonder of Life).[18] Having heard about the Vienna Method, and knowing that Neurath was now in The Hague, Kleinschmidt made a detour to visit him there. Kleinschmidt returned home convinced that Isotype could be applied to health education in the USA, and he secured some funds from the NTA to help bring Neurath to New York for a collaboration.[19]

Neurath set off in September 1936 for what turned out to be a six-month sojourn in America. The main objective was to design a public information campaign about tuberculosis for the NTA, and Marie Reidemeister joined Neurath in November for this purpose (in her first and only visit to America). She recalled working in the NTA office at Rockefeller Center, in a fruitful dialogue with experts.[20] The result was an exhibition of large posters, produced in an edition of 5,000 copies, that was shown all over North America, with accompanying publications (fig. 4.6).[21] Versions of the posters were even produced in French for parts of Canada. Neurath and Kleinschmidt also wrote a booklet together, *Health Education by Isotype* (1939).

In January 1937, *The New York Times* published a feature about Isotype by Waldemar Kaempffert, who was the newspaper's science editor.[22] Such press coverage about Neurath, and his gregarious presence in the USA, led to significant commissions. Towards the end of that month, he met with publisher Alfred Knopf, and they signed a contract for a book 'with pictures, [on] a splendid sociological topic', with advanced payment.[23] Neurath had already proposed a book about the 'Pilgrimage of Man' to Knopf in November 1933, and this developed into *Modern Man in the Making*.[24] Immediately after signing that contract, he received a request to provide charts and diagrams for the next edition of *Compton's Pictured Encyclopedia* (Chicago). Neurath was relieved that these commissions guaranteed paid work in Isotype for at least the next two years.[25]

Yet another exciting prospect developed several days later: a formal invitation from the Mexican National Council for Higher Education and Scientific Research to collaborate on developing a newly founded museum for science and industry. The National Council had been established at the beginning of 1936 as part of a programme to nationalize education, and was directed by social anthropologist Miguel Othón de Mendizábal. An old friend of Otto Neurath, the writer and psychologist Alice Rühle-Gerstel, was working as an interpreter there, and she had suggested him as a consultant for the new museum. Neurath and Reidemeister had already booked a passage back to Europe for March 1937, but they managed to squeeze in a working visit to Mexico before their return. They made the three-day train journey to Mexico City and spent three weeks there giving advice and instruction. Marie Neurath recalled later that 'here for the first time we were in a country with an ancient tradition of pictures and numbers'.[26] Developing a new Museum on the basis of Isotype was a desideratum for Otto Neurath, and he and Reidemeister enjoyed their time in Mexico so much that they later toyed with the idea of emigrating to Latin America.

Back in The Hague, work began on *Modern Man in the Making*. Reidemeister proposed that it be conceived as an intimate integration of text with pictorial charts, so that the latter function almost as paragraphs in themselves. The resulting book is one of the most accomplished examples of Isotype work, reflecting a close collaboration between author, transformer, designer and publisher. It was published on the eve of the Second World War and was soon issued in Dutch and Swedish translations. Reidemeister commented later to Arntz that she felt it represented the pinnacle of their work in making books.[27]

Pioneering exhibition work

By the late 1930s, more commissions began to originate in the Netherlands, including some work for the Ministry of Social Affairs. The IFVE provided this ministry's section (mainly on the subject of health) for the exhibition marking forty years of Queen Wilhelmina's reign, and also its section at the New York World's Fair (1939–40).[28] The large department store De Bijenkorf asked the Institute to curate and design an exhibition to be shown in triplicate at its branches in Amsterdam, Rotterdam and The Hague; moreover, the Isotype team were free to choose the subject. Reidemeister suggested Rembrandt as the theme: 'frequent visits to the Mauritshuis, and above all to a room there with three Rembrandt pictures and Vermeer's "View of Delft", had become almost a necessity of life to me', she remarked later.[29] This would be the first Isotype exhibition about art, but it could not include original artworks; instead it examined the socio-historical context of the artist's work – hence its title, 'Rondom Rembrandt' (Around Rembrandt, 1938). Reidemeister consulted Viennese art historian Horst Gerson, who was then living in the Netherlands and working on a catalogue raisonnée of Rembrandt's works. (Reidemeister's interest in Rembrandt may also have been sparked earlier by visits to her grandmother's brother Wilhelm von Bode, former director of Berlin museums, and an expert on the artist.) Some photographic reproductions of paintings were included in the exhibition (notably some enlarged details charting the evolution of brush technique) but, as Neurath explained to American art historian Meyer Schapiro, it would also

> give our visitors an opportunity of seeing Rembrandt's career and social life of his time. E.g., the period of explorers, of the 80 years' war between Spain and the Netherlands, and the journey of the Pilgrims to America. A short systematic demonstration of statistical data might explain the historical situation; we could show the plague in Amsterdam, Leyden and other Dutch towns.[30]

The value of paintings as commodities was also addressed: one particularly inventive chart showed the increase in the price of a Rembrandt picture over the centuries (fig. 4.7)

In 'Rondom Rembrandt', the Isotype team pioneered multimedia techniques for engaging the public, which have since become much easier to achieve technically and are now commonplace. For example, a set of alternative groups of images (each including a building, a ship and a painting) were offered for visitors to choose which groups they thought belonged to the same historical period. When a button underneath a column was pushed, a recording of 'right' or 'wrong' was set in motion. Even greater opportunities for interactive exhibits were offered by a second exhibition designed for De Bijenkorf to commemorate 100 years of Dutch railways. Titled 'Het Rollende Rad' (The Rolling Wheel, 1939), it included an apparatus which could be activated by visitors to set wheels in motion (fig. 4.8).

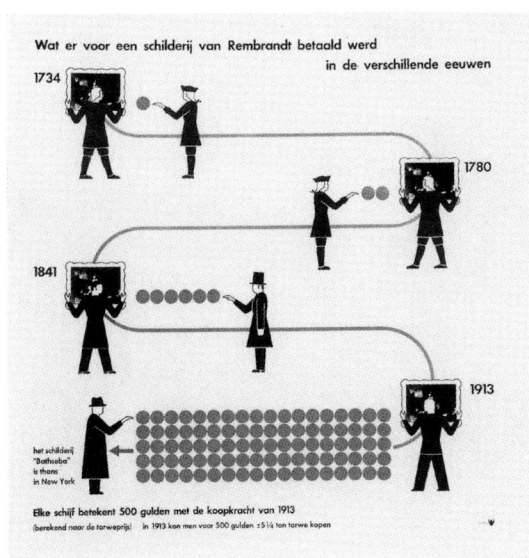
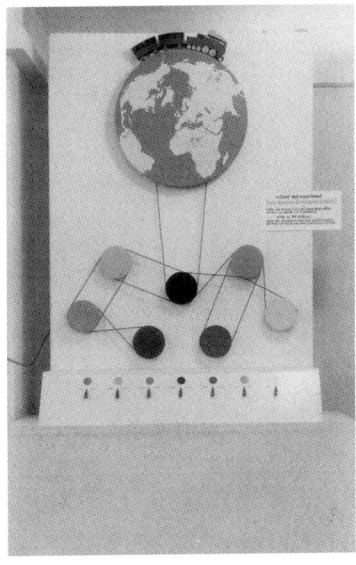

4.7 'What Was Paid for a Painting by Rembrandt at Different Times' (IC T1703), 1938. Each disc represents 500 guilders with the purchasing power of 1913.

4.8 Interactive apparatus designed by the Isotype team for the exhibition 'The Rolling Wheel', 1939.

ISOTYPE IN EXILE

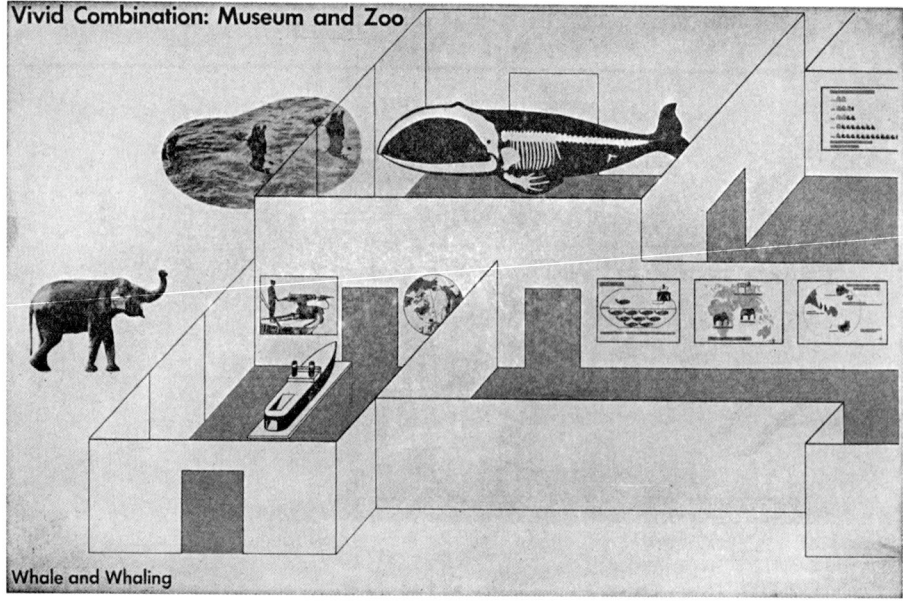

4.9 Photomontage envisioning a museum containing natural history exhibits combined with contextual information charts, c. 1939.

Such commissions were no doubt a welcome return to exhibition work, which had been central in Vienna. During his time in The Netherlands, Neurath seemed to have been developing ideas for 'Museums of the Future', which he had outlined in an article of that name in 1933. An example he gave to illustrate his concept was whaling, partly spurred by the lacking context of a great whale displayed in the New York Natural History Museum. In The Hague, the Isotype team made designs for a speculative exhibition, 'Around the Whale' (fig. 4.9), as Neurath explained (beginning with a suggestion that prefigures the infamous shark exhibit by artist Damien Hirst):

> How to make the whale a little more attractive? One presents only half of this animal, then you may look into his skeleton from his one side and at his skin from the other side. You may use one whale for two exhibitions in different places. Further, we may present the whale's ancestors and relatives, a family exhibit, then we may look at his body as a technical implement and compare his body with the body of fishes and other water animals, with submarines. We may show something of aerodynamics, too, presenting similarities and dissimilarities. We may present something about the distribution of whales on the earth. We prepared a simple world map for children, where they may see that the majority of the whales live in the southern seas. Then one may show how the Norwegians, the British and

others are hunting whales south of the equator. The amount of whale oil may be presented too, related to fat and oil from other sources. The various parts of a whale presented not from an anatomical point of view, but as sources of stays [corsets] of a lady, for perfumes, boots, and so on.[31]

The 'Around...' concept for showing socio-historical context was pursued with many suggested topics into the 1940s, mainly for publications, because no possibilities for such ambitious exhibition design ever arose again.

Escape to England

Near the end of 1939, Neurath wrote to Rudolf Carnap: 'I gladly take precautions, but I dislike retreating before I have to.'[32] He and Reidemeister stayed as long as possible in The Hague, considering it a kind of defeatism to leave in fear of invasion.[33] (Olga Neurath had died in 1937.) When Germany attacked the Netherlands on 10 May 1940, it became dangerous for foreigners to venture into the streets, and they no longer went to their office. When the Dutch surrender was announced on 14 May, they decided to leave, walking with conscious nonchalance to Scheveningen harbour to see if they could escape. (Gerd Arntz and other members of the team remained behind.)

Their passage to England was adventurous and perilous. They walked through the crowds of people attempting to purchase a place on a boat and, almost at the end of the harbour, they saw a small motorized lifeboat that was filling up with refugees. They recognized acquaintances among them and Neurath said 'that boat is the right one for us'.[34] They jumped into it from the quayside, among the last of forty-six passengers aboard a boat designed to hold a maximum of twenty-five people. It had been commandeered by some engineering students, who proceeded to set off in the general direction of Great Britain. During the night, passengers took turns looking out for mines: at least one suspicious, barrel-like object was spotted, and they steered clear of it. Neurath tried to keep spirits up by saying that England would need them all for the war effort – which, in his and Reidemeister's case, turned out be an accurate prediction.

Early the next day, a warship was spotted: luckily it was the British Royal Navy destroyer HMS Venomous, which took everyone on board. The captain confirmed that they had indeed passed through several minefields strung just below the surface of the water; the shallow draft of their boat had saved them. Venomous set the refugees ashore in Dover. They arrived just as mass internment of 'enemy aliens' began in Britain: both Neurath and Reidemeister were now reluctant citizens of the Third Reich and were taken into custody immediately. They were sent to separate internment camps on the Isle of Man, a small island in the Irish sea – a further perilous journey through rough waters. From the British government's point-of-view, they were kept at a safe distance from the mainland there, and internment camps were established in existing holiday houses, cordoned off by barbed wire.

In these camps, a remarkable microcosm of Central European culture congregated, with leading scientists, artists and writers among those in custody. Neurath and Reidemeister met some previous acquaintances there and made new friendships that continued after their release. Both of them were active in educational initiatives within the camps: Neurath lectured in the so-called 'popular university' organized by inmates. They made plans to get married (so that they would not be separated) and to carry on their work in visual education together. They were assisted by the Society for the Protection of Science and Learning, which campaigned for the release of exiled academics through the official channels. Yet their case was not so simple, and it took nearly eight months before they could be released; the decisive cause was an invitation for Neurath to give some guest lectures at Oxford University. In February 1941, they were freed from the camps and travelled to Oxford, where they remained for the duration of the war.

Making films for the British war effort

On being released, Neurath and Reidemeister wasted no time – first of all in getting married almost immediately, and then in starting to re-establish their Isotype work. Neurath wrote to Fleddérus:

> Here we are rebuilding our office, we found technical collaborators, bought now our own letter [printing] types, we are making scientific research, transformations etc, 'as once in May'. We received photostats from American friends and were therefore immediately after our release in a position to continue all our activities. We have many contacts with people here who are really interested in our visual, our logical and our scientific work. ... We like Oxford very much. We would prefer to stay and work here and to visit the U.S. from time to time only.[35]

No real jobs had yet materialized when he wrote this, but less than a month later Neurath was contacted by documentary filmmaker Paul Rotha with a request for help in making an 'animated symbolic explanation' of blood transfusion for a short information film:

> Having admired your work in pictorial symbolism for many years I feel that there is no-one more qualified to help us in this matter than yourself. If you are free to undertake such work, I should be glad if you would get in touch with me to discuss the matter.[36]

 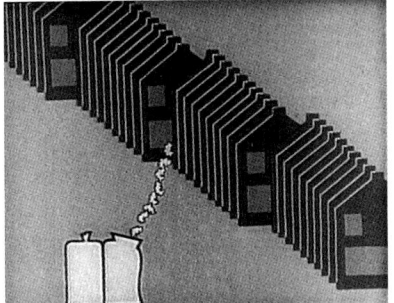

4.10 Stills from the animated film *A Few Ounces a Day*, 1941.

The Neuraths' advanced reputation now provided an opportunity for collaboration on films sponsored by the British Ministry of Information. Rotha knew *Modern Man in the Making*, and he perceived similarities between graphic design and filmmaking. Perhaps he was not aware that some films of animated Isotype had already been made in Vienna, and were once shown in London.[37] Neurath was interested in the potential of movies for mass communication, so he did not hesitate to agree to Rotha's request. After three years of working together, he told Rotha: 'We think the screen is an important part of our realm.'[38]

During the 1930s, there had been some resistance within the British film industry to émigrés being given work in film production. Rotha, however, welcomed their contribution; he was also a historian of film, having written *The Film Till Now* (1930), and no doubt his broad knowledge of continental film alerted him to important figures when they arrived in England. In addition to the Neuraths, he employed cinematographer Wolfgang Suschitzky, screenwriters Carl Mayer and Wolfgang Wilhelm, and composer Ernst Meyer.[39] (Rotha's surname implies that he was also not British, but he was in fact an Englishman, born Paul Thomson.)

The Neuraths designed animated inserts for short films in the documentary series *Worker and Warfront* (1942–6). These were not shown in cinemas, but in factory canteens to workers engaged in war production. An urgent project that initially took priority was a film about salvage for the MOI, to convince British householders not to waste material that could be useful for the war effort. This film, *A Few Ounces a Day*, consisted entirely of animation designed by the Neuraths, and was completed in a remarkably short time – it was released in October 1941 (fig. 4.10). Indeed, their work on it started so soon after their release from internment that they needed a special labour permit, which Rotha justified by writing that their services were 'indispensable' for this film, for which they would 'carry out 99% of the design work'.[40] The MOI agreed that the Neuraths' 'skilled services' were important for the production, reflecting a certainty in official circles of their loyalty to the British cause. The animation work itself was carried out under the supervision of Norman MacQueen at Science Films, which mainly worked for the Air Ministry.⁴¹ From early in their collaboration, Rotha and Neurath discussed the desirability of taking control of the animation procedure themselves by setting up their own animation table, but this never happened.

After the completion of *A Few Ounces a Day*, Arthur Elton of The MOI Film Division wrote to Rotha that Isotype was 'delightful' and that he was keen to use it again, although he became disenchanted when he discovered how costly it would be to include Isotype in subsequent productions.⁴² Elton spoke at the First Scientific Films Conference, held in August 1942 in London, at which Rotha films featuring Isotype were shown. A few months later, Neurath gave a talk in London to Elton, Arthur Calder-Marshall (a left-wing novelist and screenwriter, who handled MOI film production from 1943), Basil Wright and Edgar Anstey (both leading documentarians), and members of Rotha films. The idea was proposed by Rotha so that his colleagues could learn about Neurath's ideas and methods directly from him.

The two most substantial films directed by Paul Rotha including Isotype animation were *World of Plenty* (1943) and *Land of Promise* (1945), the first two parts of a loose trilogy about planning for wartime and its aftermath (the third was *The World is Rich*, 1947). In these films, Rotha originated a distinctive, dialectical style based on a tight combination of newly filmed scenes and interviews, stock footage, animated diagrams and multi-voice commentary. *World of Plenty* was mainly inspired by the views of Scottish nutritionist John Boyd Orr: its working title was 'Strategy of Food', and it dealt with the efficient exploitation and distribution of global food resources. A group of people contributed to the script, including Carl Mayer and Eric Knight, an Englishman then based in the USA, where the Hollywood film of his book *This Above All* was about to be released. Knight's voice can be heard on the soundtrack of *World of Plenty* as the 'man-in-the-street', a phrase often used by Neurath when writing about Isotype (fig. 4.11).⁴³ Indeed, Neurath was paid a monthly 'consultancy fee on script-work' for *World of Plenty*. Rotha later explained: 'The work of Dr. Neurath and his associates was not restricted to the designing of the Isotype sequences, their knowledge and experiences being invaluable in the general construction of the film.'⁴⁴ Neurath wrote to Rotha about his concept for the film:

> All material available is rough and often doubtful, but not, when we try to speak only in grand lines to the eyes. Food, Shelter, Entertainment, Education, etc. One could combine documentary material with animated diagrams, forming together a gigantic picture of the world. *Great Britain and the world*.⁴⁵

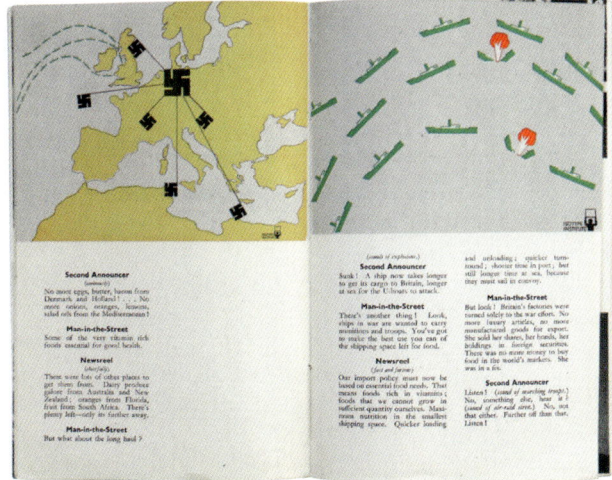

4.11 Cover and pages of *World of Plenty: the Book of the Film*, 1945. 227 × 147 mm. Animated charts from the film were adapted here for printing in colour, and were combined with the script and photographic stills.

Around the same time that *World of Plenty* was in production, Walt Disney produced a short movie on the same subject, *Food Will Win the War*. When Neurath saw it, he reported: 'I am depressed by seeing how he does not use the power that he has' but instead uses 'cheap jokes'.[46] Although both Rotha and Neurath appreciated the entertainment value of Disney's work, they felt that jokey treatment was inappropriate for educational graphics in movies. Rotha declared: 'Disney has no scientific mind or understanding of the diagram technique for education. Eric Knight wrote me that last year while he was with the Disney studios supervising some instructional films, but Knight also marvelled at the superb machinery at Disney's disposal and sighed to think what we could have done with it.'[47] It may have partly been Knight's experience there that inspired ironic comments in *World of Plenty* made by the doubting 'man-in-the-street': 'Healthy world trade! Yeah, you can prove anything with diagrams. Give me a half hour with Walt Disney and I could pay my income tax and never feel it.'[48]

World of Plenty was a very complex production logistically, with some scenes being filmed in America, and permissions required to excerpt scenes from other existing films. Isotype was an added complication, but Rotha felt it was an essential part of the film's rhetoric. Rotha requested extra budget to cover Isotype, but MOI officials were indignant that he had gone ahead and produced more Isotype animation than the budget allowed.[49] Calder-Marshall thought that animations in some of Rotha's short films were not 'worked out

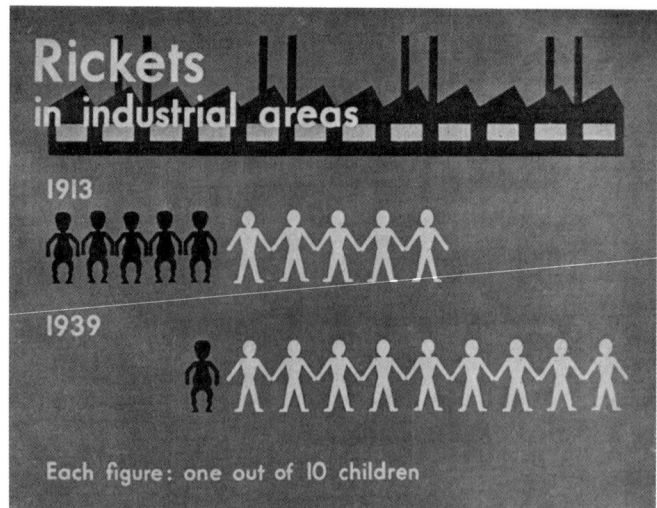

4.12 Still from an Isotype sequence in the film *World of Plenty*, 1943.

correctly visually' and that Isotype should be used sparingly, as a last resort, in *World of Plenty*.⁵⁰ Rotha retorted:

> We would point out that the Isotype sequences are not diagrams 'added to the film' because there was no documentary method expressing our meaning. They are an integral part of the film and dovetail in with the documentary sequences producing a new kind of visual technique. ... The Isotypes throughout are carefully fitted to the commentary.⁵¹

Some Isotype sequences could be tailored to fit existing dialogue, but others depended on commentary yet to be recorded, and so extra film had to be shot for insurance. Elton was not unsympathetic, but he objected to Rotha spending government money without prior authorization. The MOI refused to pay the Isotype Institute's fees for preliminary research on its work for films, so Rotha's company covered that expense. Elton considered Rotha to be too indulgent of Neurath and Isotype, describing his condition punningly as 'Neurathemia'.⁵² After the war, Rotha paid tribute to Neurath, 'who of all others I have met, understood most fully how the film could extend the consciousness of the international man-in-the-street'.⁵³

It was fortunate that Rotha appreciated Isotype work so highly and advocated its use for MOI films, but the division of labour involved in making the animation meant that Neurath was rarely satisfied with the results. He was not convinced that movement was always an educational advantage, sometimes complaining that the Isotype action moved too quickly. 'Isotype should avoid vague and "sliding" shades', he declared, in resistance to the inherent potential of movies.⁵⁴

In early May 1943, a special screening of *World of Plenty* was held at Colwyn Bay for senior officials on the supply side of the Ministry of Food. F. J. H. Corbyn (an administrative official at Unilever) reacted that it was 'magnificent ... so simple and yet so compelling ... Surely to goodness a film like that should be shown in every cinema in the country.'⁵⁵ The public premiere of the film took place at the United Nations Conference on Food and Agriculture in Hot Springs, Virginia (18 May to 3 June 1943), where it was greeted with much applause and approval.⁵⁶

At the end of May 1943, a private screening for the press was organized by the MOI, resulting in many positive newspaper reviews. The *New Statesman* represented the general tone:

> *World of Plenty* is much more than a first class documentary. It is a political event. It is the first satisfactory use of modern technique to explain to the public one of the great world problems about which common people as well as statesmen and technicians must be compelled to think. *World of Plenty* is a front-page story and a leading article thrown at the heads of cinemagoers.⁵⁷

The Minister of Information, Brendan Bracken, recommended in parliament that *World of Plenty* be shown widely in cinemas. The MOI paid a sum equivalent to one tenth of the film's budget to Paramount for its commercial distribution.⁵⁸

In October 1943, preparation began for a 'planning film', which became *Land of Promise*. Wolfgang Wilhelm and Ara Calder-Marshall (wife of Arthur) were working on a draft of the script, but Rotha planned to visit Oxford to consult Neurath about it. Neurath hoped that the 'planning film ... will be something of importance', but he added cautiously, 'this time, we should try to make the Isotypes walking more slowly' [sic].⁵⁹ The film suggests that wartime economic measures could be effectively adapted to peacetime, an idea which Neurath had first written about decades earlier with respect to the First World War. *Land of Promise* is less international in scope than *World of Plenty*, concentrating largely on proposals for post-war housing: it was finally subtitled 'an argument about our homes and houses', echoing the way Neurath referred to Isotype charts as 'visual arguments'. It featured the same multi-voice commentary technique and dialectical structure as the earlier film, but this time Isotype itself was given a voice. Neurath wanted this to be an 'artificial' voice created by a Vocoder – there was one such device in the UK, but this idea proved unworkable and Isotype was instead given a dispassionate, male voice (similar to another voice in the film that utters facts from parliamentary records).⁶⁰

Land of Promise was not shown as widely as *World of Plenty*, but it received generally positive press notices: the *News Chronicle*'s reviewer felt that the

Isotype diagrams 'stole the film', while *The Times* noted how the animated diagrams were woven tightly into the film's argument.[61] Rotha attempted to use the film to influence policy in the new Labour government that was elected soon after the war. He showed it to the President of the Board of Trade, Stafford Cripps, who especially praised the Isotypes, and he hoped to arrange a showing to Aneurin Bevan, Health Minister (also in charge of housing), and Prime Minister Clement Attlee.[62] But the film was not utilized by the Labour leadership due to political uncertainty and indecision.

Wartime books of 'soft propaganda'

The Isotype animation of the 1940s seems more dated now than contemporary printed work, despite film being a more modern medium: the black-and-white films have survived in scratchy prints (the celluloid available during the war was often of poor quality), whereas colour Isotype charts that appeared in books during wartime still seem fresh and contemporary. The Isotype Institute did such work almost exclusively for one publishing enterprise, Adprint, which also received a subsidy for its publications from the MOI. However, it was not a publisher in the traditional sense: it was one of the first 'book packagers', planning and producing an illustrated book, which was then sold for an agreed price to a publisher that stocked and marketed it. Adprint commissioned an author and an illustrator or photographer, who worked with an in-house team in producing a book. Adprint treated the Isotype Institute as something more than just an illustrator, instead recognizing it as a kind of author (as Rotha had done); indeed Neurath often demanded such recognition. He was fortunate to find sympathetic ears in the directors of Adprint, who were also Austrian émigrés – Wolfgang Foges and Walter Neurath (no relation to Otto). Foges, in particular, ensured that the Institute was well paid for its work, and Walter Neurath brought expertise in print production (he went on to establish the publisher Thames & Hudson with his wife Eva).

Adprint first approached the Isotype Institute in March 1942 about a projected series on 'America and Britain', to explore the commonalities and differences between these allies (fig. 4.13). The MOI considered such publications to be useful for the British war effort: they were a kind 'soft propaganda', giving cultural information to readers in Britain and in allied and neutral countries. This was not 'black propaganda' purporting to be produced in Germany and intended to undermine the enemy. That kind of material was produced by secret organizations, not by the MOI, which preferred the term 'publicity' over 'propaganda', in order to distinguish cultural content from political content. The MOI covertly subsidized certain books by providing paper, which was strictly rationed during the war. It favoured pictorial editions with mass

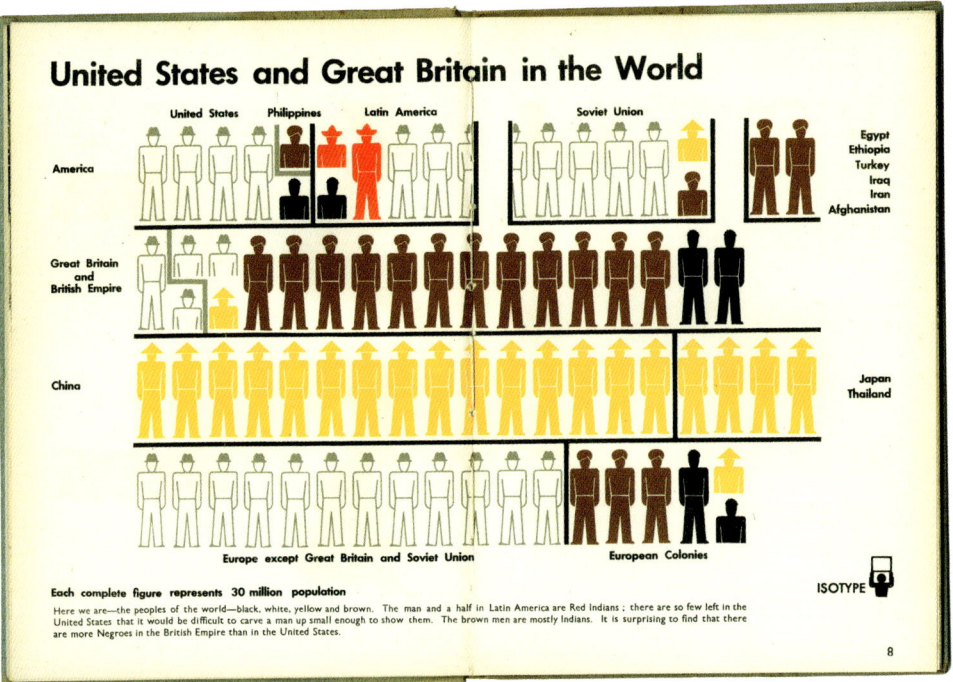

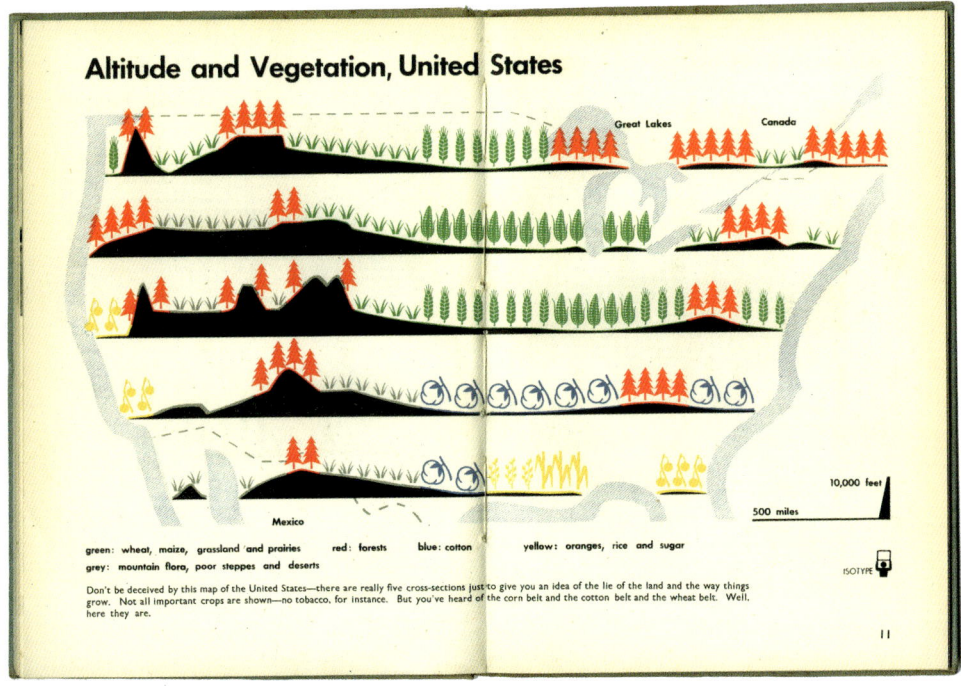

4.13 Pages from the first book in the series 'America and Britain': Lella Secor Florence, *Only an Ocean Between*, 1943. 228 × 167 mm.

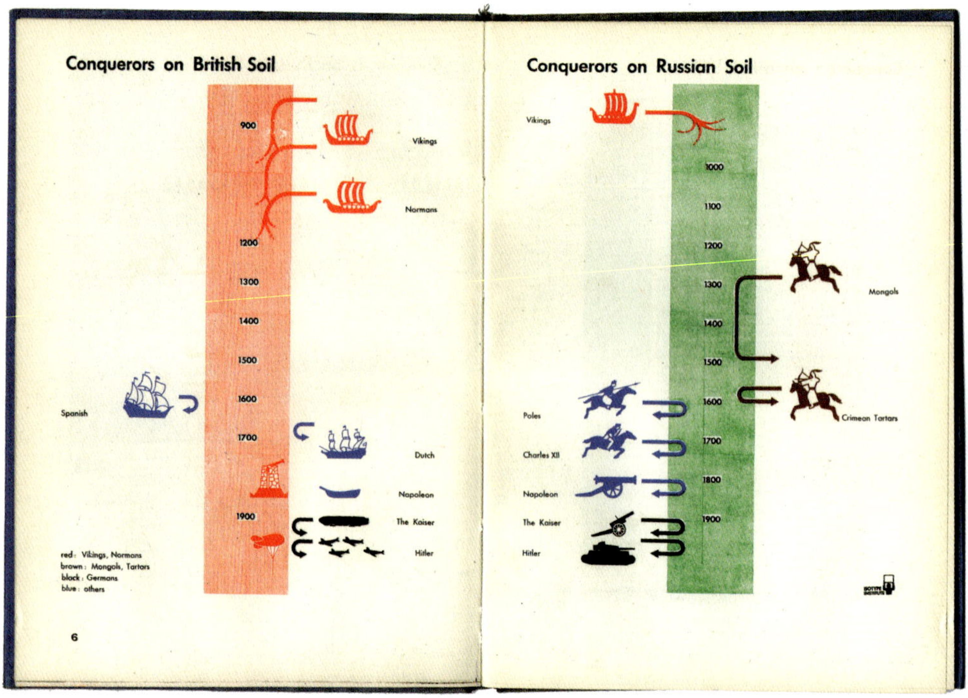

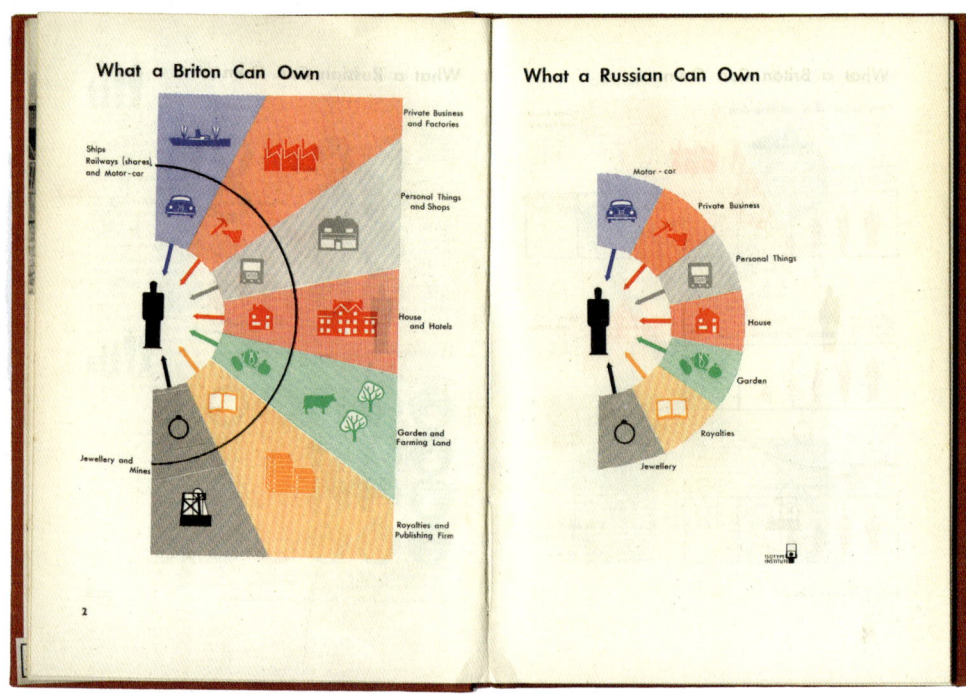

4.14 Pages from books in the series 'The Soviets and Ourselves': Maurice Lovell, *Landsmen and Seafarers*, 1945; and Ralph Parker, *How do you do tovarish?*, 1947. 228 × 167 mm.

appeal – precisely the kind of book that Adprint hoped to produce, containing Isotype charts and photographic illustrations.

The US Embassy also seems to have subsidized these publications, and the American writer and feminist Lella Secor Florence, who was assistant to the ambassador, wrote two of the three books in the series; her husband Philip Sargant Florence, also an American and a professor of commerce at Birmingham University, served as editor of all three. The Isotype Institute worked together happily with the Florences, and there was a mutual exchange of useful ideas. The Isotype charts for the series presented not only picture-statistical information about population and economy, but also cross-section maps and climate diagrams. The official subsidies allowed extensive colour printing, with up to six colours (solid, unmixed inks, not four-colour process) used for certain Isotype charts. Neurath insisted: 'I see no way to reduce these colours without reducing the stimulating power of the charts.' He gave his book *Modern Man in the Making* as a reference for the desired colours.[63]

In summer 1943, a second series of books was initiated to compare and contrast Britain with its other major ally at that time, the USSR. 'The Soviets and Ourselves' was similarly sponsored by the MOI, which had been producing positive information about the USSR since it joined the Allies in summer 1941 (fig. 4.14). This was a more delicate matter than it was with the USA, because the British government retained a view of communism as being dangerous. Its objective was partly to 'steal the thunder' of propaganda from the British Communist Party, thereby avoiding overtly political indoctrination of the British public in favour of Soviet Communism. The Soviet Relations Division of the MOI liaised with Adprint and Isotype about these publications through its director Peter Smollett.[64] He seems to have been inspired partly by the Izostat publication *USSR*, produced for the 1939 New York World's Fair, with pictorial statistics by El Lissitzky (after the Viennese connection with Izostat had been severed). The three editions of the Adprint 'Soviets' series encountered some delays in production, with the first being published in 1945.

Before any editions of these two series were completed, another job took priority in Isotype work for Adprint: a pictorial booklet summarizing the Beveridge report, the blueprint for the welfare state that would develop in Britain after the Second World War. From the moment of its publication in November 1942, the report – titled *Social Insurance and Allied Services* – began to rally public opinion in favour of state-supported welfare. It recommended a comprehensive insurance scheme for health, unemployment, and old-age pensions, along with universal family benefit payments. Its author, Sir William Beveridge, became a national hero overnight, and his name remains synonymous with this report. An abridged version of it (published by the government) became a bestseller, and the MOI obviously recognized that such a remarkable

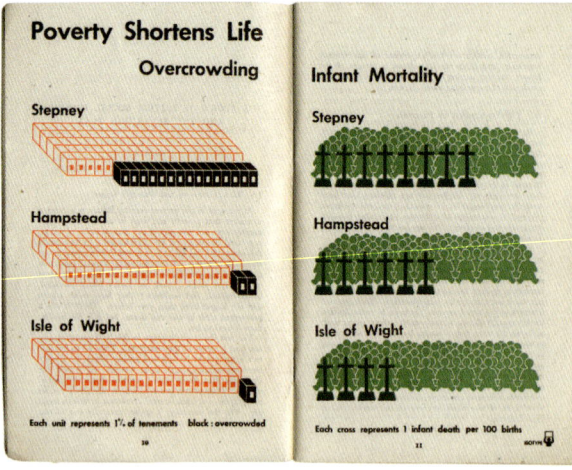
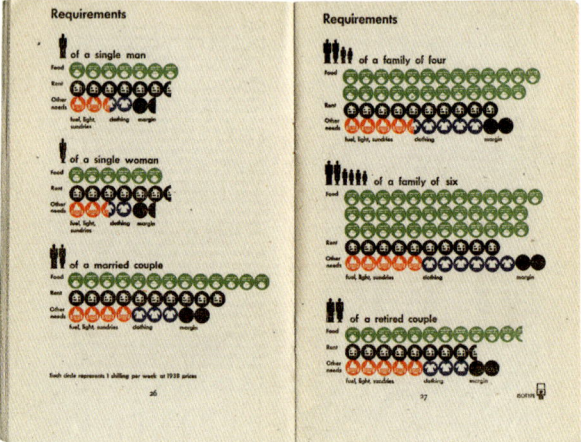

4.15 Cover and pages from *Social Security: the Story of British Social Progress and the Beveridge Plan* (London: Harrap, 1943). 185 × 124 mm.

piece of planning, carried out at the height of war, had positive propaganda value.

Discussions for a pictorial summary of the report began almost immediately, and it was published in 1943 with the title *Social Security*. The text was written by Ronald Davison, a senior civil servant, and the cover stated prominently 'visualized by Isotype' – an early use of the term 'visualize', perhaps, with reference to graphic design. The Isotype charts created a kind of parallel narrative running alongside Davison's text, including a historical dimension about the change in living standards since 1900. The theme of social welfare connected it directly to early examples of the Vienna Method produced for the Viennese municipal government.

Social Security was the first significant example of Isotype printed in Britain, and it shows signs of working out technical issues of reproduction on a new basis (fig. 4.15). The Isotype team were lucky to have the expert assistance of Walter Neurath in shepherding their designs into print. The booklet was printed

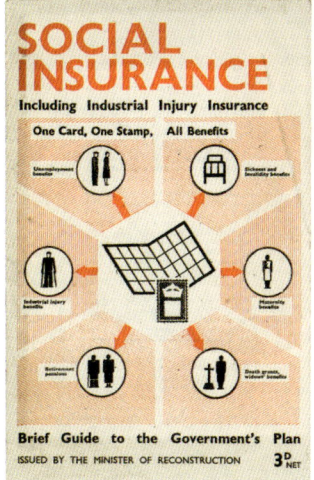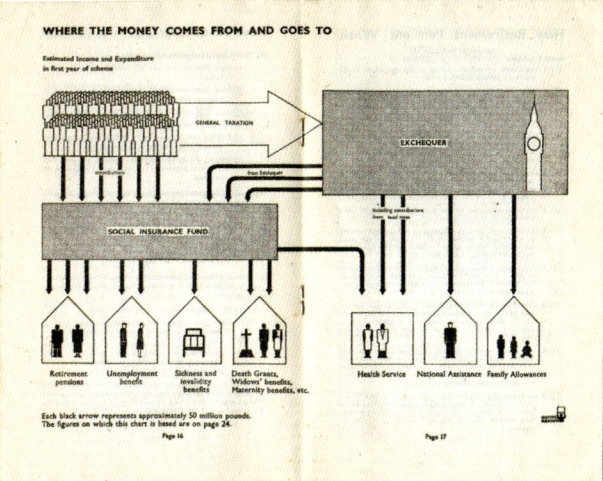

4.16 Cover and pages from *Social Insurance, Including Industrial Injury Insurance: Brief Guide to the Government's Plan* (London: His Majesty's Stationery Office, 1944). 210 × 138 mm.

on rather rough paper, no doubt due to wartime shortages, but this was remedied in several translated editions that were published in 1944. French, Dutch and Italian versions (all with the same Isotype charts) were issued in rather large numbers, apparently in preparation for the reoccupation of Europe.

Prime Minister Winston Churchill was at first reluctant to commit to implementing Beveridge's plan, but he finally acceded, resulting in the government White Paper on social insurance in 1944. The Isotype Institute also provided charts and diagrams for an official summary of this White Paper, published by the government under the imprint of His Majesty's Stationery Office (HMSO). Adprint was again the mediator, and on 17 April 1944, Foges summoned Neurath to a meeting the next day at the Home Office to discuss an 'urgent government job'. Charts and diagrams for the booklet *Social Insurance* had to be designed and printed during the next two months: the resulting booklet was less lavish, with a second colour only on its cover, but nevertheless it sparked some controversy in parliamentary discussions (fig. 4.16).

Imitators in Britain

An Isotype chart from *Social Insurance* was adapted and modified for publication in the tabloid newspaper, the *Daily Mail*, with some cartoonish details added. Neurath was annoyed about this: 'Our matters are much hurt by the vulgarization of our charts … What could be done in this case?', he asked Foges.[65] The work on publications and films sponsored by the MOI had raised the profile of Isotype and certainly encouraged some imitations. In the 1930s, before the Neuraths arrived, statistical graphics showing the vague influence of Isotype had already been produced in Britain. For example, some illustrations in the multi-volume *History of English Life* (1936) utilized the principle of repeated pictograms, but diluted it with contradictory illustrative devices (fig. 4.17). Neurath always complained that such work generally lacked the depth of research and rigour behind Isotype, which was ensured by the central task of transformation – now almost exclusively performed by Marie Neurath.

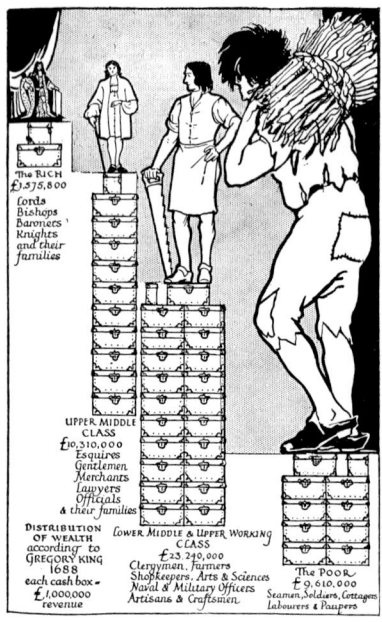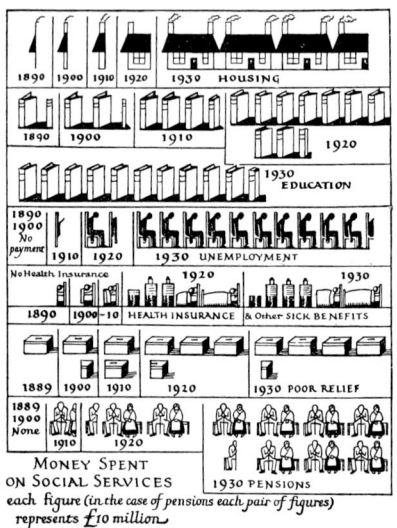

4.17 Two examples of 'graphic statistics' by Wilma Hickson from A. Williams-Ellis and F. J. Fisher, *History of English Life* (London: Methuen, 1936).

Stills of Isotype charts from *World of Plenty* were reproduced in a book by John Boyd Orr, *Food and the People* (1943), published by Pilot Press in its series 'Target for Tomorrow'. Neither Rotha nor Neurath had granted permission for this, and both were annoyed by it – especially given that the editorial board for this series consisted of Orr, Julian Huxley and William Beveridge. This book also featured pictorial charts in pseudo Isotype-style, but lacked Isotype's consistency. Other books in the series included more pictorial statistics, some co-designed by Leonard Beaumont, a pioneer of linocut technique in Britain, and J. F. Horrabin, a socialist writer and artist who had previously illustrated books by H. G. Wells and Lancelot Hogben (fig. 4.18).

Some interest in Isotype work was shown by F. H. K. Henrion, who went on to become one of Britain's most successful graphic designers. Neurath had met Henrion in internment on the Isle of Man, and met him again in London

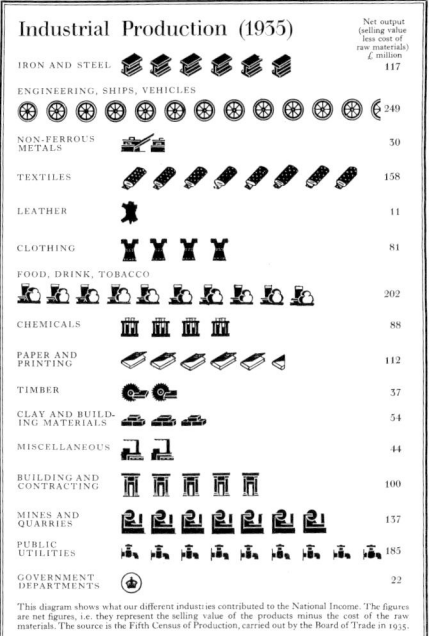
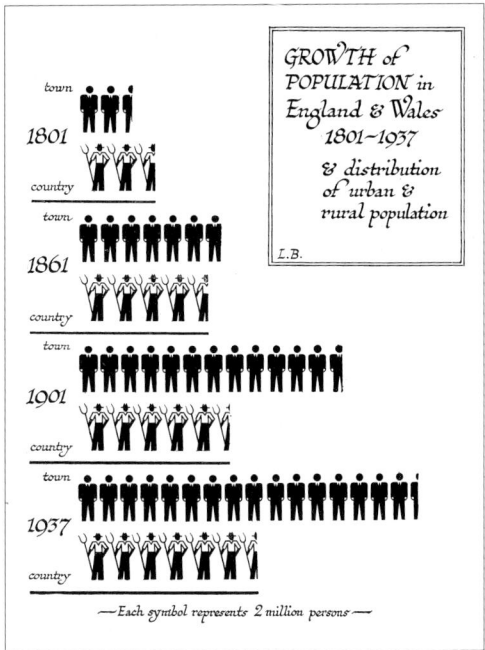

4.18 Charts from books in the series 'Target for Tomorrow': (left) designed by Douglas Robertson, from Charles Madge, *Industry After the War* (1943); and (right) designed by Leonard Beaumont, from P. Poole and F. Stephenson, *A Plan for Town and Country* (1944), where the pictograms have stylistic affinities with those in work by Rudolf Modley (see fig. 7.9).

while they were both doing work for the MOI during the war. Henrion wanted to know what charts the Isotype Institute had 'in stock' so that he could use 'appropriate ones and so avoid duplicating both research and designing'.[66] Nothing came of this, but Henrion went on to collaborate with the Isotype Institute on the periodical *Future* after the war (see chapter 6).

Charts on the subject of urban planning that emulated Isotype were featured in the popular booklet of *The County of London Plan* (1945) by E. J. Carter and Hungarian émigré architect Ernő Goldfinger, who is likely to have known earlier examples of the Vienna Method. Statistical graphics close to the spirit of Isotype had also been included in the book *When We Build Again* (1941), based on research into living conditions in Birmingham by the Bournville Trust (fig. 4.19). Bournville was a model community created to house workers of the Cadbury's chocolate factory, and Otto Neurath had given a talk there in 1933. Since then, he had been in contact with the Cadbury family about visual presentation of statistics in its publications. He wrote to Paul Cadbury:

> The style of your books is based on the principle: pictures explain text and depend upon it. Our style is different. That is the reason, why a specially

4.19 Chart from *When We Build Again*, 1941.

skilled staff is needed for making ISOTYPES, who learned our language for 'writing purposes' (the reading of Isotypes is very simple, as you have seen). Isotype making is like map making. It needs years of training, like the learning of a foreign language (as I see everyday, unfortunately).[67]

Examples of pictorial statistics that closely resembled Isotype were produced by Research Services Ltd, a mysterious organization in London, which apparently recognized the importance of the research behind its work. It produced a series of posters in the 1940s on economic and social themes, adopting certain organizational principles from Isotype (fig. 4.20). There seems to have been no exchange between this enterprise and the Isotype Institute, which nevertheless collected many examples of its rival's work. Work that borrowed some elements of Isotype continued to be produced by others into the 1950s, often to the annoyance of Marie Neurath, but there was no legal protection of the method, which raised some interesting issues (see chapter 6).

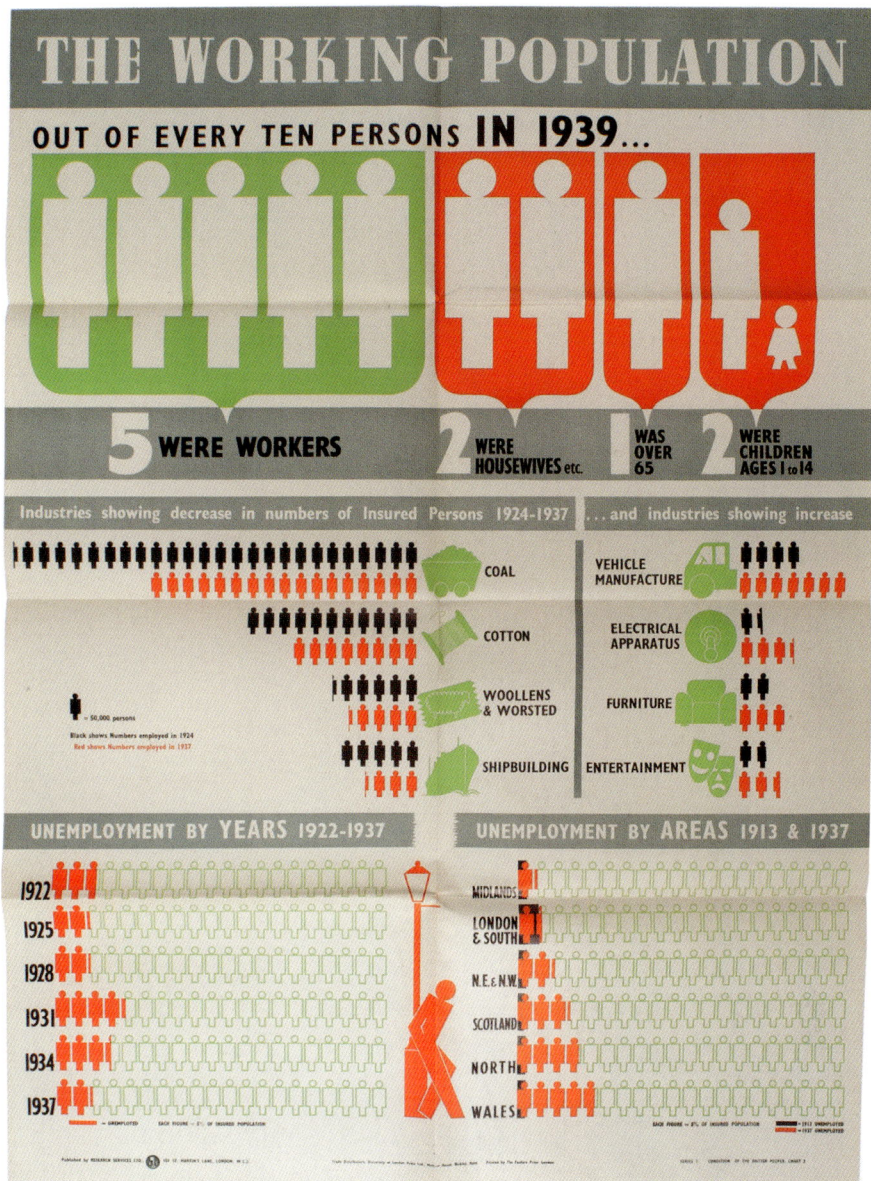

4.20 Large-format poster by Research Services Ltd, c. 1946.

5 The Austrian Social and Economic Museum after 1945

Re-establishment: conflicts, controversies and continuities

On 9 May 1945 – one day after the Second World War ended in Europe – Eduard Trautenegg convened a general assembly to reactivate the Austrian Institute for Pictorial Statistics, which had been founded under Austrofascism and renamed under National Socialism, when he became its director. However, since the Nazi functionaries who had been active at the Institute disappeared at war's end, only a secretary seemed to have been present apart from Trautenegg. Due to his involvement in National Socialism, but also for reasons of association law, there was mistrust of this project at the Viennese municipal authority. The head of the department responsible for culture stated that Trautenegg was obviously still 'completely caught up in the *Führer* principle of the past era', pointed to his role in Nazi propaganda and made a motion to remove him as director of the re-established institute.[1] Yet this did not happen. With the support of the conservative-dominated Ministry of Education, Trautenegg was able to resume his activities in post-war Vienna as director of the Austrian Institute for Pictorial Statistics.

Parallel to these developments, former staff of the Social and Economic Museum tried to reconnect with the visual education work of inter-war Vienna. Custodian Josef Jodlbauer and architect Edith Matzalik (who had worked there as a graphic technician) attempted to resume the work of the former Museum soon after the end of the war by approaching various offices and organizations – in particular, the Social Democrat Party of Austria (SPÖ), the Vienna city government and the Chamber of Labour.[2] The Viennese Deputy Mayor and SPÖ member of Parliament Paul Speiser, who had been chairman of the Social and Economic Museum until 1934, was entrusted with the reactivation of the Museum's association; but, due to his death in November 1947, the initial deadline for this was missed. However, Eduard Trautenegg, as director of the successor institute active up to 1945, also obtained the right of disposal over the association's assets.[3]

In order to oppose Trautenegg's claim to legal succession and to the association's assets, the Austrian Institute for Social and Economic Statistics was founded in June 1948 on the initiative of Franz Rauscher, a Social Democrat politician, resistance fighter and former student of Otto Neurath. The new institute's chairman was Vienna's deputy mayor Karl Honay (SPÖ), and Rauscher himself became director. Thus two prominent socialist politicians advocated the re-foundation of the Social and Economic Museum from the years of 'Red Vienna': the visual education work of that time, not the propaganda work for the dictatorial regime from 1934 onwards, was to be continued.[4] Only three days later, Franz Rauscher described the complex set of events and problems to Marie Neurath. He told her that the sponsors of the association until 1934 had to re-establish it because it was not yet legally possible to withdraw the claim to succession of the Social and Economic Museum from Trautenegg's association. However, he let it be known that this would happen soon. The board of the institute Rauscher had co-founded consisted of functionaries from the workers' movement and former students of Otto Neurath – namely the economic advisor to the Chamber of Labour Stefan Wirlander, the SPÖ city councillor Adolf Planek and the member of Parliament Alfred Porges.[5]

According to a document presumably written by Rauscher himself, the assets of the Social and Economic Museum were located in two places: in the Neue Hofburg (Imperial court buildings) in Vienna's city centre, where the Trautenegg Institute was based, and in premises at the municipal building Am Fuchsenfeld, where a branch of the original Museum had been established under Neurath.[6] Rauscher explained that a 'lot of material and furnishings' had survived and these were now in the possession of Trautenegg's institute. Rauscher aimed to recover it for the resumption of work connected to the history of workers' education in Red Vienna, but discussions between the two rivals were uncooperative and had remained fruitless. Rauscher also intended that the People's Hall would once again serve as the Museum's exhibition space, but this seems never to have happened.[7]

So, in the immediate post-war years, there were two opposing institutes that represented the two dominant political camps in conflict after 1945: Social Democrat against Christian conservative. This became particularly clear when conservative politician Julius Raab – like Trautenegg a former Heimwehr leader and later Austrian Federal Chancellor – became president of the Austrian Institute for Pictorial Statistics, with other members of the Österreichische Volkspartei (Austrian People's Party) joining its board of trustees.[8] But only one of the two institutions was ultimately able to succeed the Social and Economic Museum of inter-war Vienna. In August 1949, Vienna City Councillor Viktor Matejka (of the Communist Party) complained in a newspaper article that the rightful successor to Otto Neurath's Social and Economic Museum

5.1 Visiting card of the Austrian Social and Economic Museum, c. 1953. It is presented here as a direct continuation of the inter-war Museum founded by Otto Neurath, and of the 'Vienna Method of Pictorial Statistics'. The reformed museum was initially based in temporary offices, as can be seen from the overprinted change of address here. (Both of these initial addresses were very close to the offices and workshops of the previous Museum in Vienna's fifteenth district.)

had still not received back the valuable holdings from before 1934, which had been unlawfully appropriated, and he asserted the need to continue Neurath's scientific and educational legacy.[9]

In the same year, a court ruled that the assets of Trautenegg's institute had to be returned to that of Rauscher.[10] This was renamed the Austrian Social and Economic Museum in August 1949, establishing the claim to heredity of Otto Neurath's Museum by name. Franz Rauscher was appointed managing director.[11] It was not until 1952 that the competing Austrian Institute for Pictorial Statistics was dissolved and its assets liquidated.[12] The previous year, an article had appeared in the communist daily newspaper *Der Abend* which criticized Rauscher's Museum for its 'amateurish methods' and accused the Viennese 'City Hall Socialists' of having hesitated too long to stop the activities of Trautenegg. The latter had, after all, used the material of the Social and Economic Museum for about fifteen years and was now receiving 40,000 schillings for it from 'excessively good-natured director Rauscher'.[13] It is unclear where such detailed information came from, but the unidentified author seemed to have access to an internal source.

The Austrian Social and Economic Museum was in search of a new location for many years: it had occupied three different addresses in Vienna before it moved in 1962 to a former school building in Vogelsanggasse in Vienna's fifth district, where it is still located today (fig. 5.1). A business studio was attached

5.2 Contemporary postcard of Otto Wagner's Kaiser Pavilion at Hietzing city railway station, a venue for special exhibitions of the Austrian Social and Economic Museum. Sent by Franz Rauscher to Marie Neurath.

to the Museum, and there was also a secondary location for special exhibitions in the Hietzing city railway station. The Kaiser Pavilion there was set up as a popular education centre with the support of the Lower Austrian Chamber of Labour and the Austrian Federation of Trade Unions. The Österreichische Forschungsstelle für Gemeinwirtschaft (Austrian Research Centre for Social Economy), in which Rauscher was active, also cooperated with the Austrian Social and Economic Museum and was based in the Hietzing pavilion (fig. 5.2).

Three years before the (re)founding of the Austrian Social and Economic Museum, the exhibition 'Niemals vergessen!' (Never forget!) had been shown in the Vienna Künstlerhaus from September to December 1946. This exhibition presented the German occupation of Austria in a negative light and, peculiarly, Trautenegg's Austrian Institute for Pictorial Statistics was significantly involved in it.[14] Günter von Baszel and Alois Fischer both worked on this anti-fascist project, as they had on the Nazi propaganda exhibition 'Das Sowjetparadies' during the war.[15] This reflected the contradictory and problematic nature of this exhibition, for which Viktor Matejka (Vienna city councillor for culture) bore the main political responsibility, and the artist and graphic designer Victor Slama bore the main creative responsibility. 'People who had been involved in anti-Bolshevik exhibitions of Nazi propaganda were now drawing, pasting and mounting an anti-fascist exhibition under the direction of the socialist [Slama] appointed by a communist city councillor', is how Heidrun-Ulrike Wenzel succinctly and aptly describes the scene.[16] After Vienna, the exhibition was shown in Linz and Innsbruck. In Vienna alone it was seen by around 250,000 people, including 50,000 registered National Socialists.[17] Even *The Times* of London took note of the exhibition; its correspondent described it as an evident legacy of Otto Neurath's work: 'The Viennese skill in pictorializing fact, which the late Professor Neurath pioneered and which has since been copied everywhere, has produced something, in the Anti-Fascist Exhibition, which Austria should take a long time to forget.'[18]

The case of Alois Fischer

The Social and Economic Museum and the Vienna Method of Pictorial Statistics formed an emancipatory project that was linked to Red Vienna in many ways. It was about access to education, social enlightenment and improving the living conditions of working people. With the events of February 1934, the suppression of the workers' uprising and the final establishment of a dictatorship, the possibilities of such visual educational work came to an end. 'None of our long-standing collaborators agreed to work under the new regime,' wrote Marie Neurath in retrospect.[19] She was wrong on this point, because obviously not all of Neurath's collaborators were anchored in the Social Democrat camp, and at least some joined authoritarian and fascist tendencies.

A look at continuities and discontinuities of personnel reveals a contradictory picture: for example, Josef Scheer and Alois Fischer, former members of Neurath's team, worked at the Austrian Institute for Pictorial Statistics, which was re-established in 1945. Scheer wrote to Marie Neurath in 1947 that he had returned to the 'old parent institute', which contradicted the facts. His sympathies for National Socialism had apparently been known to the Isotype team, with which he had worked in the Netherlands. Marie Neurath wrote to Gerd Arntz in 1946 that when the Germans marched into the Netherlands, she herself had said to Scheer 'there are your friends'.[20]

The economic statistician Alois Fischer had been a long-time collaborator of Otto Neurath, and subsequently worked with both dictatorial regimes that followed the end of parliamentary democracy in Austria: Austrofascism until 1938, and National Socialism until 1945. However, he continued his work without interruption even after 1945. His career appears to be a prime example of politically opportunistic behaviour: successive, opposing political systems never caused an interruption of his work, but instead brought about a continuous process of adaptation to new political requirements, which apparently went smoothly. According to Franz Rauscher, Fischer was one of the 'first collaborators' in Neurath's team.[21] Among other things, he was involved in the work for the atlas *Gesellschaft und Wirtschaft* (1930), and Neurath seemed to value his statistical expertise. In both Neurath's lecture to the Amsterdam congress on 'World Social Economic Planning' (1931) and his article 'World Planning and the USA' (1932), Fischer's agricultural calculations are cited approvingly.[22] Furthermore, in the preface to his book *Bildstatistik nach Wiener Methode in der Schule* (1933), Neurath explicitly mentioned Fischer as one of the specialists who worked for the Social and Economic Museum.[23] So this was obviously a loyal employee who accompanied Neurath's Museum from its beginnings to its end.

Fischer's activities under Austrofascism and National Socialism have already been examined in chapter 3. However, it should be reiterated that his work between 1934 and 1945 did not merely entail statistical calculations or graphic processing of more or less 'neutral' content, but rather active participation in Nazi propaganda, which became clear not least through his textual contributions written in the language of the Third Reich.

A two-part article by Fischer published in 1925, 'Zur Tragfähigkeit des Lebensraums' (On the Sustainability of Living Space), already shows his closeness to distinctly *völkisch* concepts. Prompted by declining birth rates in Berlin and Vienna, he names 'greed for money' and 'laziness' as 'the real causes of the death of peoples', in which he sees 'the only danger for the future of the white race'.[24] Throughout the regime changes, Fischer continued his contributions to the pan-German oriented periodical *Zeitschrift für Geopolitik* (Journal for Geopolitics). His last article from 1941 harmonized linguistically and ideologically with National Socialism: Fischer welcomed the rejuvenation of 'the old cultural people of the Germans'; he also registered 'the flushing out of foreign elements in large numbers from the territory of the Reich, especially Czechs, Poles and Jews', as well as a strategy for 'reverse Germanization of the new parts of the Reich'.[25] Already in his book *Quo vadis, Europa?* (1933 – several years before National Socialism came to power in Austria), he differentiated between 'high-value', 'medium-value', 'moderately high-value', 'low-value' and 'primitive' races – unsurprisingly, the 'Nordic race' was at the top – and added reflections on the 'problem' of racial mixtures.[26]

This makes it all the more remarkable that Fischer continued his work in the early days of post-fascist Austria – in particular on the anti-fascist exhibition 'Niemals vergessen!' During the period of reconstruction, he was an employee of the Austrian Institute for Pictorial Statistics, which (as detailed previously) was re-established in 1945 with personnel from the Nazi era.[27] He also wrote the text for a brochure (published in English) by the newly founded, conservative-oriented Austrian Cultural Association, which was intended to convey the history and culture of Vienna to an international audience.[28] It was surprisingly elaborate for a publication from the war-torn Vienna of 1946. The complete omission of the two dictatorships (1934–8 and 1938–45) is particularly striking in Fischer's historical overview. His colleague at the Austrian Institute for Pictorial Statistics, Günter von Baszel, was responsible for the design of the publication.

Alois Fischer probably died in Vienna in 1952.[29]

Otto Neurath's student: Franz Rauscher

Born in Vienna in 1900, Franz Rauscher had been involved in the Social Democratic Party and trade union movement since his early youth. He studied in the first cohort of the Arbeiterhochschule (Workers' College) in 1926, where he heard lectures by Otto Neurath, among others. This was probably the most important reason why, after 1945, he would always refer to himself as a 'student' of Neurath. But he also attended the 1931 World Social Economic Congress in Amsterdam, where Neurath gave a lecture. Rauscher was active in many areas of the workers' movement, including education, as director of the Vienna Parteischule ([Social Democratic] Party school) from 1927 to 1934.

After the Social Democratic Party was banned in February 1934, Rauscher belonged to the leadership of the illegal party, and was arrested by the Austro-fascist authorities in October 1934.[30] He was one of the defendants in the 1936 'socialist trial', and was then sent to the Wöllersdorf detention camp for a year, being released in autumn 1937 after three years in captivity.[31] After the National Socialists seized power, Rauscher was first imprisoned by the Gestapo in 1938, and was arrested again shortly before the beginning of the war.[32] He spent most of the Nazi period imprisoned in the concentration camps Buchenwald, Lublin-Maydanek and Jamlitz-Lieberose. Later, he summed up that he had spent a total of ninety-nine months of his life in prisons and concentration camps.[33] At the beginning of 1945, he was transferred to Stadtroda (Jena), from where he managed to escape.

After the war, Rauscher played a leading role in building up the SPÖ in Salzburg.[34] In his curriculum vitae, he referred to the fact that he became acquainted with Dyno Lowenstein after the arrival of the US troops. Lowenstein possessed an 'Eisenhower passport' allowing free movement, and the two went on several trips in a military jeep.[35] Their meeting is remarkable because Lowenstein also worked in the tradition of Isotype. The son of a Berlin socialist, he had become an officer of the OSS (Office of Strategic Services) in the USA and, in this capacity, he organized an espionage project in the Nazi-occupied area (Operation Greenup). After the end of the war, he produced pictorial statistics for the *New York Times*, and later took over the Pictograph Corporation in the USA (for more on this, see chapter 7).[36]

In the immediate post-war period, Rauscher initially seemed to embark on a party-political career. He was part of the SPÖ government team: until December 1945 he was Undersecretary of State in the Provisional Government of Renner, and from March 1946 to January 1947 he was Secretary of State in the Federal Ministry for Property Security and Economic Planning. In 1945 and 1946 he also worked as Central Secretary of the SPÖ, and from 1945 to 1949 he was also a member of Parliament. He was involved in the policy areas of nationalization, socialization and the social economy, which were particularly important to him. Rauscher was thus an experienced, loyal and politically versed functionary in his prime, whose socialist convictions were completely beyond question. It is not clear why the Party did not assign him a central role after the early years of the Second Republic. The communist daily *Der Abend* considered Rauscher to have been 'shunted off' to the function of director of the Austrian Social and Economic Museum. Was this a strategy of the Party leadership or did Rauscher himself no longer want to play a key political role? Were his clearly formulated views on economic planning, nationalization, and democratization of the economy too radical?[37]

After 1945, Rauscher was invited to give lectures at the Hochschule für Welthandel (World Trade College, where he had been a temporary guest student during Austrofascism), and also acted as an examiner for its diploma exams. However, he resigned this function in 1965 'because of a Nazi professor (B.)', as he noted in his curriculum vitae.[38] He referred to the so-called 'Borodajkewycz affair', which climaxed in that year. Taras Borodajkewycz, a professor at the World Trade College, had been making National Socialist and anti-Semitic statements for years. During demonstrations for and against Borodajkewycz, the first political fatality of the Second Republic occurred on 31 March 1965: a former communist resistance fighter was knocked down by a right-wing extremist student and succumbed to his injuries a few days later.[39]

Franz Rauscher endeavoured to develop an approach to visual education that he presented as being in the tradition of Otto Neurath. In his booklet *Darstellungsmethoden der Statistik* (Representation Methods for Statistics, 1957; fig. 5.3), he compared different forms of visualization, emphasizing the advantages of the Vienna Method, but summarizing: 'Where quantity pictures are not quite possible for spatial and other reasons, one will represent different group sizes by symbols of different sizes' (thereby breaking a cardinal rule of Isotype).[40] In addition to statistical charts operating with pictograms, bar charts were frequently used by the new Museum. In general, its pictorial statistics fell far behind those produced prior to 1934 in terms of educational and graphic quality. In addition, Rauscher repeatedly pointed out that the designation 'museum' was only retained for traditional reasons because 'today the Museum has much more the character of a school or academy'.[41] It is possible that Rauscher did not know Neurath's position on this very well. For Neurath, social museums were places of science and education. His concept of the museum was oriented away from the traditional art museum and towards museums of the future, which were to be guided by the needs and interests of the visitors, designed in a serial fashion and internationally applicable.[42]

The teamwork of the Rauscher era was also not comparable to that under Otto Neurath. He explained to Marie Neurath that it was often he alone who had to take on different tasks: drafting, checking, presentation and more.[43] An article in the trade union magazine *Solidarität* (Solidarity) states that, by 1967, the staff of the Museum had reduced from thirteen to seven.[44] In either case, this is significantly smaller than the team at the Vienna Museum in the interwar period, which reached a maximum of fifty during its busiest period.

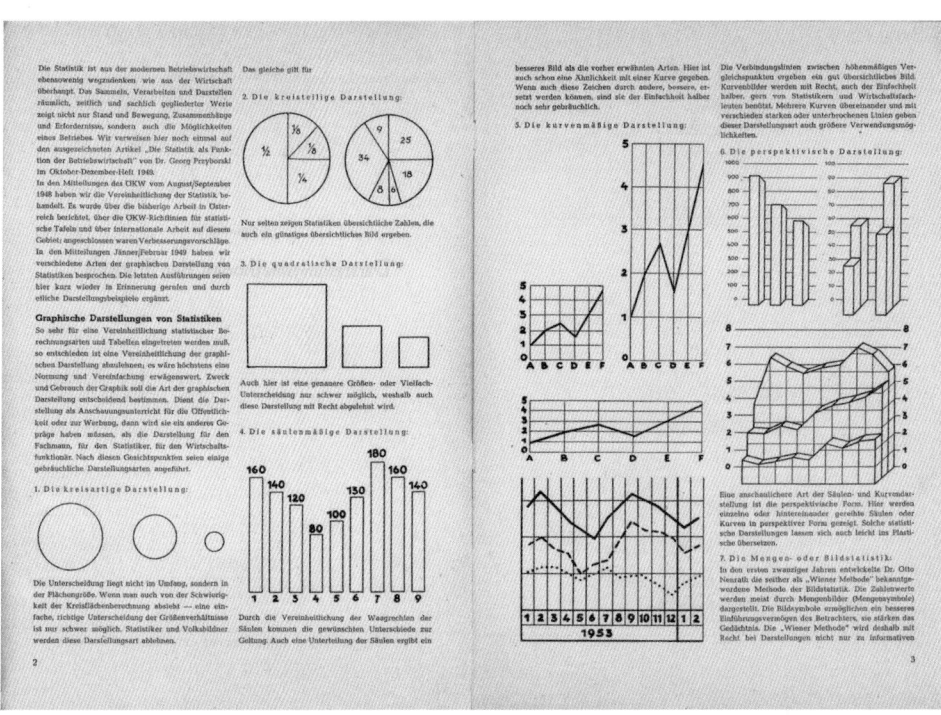

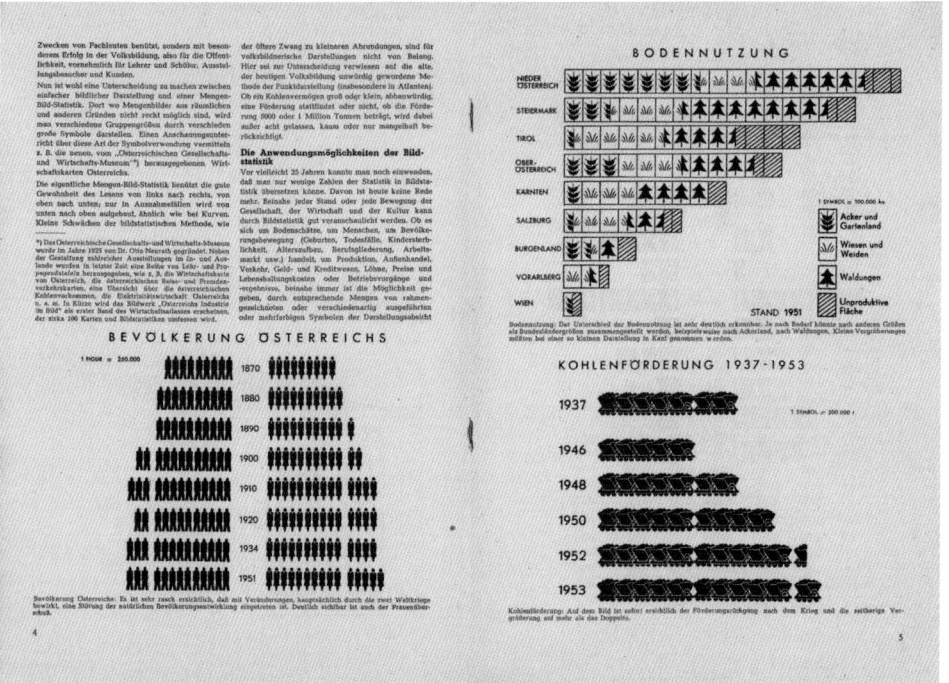

5.3 Franz Rauscher, *Darstellungsmethoden der Statistik* (Representation Methods for Statistics), 1957. Here, Rauscher discusses not only pictorial methods but also other techniques that had generally been rejected by Otto Neurath.

Franz Rauscher remained director of the Austrian Social and Economic Museum until 1972. He had been planning his resignation for a long time before that, but who was to succeed him? At the end of the 1960s he wrote to Marie Neurath to say that he had been trying in vain for three years to find a new director.[45] He considered his eventual successor to be completely miscast.

Rauscher continued to be active for the Museum after his retirement, despite advancing illness. He participated in projects such as the Isotype exhibition at the University of Reading (1975), which was brought to Vienna shortly afterwards, and the exhibition 'Arbeiterbildung in der Zwischenkriegszeit' (Workers' Education in the Inter-War Period) at the Vienna Chamber of Labour (1982). On his eightieth birthday, a courtyard in a cooperative housing estate in the Floridsdorf district of Vienna was named after him. Franz Rauscher died on 11 March 1988 at the age of 87.

Activities in the Rauscher era: teaching materials, exhibitions and publications

The activities of the Museum developed in many ways during the decades after its (re)founding. It produced educational leaflets and writings that were approved by the Ministry of Education and distributed to schools, while illuminated charts and models were used extensively in exhibitions.[46] School classes visited the Museum and guest lecturers were sent out to schools. The Museum also published numerous brochures and booklets on topics such as iron and steel or the social economy, and produced economic maps of Austria. In addition to this educational work, the Museum took on commissions from companies and organizations: for example, from the Wiener Stadtwerke, for which it designed annual reports, or from the Austrian delegation to the United Nations, for which Rauscher and his team graphically designed a book about Austria.[47]

Exhibitions on economic topics also played a key role, despite the Museum not having a permanent display space until 1962. The Museum curated two exhibitions about nationalized industry around 1950, and provided a 'Blick in die österreichische Wirtschaft' (View into the Austrian Economy) at the Chamber of Labour in 1959/60, followed by three booklets under this title in the following years. The largest exhibition project of the early years was entitled '100 Jahre Aufstieg einer Klasse' (100 Years in the Rise of a Class) and was on show in the Vienna Künstlerhaus from 15 September to 31 October 1951. The exhibition was organized by the Chamber of Labour and the Austrian Federation of Trade Unions, and the Austrian Social and Economic Museum played an important role in the design of it. With 1,350 exhibits, a history of labour and the labour movement from 1848 to the present was shown in eleven rooms. Although not indicated in the title, there was a strong focus on Austria. The exhibition was directed by Victor Slama, Fritz Konir and Franz Rauscher. Alois Fischer was also one of several expert advisors.[48] In the mid-1960s, the Museum created the travelling exhibition 'Gemeinwirtschaft' (Social Economy), and 'Die Elektrizitätswirtschaft' (The Electricity Industry), which was on display in the Hietzing Kaiser Pavilion from October to December 1965.

The three board members (in addition to the director) of The Austrian Social and Economic Museum represented the Vienna municipality, the Chamber of Labour and the trade unions respectively. The board of trustees was much broader, and was also continuously expanded. Franz Rauscher wanted to adapt the organizational structure to the new political circumstances and also cautiously open up the Museum politically. Individual institutions now nominated members to its board of directors and board of trustees who were functionaries of the conservative Österreichische Volkspartei (Austrian People's Party). Nevertheless, Social-Democratic hegemony remained intact at the Museum until the end of the Rauscher era. Minutes of the 1968 general assembly noted that the (conservative-dominated) Chamber of Commerce 'still' refused to accept membership in the Austrian Social and Economic Museum.[49]

Franz Rauscher was a loyal disciple of Neurath who strove to administer his legacy and continue his work. But neither his sociological nor his graphic understanding was sufficient to do justice to this attempt. He was also occupied by a whole range of other, mainly voluntary activities in or around the SPÖ. If one looks back over his more than twenty-year era as director of the Austrian Social and Economic Museum, it cannot be overlooked that the high quality of the work from the original Museum in 'Red Vienna' was not achieved. Perhaps it never could have been, given the change in social and political context.

Post-war publications in the tradition of Isotype

It was not only in Vienna that the visual education work of Otto Neurath's team was taken up in the decades after 1945. A former draughtsman and photographer of the Social and Economic Museum, Walter Pfitzner, founded the Institut für Geo-Graphik (Institute for Geo-Graphics) in the city of Salzburg in the mid-1950s. Pfitzner had also published several articles on photography in the magazine *Photo-Börse* in the 1930s, also using pictograms.[50] It is unclear whether Pfitzner had ever felt part of the Social Democratic milieu; in any case, during the years of Nazi rule in Austria he was responsible, among other things, for the picture service of the Nazi newspaper *Deutscher Telegraf*. As his denazification files show, he had also applied for membership of the NSDAP and of the Sturmabteilung (SA), its paramilitary organization.[51]

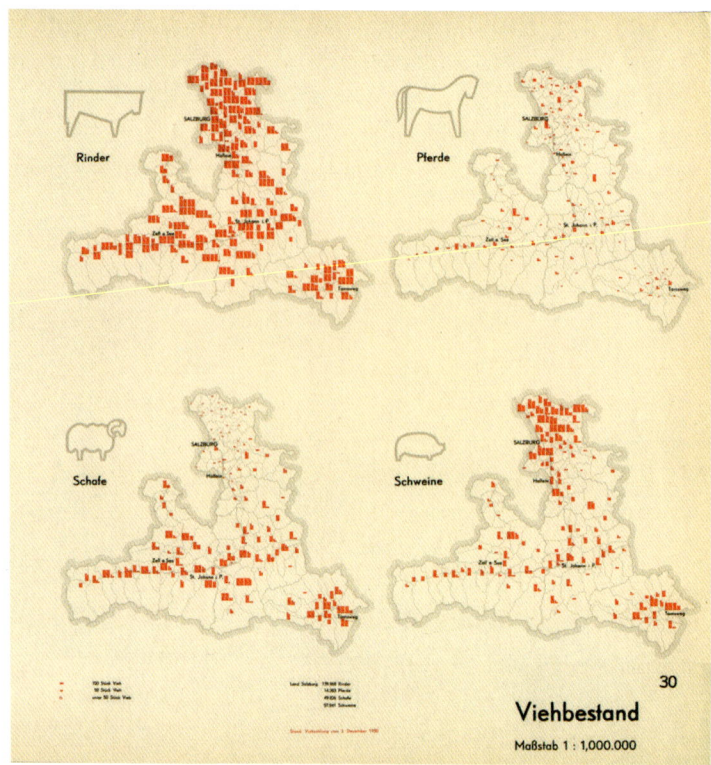

5.4 Chart from the *Salzburg Atlas*, 1955. Pictograms were not often placed on the maps that dominate this publication; here they are only used as key images, with quantities indicated on the maps using repeated squares. 350 × 350 mm.

Pfitzner worked with the artist/designer Augustin Tschinkel for around ten years. The two presumably already knew each other through their joint work at the Social and Economic Museum, where Tschinkel had been brought in to work on *Gesellschaft und Wirtschaft*.[52] Pfitzner's institute produced numerous maps for schools, and on behalf of the Salzburg provincial government. As he wrote to Marie Neurath, however, he had to close the Salzburg Institute for financial reasons only a few years after its foundation. He then continued his activities in Salzburg in the form of a working group.[53]

Perhaps the most important publication of the Institute for Geo-Graphics was the *Salzburg Atlas* (1955). Alongside Pfitzner, Kurt Willvonseder and Egon Lendl acted as editors.[54] In his introductory remarks on the methodology used, Pfitzner explicitly referred to the work of Otto Neurath's team in the years from 1926 to 1934, where 'intellectual guidelines and principles of applied cartography and especially of pictorial statistics were developed'.[55] Of course, the focus of the work was not on social and economic contexts, but on geographical representations of economy (figs 5.4 & 5.5). The atlas contains maps of the economy, soil, vegetation and climate, but also of folklore, art and education. Only a few of them contain quantitative or numerical statistics, such as those on businesses and employees, or on the University of Salzburg, where 'foreign students' are historically differentiated according to number and origin.

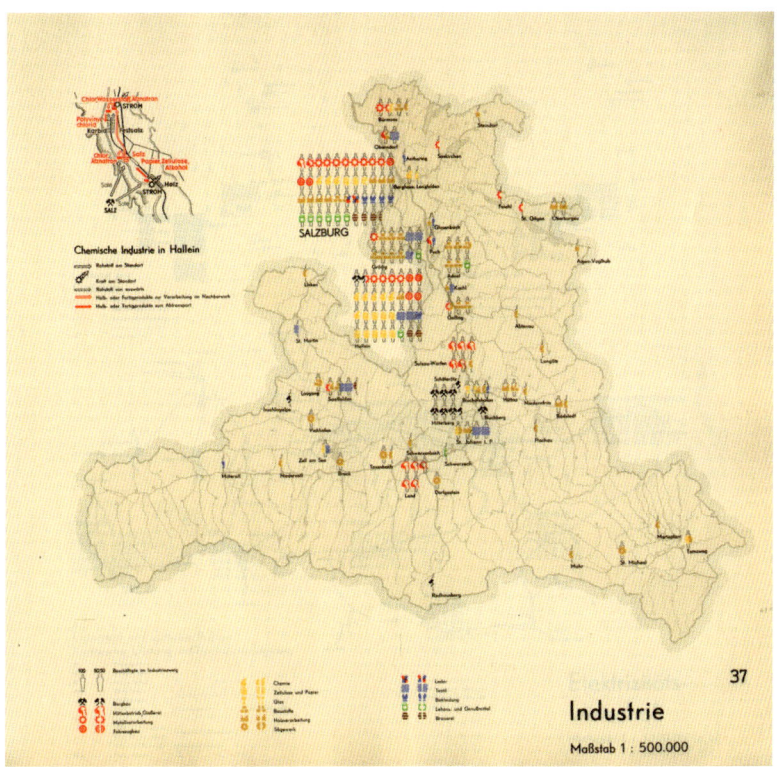

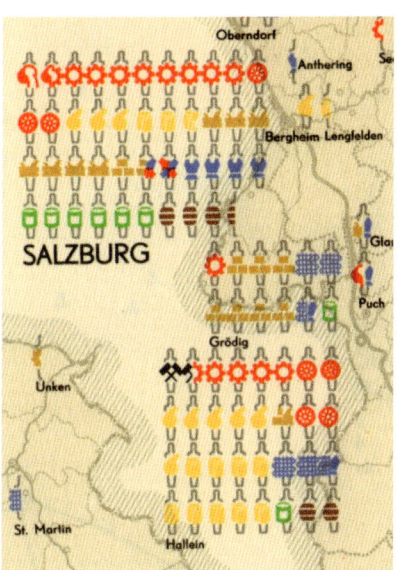

5.5 (top) Rare example of pictograms placed on a map about industry in the *Salzburg Atlas* (with detail, bottom left). Symbols of various industries are superimposed on the human figure, a technique that was pioneered in the Vienna Method between the wars, as shown in the example (bottom right) from *Gesellschaft und Wirtschaft* (1930).

AUSTRIAN SOCIAL AND ECONOMIC MUSEUM AFTER 1945

The publication, also known as the 'Salzburg Atlas of Local History', took several years to compile, and was met with a predominantly positive response, especially from local media. Marie Neurath had registered the reference to her late husband with satisfaction, and found the atlas 'really very beautiful', though also 'terribly expensive'.[56] From the point of view of the continuity of Isotype, it is instructive to compare the *Salzburg Atlas* with the publication *Österreich: Gesellschaft und Wirtschaft* (Austria: Society and Economy), published a little later by the Austrian Social and Economic Museum. It was divided into three parts: 'Population and its problems' (1958), with two following sections both on 'Energy economy' (1959 and 1961). The subtitle of this collection made it clear that its unnamed authors intended it as a continuation of *Gesellschaft und Wirtschaft*, a highpoint of work in the Vienna Method. However, there are significant differences between the two works: whereas the atlas from 1930 was internationally oriented, the follow-up publication from 1958 concentrated exclusively on Austria. Its pictorial graphics did not match its predecessor in terms of design, and the educational communication of social correlations was less compelling and memorable (figs 5.6 & 5.7).

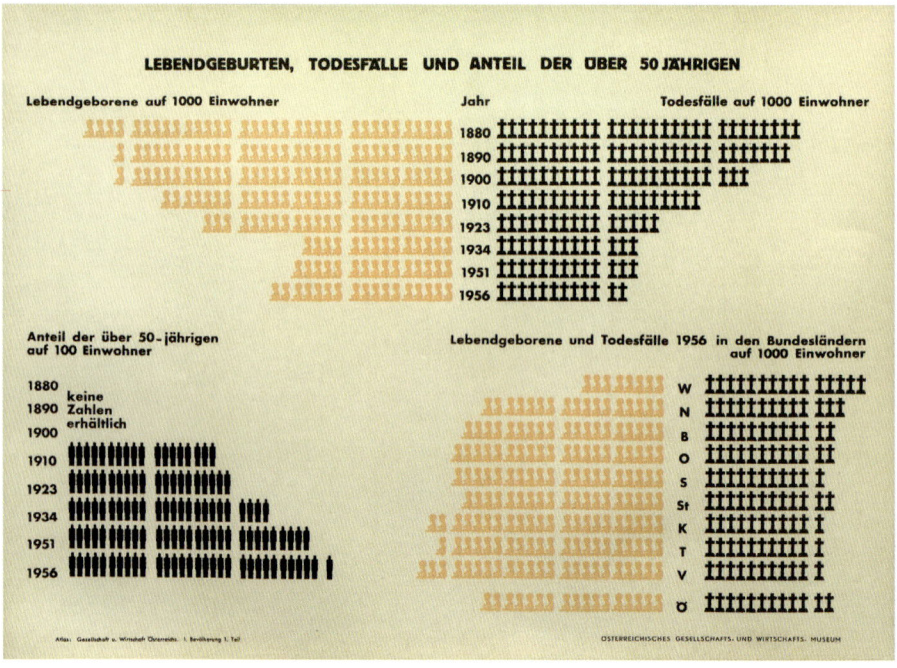

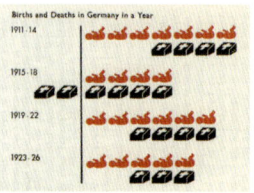

5.6 (above) Chart from *Österreich: Gesellschaft und Wirtschaft*, published by the Austrian Social and Economic Museum, 1958. 420 × 600 mm. The comparison of births and deaths is arranged around a central axis, unlike the favoured solution in earlier Isotype work, where a surplus of deaths extends beyond an axis, as in the example (left) from *International Picture Language*.

118   HISTORY AND LEGACY OF ISOTYPE

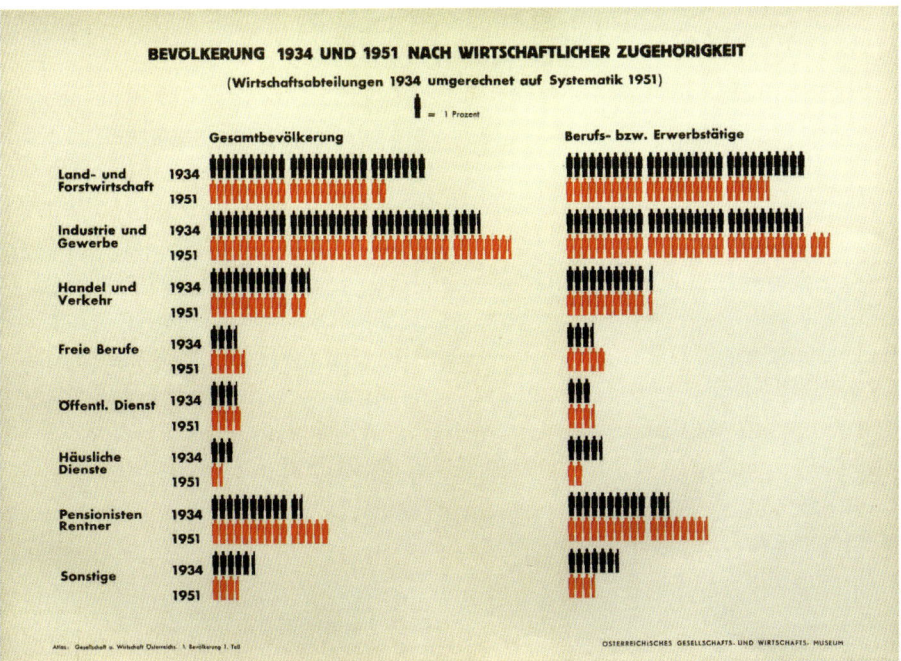

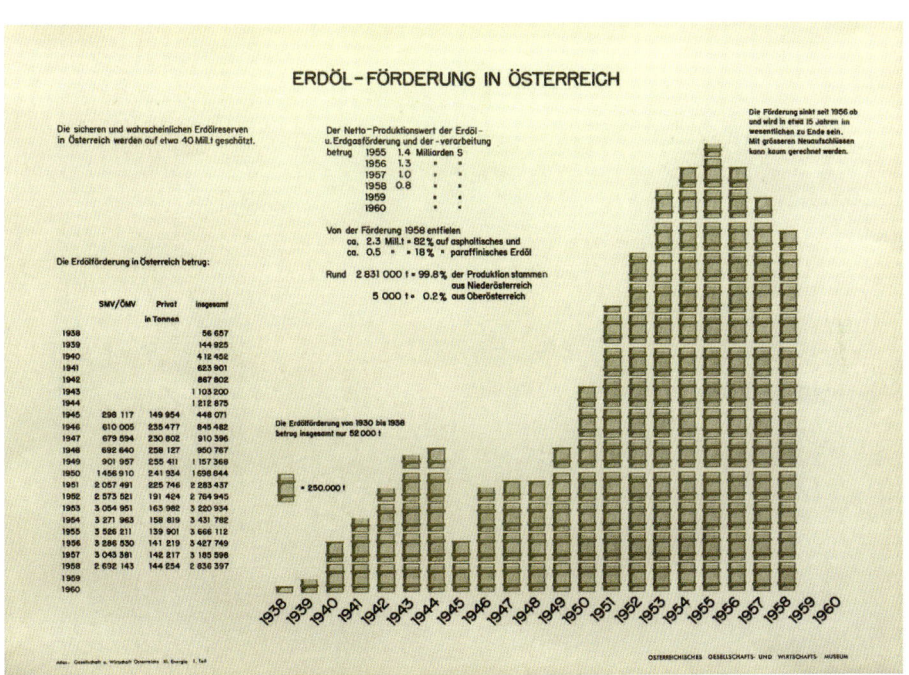

5.7 Further charts from *Österreich: Gesellschaft und Wirtschaft*, 1958–9. Considering the large format of the sheets (presumably for wall display), the scale of the pictograms and type is rather small.

The Salzburg Atlas, in turn, differed from the two publications on 'society and economy' with respect to the political orientation of its authors. For with Egon Lendl and Kurt Willvonseder, Pfitzner worked together with two former National Socialists.[57] Pfitzner's Institute for Geo-Graphics also participated in the publication *Flüchtlingsland Österreich* (Austria: Country of Refugees, 1957), edited by Adalbert Karl Gauss, to which Egon Lendl again contributed. Most of the pictorial statistics in it are to be found in the section dealing with the 'biological power of the displaced': the high birth rate of the ethnic Germans from Eastern and South-Eastern Europe are contrasted with Vienna, which had a comparatively low birth rate, suggesting that these 'displaced' are also a 'biological gain for Austria' because of their 'surplus of women'.[58] Pfitzner was still active in publishing after the dissolution of his institute: for example, he designed the illustrations in Karl Hartl's book *Wie? Wann? Wo?*, edited by publisher Walter Neurath.[59] According to Gerd Arntz, Pfitzner went back to Vienna in the early 1960s,[60] but seems to have spent his retirement in Salzburg, where he died in 1975.

Marie Neurath and the Austrian Social and Economic Museum

Marie Neurath observed the developments in Austria with interest from England. Matzalik and Scheer had informed her about the situation in Vienna, and she read about the 'Niemals vergessen!' exhibition in *The Times*.[61] Franz Rauscher first contacted Marie Neurath in the summer of 1948, shortly before the founding of the Austrian Social and Economic Museum. In his letter, he assured her that the work of the new institute, founded on an association basis, was entirely in the spirit of Otto Neurath.[62] She replied suspiciously, requesting more detail, and he pointed out that all four board members were students of Otto Neurath, three of them graduates of the Workers' College.[63] He also informed her that, on his initiative, a street in Vienna's twenty-second district had been named after Otto Neurath in 1949, which pleased Marie Neurath.[64]

On the other hand, she judged the work of the Austrian Social and Economic Museum with scepticism. When Franz Rauscher made her an offer of exchange – mutual use of each other's work – she did make the work of the Isotype Institute available to be reproduced in Vienna, in German translation and with indication of origin. For her part, however, she expressly refrained from using charts of the Austrian Social and Economic Museum in a similar way.[65] She suggested that she could offer an opinion on 'what Otto Neurath would have said' about its graphic work: 'Clarity, stimulation and variety were more important to him than blind obedience to the rules he himself had created', she reflected; and she warned Rauscher: 'Nothing is worse than confusion and boredom.'[66] Her critical attitude also proved to be an obstacle

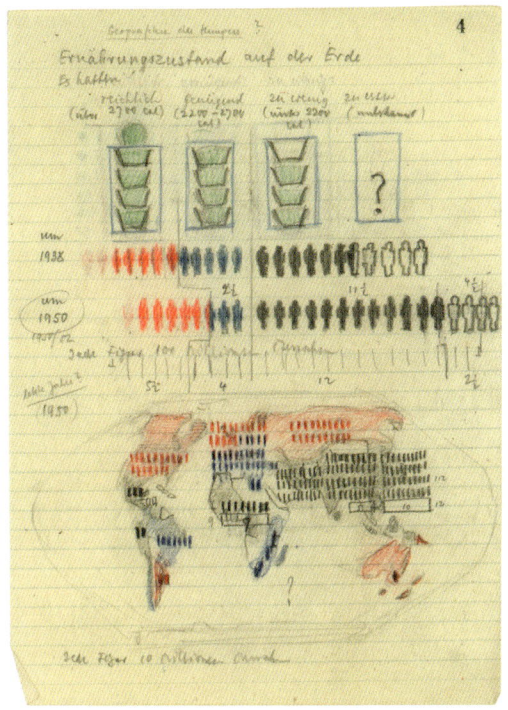

5.8 Transformation sketch by Marie Neurath for a projected exhibition at the Austrian Social and Economic Museum about world population, agriculture and nutrition, 1953 (IC 1/48).

to a possible return to Vienna. She wrote to Arntz that the work of Rauscher's Museum was 'rather paltry after all' and that she did not know 'whether an intensive effort there would be worthwhile'.[67]

So, was the Austrian Social and Economic Museum indeed the legitimate successor to Otto Neurath's Museum, not only in the legal sense, but also in the sense of a continuity of visual education work? This is where the views of Franz Rauscher and Marie Neurath differed. In a letter, she answered the question of succession as follows:

> But what have we actually inherited and continued? Otto Neurath worked and established institutes in Vienna, Holland and England. In Holland his main draughtsman continues to work at another but similar institute … and in England his main 'transformer' continues to work at an institute he himself founded. And in Vienna? The name, the location, the furniture, the circle of friends and interested parties, but hardly any pictograms, no staff, etc.[68]

Despite this difference of opinion, Rauscher and Marie Neurath continued to correspond and visited each other in Vienna and London; and there was also some cooperation. Near the end of 1953, Marie Neurath prepared some transformation sketches for a projected exhibition at the Museum about world population, agriculture and nutrition (fig. 5.8).

A facilitating link between Marie Neurath, the Museum and other offices in Vienna was offered by Philipp Rieger.[69] He had become acquainted with her work in pictorial statistics as a young man in Vienna and, like the Neuraths, had fled to England to escape National Socialism. After his return in 1957, Rieger worked at the Chamber of Labour until 1965, before moving to the Austrian National Bank. For a possible cooperation between the Austrian Social and Economic Museum and the Isotype Institute, he developed a plan for a branch of the latter to be established in Vienna. The cooperation with the Museum, which was partly supported by public funds, would also provide the Isotype Institute with the opportunity to conduct more research on visual education.[70] Rauscher even offered Marie Neurath a 'life position' and emphasized that he was speaking for the Austrian Social and Economic Museum's board of trustees.[71] She had many questions, but remained undecided.

From 11 December 1957 to 18 January 1958, a small exhibition was shown in the Vienna Library to celebrate the seventy-fifth birthday of Otto Neurath, giving an impression of his life and work.[72] Most of the material came from Marie Neurath and, as a result of this exhibition, there was some press and radio coverage of her late husband, who had otherwise been largely forgotten in Austria by the late 1950s.

The most significant project on which Marie Neurath and Franz Rauscher cooperated was an exhibition shown at the Vienna Chamber of Labour in 1962. She stayed in Vienna for three weeks to perform her work of 'transformation': 'out of a jumble of material [I] sketched together an exhibition, which I then left with Rauscher and his draughtsmen for execution, which Philipp Rieger, the Chamber of Labour's statistician, will have his eye on.'[73] The exhibition opened under the title 'Der Hunger in der Welt – auch unser Problem' (Hunger in the World – Our Problem Too) in January 1962. The theme was closely related to a campaign of the Food and Agriculture Organization of the United Nations.

In a historical article about Isotype for the magazine *Graphic Design* in 1971, Marie Neurath summarized her experience with the Austrian Social and Economic Museum: 'The question of my return to Austria was raised, it was even tempting for some time when there was a crisis within the firm of our publishers. But I decided for England and do not regret it.'[74] In 1977, the Austrian Federal President awarded Marie Neurath the title of 'Professor' and the Socialist Minister of Science, Hertha Firnberg, presented her with the certificate.[75]

The Austrian Social and Economic Museum after Rauscher

In 1972, Franz Rauscher resigned as director, although he continued working in the branch of the Kaiser Pavilion. His successor, Josef Docekal, had previously

5.9 View of the exhibition 'Graphic Communication through Isotype' at the University of Reading, 1975.

been active in socialist organizations such as the Kinderfreunde (Children's Friends) or the Rote Falken (Red Falcons), but he had no connection to Otto Neurath and his visual education work.[76] There was no collegial or even friendly relationship between Docekal and Rauscher. Docekal repeatedly claimed to have taken over the Museum in a critical state, without financial foundations, and to have rebuilt it into a functioning institute.[77] Rauscher, in turn, saw in his successor someone who did not know how to adequately continue the long tradition of visual education work, and he demonstratively stayed away from events that the latter organized. He advised Marie Neurath to do the same.[78]

In 1975, the exhibition 'Graphic Communication through Isotype' took place at the University of Reading, England. Under the direction of Professor Michael Twyman, and with the collaboration of Marie Neurath, the largest exhibition to date was organized to commemorate Isotype and its history on the fiftieth anniversary of the founding of the original Social and Economic Museum (fig. 5.9). The successor Museum also provided materials for the event, and former director Rauscher was invited to give a speech at the exhibition opening. Rauscher seemed to have been embarrassed that he was given precedence over Marie Neurath: 'I only came to this honour innocently. You exaggerate your modesty and put yourself too much in the shade. I feel ashamed! You have so much merit for the cause!' Rauscher also had the idea of bringing this exhibition to Vienna and 'setting up at least an equally large, worthy exhibition in the always well-attended large hall of the Central Savings Bank'.[79] In 1977, the Isotype exhibition was indeed shown in Vienna.

Josef Docekal had to begin his work as Museum director under difficult conditions. Due to water damage, the Museum building was closed shortly after he took office and its activities necessarily shifted elsewhere in the period between 1973 and 1986. In 1975, the Museum organized the exhibition 'Österreich und der 30jährige Friede' (Austria and the 30 Years' Peace) in a newly created pedestrian zone in the centre of Vienna. A series of other economic and contemporary history exhibitions followed, such as the open-air exhibition 'Von der Monarchie bis zum Anschluss' (From the Monarchy to the Anschluss), which was shown in numerous Austrian cities, 'Um den Schilling dreht sich alles' (Everything Revolves Around the Schilling), '25 Jahre Staatsvertrag' (25 Years of the State Treaty) and 'Österreich und der Marschallplan' (Austria and the Marshall Plan).[80] From 1978, the Austrian Social and Economic Museum also participated in the design of the Karl Renner Museum in Gloggnitz, Lower Austria. This was followed in 1985 by 'Zug der Zeit' (Train of Time), a contemporary history exhibition shown in train carriages that stopped at various railway stations.

After the Museum regained its own building, an economic-educational trail was built there. In 1987, it showed the socio-historical exhibition 'Von der Großmutter zum Enkel – Leben und Wohnen in Wien von der Jahrhundert bis zur Jahrtausendwende' (From Grandmother to Grandson – Life and Living in Vienna from the Turn of the Century to the Turn of the Millennium). During the Docekal era, there were many smaller exhibitions and cooperation projects with schools; economic maps were produced, and folders and brochures such as *Wirtschaft im Überblick* (Economy at a Glance) were published. Furthermore, there was an intensification in the production of material to be used in schools; in this respect, the Museum was following its forerunner of the 1920s. Docekal also continued to open up politically by bringing representatives of the Chamber of Commerce and the Federation of Austrian Industries onto the Museum's board of trustees.[81]

But what increasingly faded into the background and became forgotten was Isotype. Docekal wrote that the Museum liked to use 'Neurath's pictorial statistics' where, for example, the development of the number of tractors and horse-drawn carriages, or the decrease in infant mortality was concerned; today, however, the cost-of-living index could be 'made just as easily recognizable with a simple curve'. As a reason for this change in the graphic forms of representation, he said that 'the level of education of the people has risen considerably compared to that of the inter-war period'.[82] Of course, such thoughts had little to do with Neurath's detailed reflections on visual education. While Neurath acknowledged that pictorial statistics could appeal to less educated groups in particular, he believed that this method could also impart knowledge in a form that was commonly accessible to all social strata.[83]

 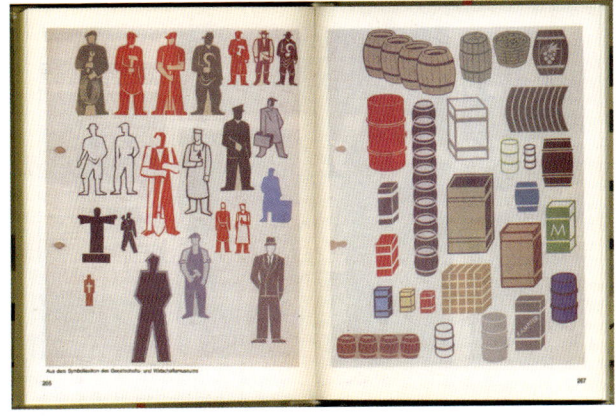

5.10 Cover of *Arbeiterbildung in der Zwischenkriegszeit*, 1982, with pages from the book showing pictograms created in Vienna during the fascist period.

The historical memory – and thus also the question of reactivating the emancipatory educational tradition – was instead brought to the Museum from outside. The exhibition 'Arbeiterbildung in der Zwischenkriegszeit' (Workers' Education in the Inter-War Period), shown at the Vienna Chamber of Labour in 1982, was a pioneering project to rediscover the educational tradition in Vienna.[84] A young generation of researchers led by the historian and philosopher Friedrich Stadler entered into dialogue with surviving witnesses who had been active in Red Vienna. The exhibition was also an important cornerstone in the interpretation of the history of Viennese pictorial statistics. What is striking here is the clearly more prominent role that Gerd Arntz now assumed in comparison to Marie Neurath. However, Stadler invited Marie Neurath to the exhibition opening and offered her the opportunity to proof-read all the texts in the exhibition catalogue *Arbeiterbildung in der Zwischenkriegszeit*, which she did (fig. 5.10).[85]

Overall, there are few indications that the Austrian Social and Economic Museum still consciously kept its legacy in mind after the end of the Rauscher era. Josef Docekal's successor even openly admitted once in a retrospective lecture at the Museum that, when he took office in 2000, he simply knew nothing about the pictorial statistics of Red Vienna, nor about the person of Otto Neurath.[86] Although a Neurath memorial room was set up in the Museum in 2012 under the title 'Speaking Signs', this hardly played a role for the visual education work.

In 2019, under new management, the Museum displayed 'Geschichte und Gegenwart von Isotype' (History and Present of Isotype) as part of a larger Viennese exhibition on Red Vienna, implying that this historical tradition could also be taken up again more strongly in the future.

AUSTRIAN SOCIAL AND ECONOMIC MUSEUM AFTER 1945

6 Following Otto Neurath: Marie Neurath and Gerd Arntz on separate paths

In the first letter that he wrote to Gerd Arntz after the Second World War, Otto Neurath gave a characteristically terse summary of his and Marie Neurath's experiences since the German invasion of the Netherlands:

> In short our adventures. You remember 14 May 1940, resistance stopped – Nazis invaded the remaining Holland. We could not reach you and tried to escape. Some shooting in the streets. We reached the harbour, no preparation for evacuation. We finally saw a motor-life-boat and jumped into it. 50 persons instead of 25. Burning Rotterdam, exploding ammunition dumps at the Hague. Calm sea. Next day in the neighbourhood of Dover a British destroyer picked us up. First interned. Famous people intervened, Einstein, Huxley, Earl Russell etc. Finally the Oxford University invited me to lecture. Released, we married. English friends, Stebbing as chairman (she died in the meantime) organized the Isotype Institute. We prepared book illustrations, made films, etc in grand style. … Now we have to get you back.[1]

On learning that Arntz was an American prisoner of war, Neurath wrote to Arntz's wife, Agnes, and assured her that he would do everything possible to secure his release and to organize employment for him. Neurath asked a friend at the American Embassy in London to intervene and sent him a testament to Arntz's character as a 'staunch anti-Nazi' and 'an artist of high standing with peculiar abilities which are needed in our Isotype work'.[2] Neurath was informed that the IFVE had been hidden (and its material preserved) behind a new Dutch organization, the Nederlandse Stichting voor Statistiek (Dutch Foundation for Statistics). Arntz had continued work for this organization before being conscripted into the German army, and Neurath hoped to arrange post-war cooperation between the Dutch and British institutes 'in the most friendly way'.[3] This proved to be more complicated than he imagined, however, and would not be resolved before his death in December 1945.

Gerd Arntz's experience during the Second World War

The Dutch Foundation for Statistics (NSS) was established soon after the German occupation of the Netherlands, in August 1940, through quick thinking by influential friends of the Isotype team. The lawyer Peter de Kanter, who was chairman of the IFVE, arranged for the new institute to be established as an affiliate of the Central Bureau voor de Statistiek (CBS) – the governmental office of statistics. The director of the CBS, Philippus Jacobus Idenburg, was interested in Isotype and he became chairman of the new foundation. The NSS was intended to popularize statistics, partly in graphic form. Among its board members was Jan Tinbergen, a renowned economist (and an administrator at the Central Bureau), who had also been on the board of the IFVE. Jan van Ettinger, an engineer and statistician, became the director of the new foundation, and Arntz was appointed as head of the graphic department. Arntz recalled that he was the only paid employee of the NSS; he could not have been employed directly by the CBS because, as a foreigner, he was not allowed to be a Dutch civil servant.[4] His work involved much discussion with civil servants, however, and he was forced to improve his skills in speaking Dutch.

De Kanter explained later to Neurath that he took this action to 'keep Isotype method and material out of German hands' and to provide work for Arntz and Josef Scheer, the two members of the Isotype team that remained.[5] (Erwin Bernath had left before the war to manage a printing house in his native Switzerland.) According to Arntz, Scheer was in favour of putting Isotype material at the disposal of the Germans, and he did not make the transition to the NSS.[6] The Arntz family, as 'Aryans', could have collaborated with the occupying forces and made life easier for themselves, but they never did, as Neurath was reliably informed by mutual Dutch friends.[7]

Arntz worked initially for the NSS for a little over two years, until the beginning of 1943, when he was pressed into military service. But in that short time, he designed a number of attractive booklets with the series title 'Boeinde Statistiek' (Fascinating Statistics), which are a direct continuation of the spirit and graphic idiom of Isotype. Some of the texts, on themes of population, economy and trade, were written by Van Ettinger or Tinbergen, and feature subtle charts of equal quality in transformation and design to previous work. In the introduction to the pilot booklet on 'Welfare in industry in the Netherlands' (published in both Dutch and German editions), Idenburg stated:

> It is wrong to assume that the masses of people are not interested in the results of statistical research. On the contrary, I am convinced that it is possible to arouse the interest of many thousands for quantitative data about the most essential parts of our national economy. The prerequisite, however, is that one masters the art of expressing these data in a vivid way. The 'Dutch Foundation for Statistics' is active in this sense. Its rich program

> also includes the publication of popular writings in which the fruits of statistical research are made accessible to the broad strata of the Dutch population. For this purpose, pictorial statistics are used according to the Isotype method, which was developed from the cooperation of experienced statisticians and graphic artists. Simple pictures, as experience teaches, are more easily grasped by the human mind than precise figures.[8]

There are strong echoes here of Neurath's previously published views on the potential of pictorial statistics.

A staple task for the NSS became the *Statistisch Zakboek* (Statistical handbook) published annually by the CBS, predominantly containing tables of figures. In 1940, pictorial statistics (in black and white) were included for the first time, and in the handbook for 1941, charts in as many as three colours were produced by the NSS to enliven the monotonous pages of tabular data. Again, the hand of Arntz can be clearly discerned in these examples, which connect directly to Isotype work. In consecutive editions, many of the same charts were simply updated with new data, and the NSS contribution to this publication continued well into the 1960s.

These tasks kept Arntz fully occupied in the early years of the war, and he had no spare time to spend on his 'free' artwork. When the Germans invaded, he destroyed some of his artwork with anti-fascist themes, which could have led to trouble for him. (He had contributed to the 1936 exhibition 'Olympics Under Dictatorship' in Amsterdam, disguised by the pseudonym 'Dubois'.) Later, he explained that he did not flee the Netherlands in 1940 because he would have lost all of his artwork;[9] whereas the Neuraths fled with nothing except the clothes that they were wearing.

In 1943 Arntz was forced to wear the 'hated uniform' of the Wehrmacht and was sent to serve as a driver in a tank division at the front in Normandy. He later recalled that, fortunately, he 'never had to shoot'. He surrendered to the French resistance in August 1944, and was handed over to the Americans, who put him to work as a POW in Cherbourg harbour. He was then briefly held in Germany before being released at the end of April 1946.[10] He returned to the Netherlands, but it seems that the way he re-entered the country was deemed to be illegal; so Idenburg felt it imperative to reinstate him to his position at the NSS, in order to secure his legal status.[11]

Legal complications between Dutch and British institutes

Before Arntz returned, contact resumed between the Isotype Institute and former colleagues in the Netherlands. Neurath was at first pleased that the working material of the IFVE could be saved, and its work partly continued by the new foundation; and he was glad 'that they were even in a position to shelter

Arntz as collaborator of the Stichting with such a fine official name'.[12] The IFVE had largely operated under its English name, and De Kanter felt it advisable to let both it and the Mundaneum 'go to sleep as their continued existence might arouse unwelcome German attention'.[13]

Neurath appreciated the friendship and kindness shown in making these arrangements, but he soon realized the complexity of the situation. De Kanter and Tinbergen had assumed that a 'copyright in Isotype methods and symbols' belonged to the IFVE or the Mundaneum, and they decided (as board members of those organizations) that these putative rights should be sold to the NSS in 1940, along with the working material. De Kanter added: 'Not to give the Germans any handhold over us we considered you and your present wife as having resigned from your offices in both foundations. These then went to sleep.' Neurath considered this agreement to be invalid due to defects in the procedure, but he felt it more important to find a way that work could continue on both sides, without competition. De Kanter admitted: 'When the Germans threatened your lifework we did not care much for legal finesses, but our one care was to save the work and find a living for Arntz'.[14]

It was proposed that the IFVE be revived and relocated to England, serving as a coordinating body for the Isotype Institute and the NSS. Both Marie Neurath and De Kanter seemed to agree on this soon after the death of Otto Neurath, and both felt it best to avoid approaching the matter in a legalistic way. Marie Neurath stipulated that much of the material (including some from the Viennese period) had only been held on trust by the IFVE, and demanded that it be sent to the Isotype Institute. This eventually happened, but only due to the continued friendly connection between her and Arntz; more official negotiations between the Isotype Institute and the NSS broke down without a firm resolution. Marie Neurath could not accept equal status for the NSS and the Isotype Institute: in her view, it was necessary for her to train somebody in the skills of transformation to work at the Dutch institute. Both sides seemed attached to their respective autonomies and could not compromise. Marie Neurath explained to Mary Fleddérus: 'Our co-operation with the Nederlandse Stichting voor Statistiek does not come to much; we are just fixing somehow our spheres of interest, going on separately, though maintaining some lose [sic] friendly contact I hope.'[15]

One way of distinguishing the activities of the two organizations was by the brand mark used to sign graphic work. Both had initially adopted the symbol designed for Isotype by Arntz in 1935 – a schematic human torso holding up a chart. It was agreed that the Isotype Institute should continue using this and Arntz designed a new symbol for the NSS: a full-length figure supporting a chart from an outstretched arm, which contained the name 'Ned[.] Stichting voor Statistiek'.¹⁶ (Peculiarly, the NSS reverted to the original symbol around 1965, almost at the end of Arntz's time working there).

The disagreement with NSS created difficulties for Marie Neurath when re-negotiating a contract between the Isotype Institute and Adprint in 1946. It contained a standard clause about copyright, which was now cast into doubt by the NSS having raised that matter. Paul Rotha, as the other principal client of the Isotype Institute, was similarly concerned. They suggested the formation of a commercial company that would administer (and defend) copyright in Isotype work. The discussions centred on the pictograms, which Marie Neurath did not consider the most important aspect of Isotype, at least not in isolation; they were generally designed for specific functions in a larger design. She was advised that publishing them in an itemized catalogue would protect them legally; but the same legal advisor explained that copyright could not be applied to the method or 'idea' of Isotype – and it was this that mattered to Marie Neurath. She resisted involvement in what she described as a 'capitalistic, monopolistic' enterprise; 'Foges was furious, but I kept my head', she recalled later, and their cooperation continued, unimpeded by the phantom of copyright. Similarly, no further disputes arose between the Isotype Institute and the NSS: 'We found that the world was big enough for the two of us.'¹⁷

In their long, post-war correspondence, Marie Neurath and Gerd Arntz did not discuss the issue of copyright in Isotype or its pictograms. After they had both retired from work, she wrote to him: 'We don't need to protect our rights any more. A monopoly usage no longer interests me, and you neither probably. Better that we provide everything for use in posterity.'¹⁸

Her approach to protecting Isotype from imitation is exemplified in her complaints about the *World Geo-Graphic Atlas* (1953), published by Container Corporation of America, and designed by Herbert Bayer. It is clear that the pictorial statistics and some other graphics in this atlas owed a debt to Isotype, but it is not acknowledged among the credits in its preface. In particular, a chart from *Modern Man in the Making* had been adapted (and noted as such),

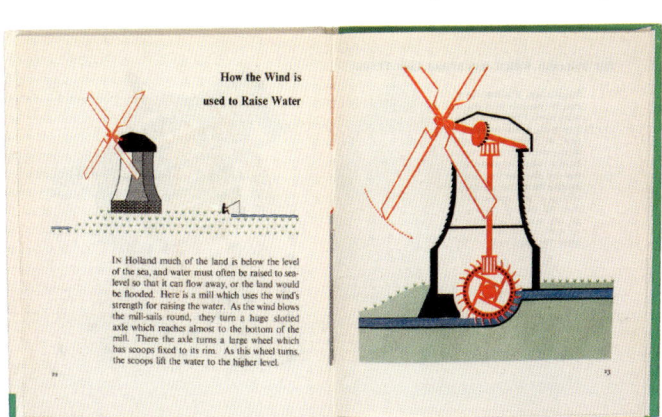

6.1 Illustration from Marie Neurath's book *If You Could See Inside* (1948) that was modified for inclusion in the *World Geo-Graphic Atlas* (1953).

and a cutaway illustration of a windmill had been modified from an illustration in Marie Neurath's book *If You Could See Inside* (1948; fig. 6.1). She wrote to Waldemar Kaempffert for advice, remarking: 'I think it is not according to the rules of common politeness to do such a thing without even trying to get our agreement.'[19] Kaempffert passed on her complaint to the publisher of *Modern Man in the Making*, Alfred Knopf, framing it as a matter of copyright (which Marie Neurath had not). Knopf was sympathetic but saw no issue of legal infringement. Marie Neurath was mainly indignant about appropriation without due credit. When a German edition of the atlas was published in 1955, she wrote again to the Container Corporation:

> I have not asked for more than a fair acknowledgment of the indebtedness to our work of which you are obviously aware. To give the credit which is due to my husband's work would remove all ill feeling without costing anyone a penny; it would not damage Herbert Bayer's reputation but improve it.[20]

Marie Neurath shared the attitude of her late husband to such matters: 'Of course he never felt powerful enough to fight all these imitators; … let us do the best work possible to be different from them.'[21]

Marie Neurath takes Isotype in new directions

One of the first projects continued by Marie Neurath after her husband's death was *Future*, a magazine that had been in planning with Adprint for two years before its first number appeared in 1946. It was published initially as a book series, in order to disguise its nature as a periodical, due to a ban on new magazine titles as a way of rationing paper. The American magazine *Fortune* served as some kind of model, but the name and contents of *Future* were intended to reflect the spirit of reconstruction after the Second World War. Otto Neurath had hoped that there would be scope within it for articles conceived and edited by the Isotype Institute, but this hope was soon frustrated by discussion with Adprint of ideas for Isotype involvement. Nevertheless, some accomplished and varied examples of Isotype appeared in *Future Books* and in the subsequent magazine, up to 1952 (figs 6.2 & 6.3). Eric Kindel remarks that some of these examples 'employed features untypical of Isotype, suggesting a loosening (or compromising) of its rules in search of novelty and impact'.[22] *Future* also featured more illustrative information graphics by Abram Games and F. H. K. Henrion; the latter was a consultant art editor for the magazine, a position he also occupied for a contemporary periodical with similar motives, *Contact*, published by Austrian émigré George Weidenfeld.[23]

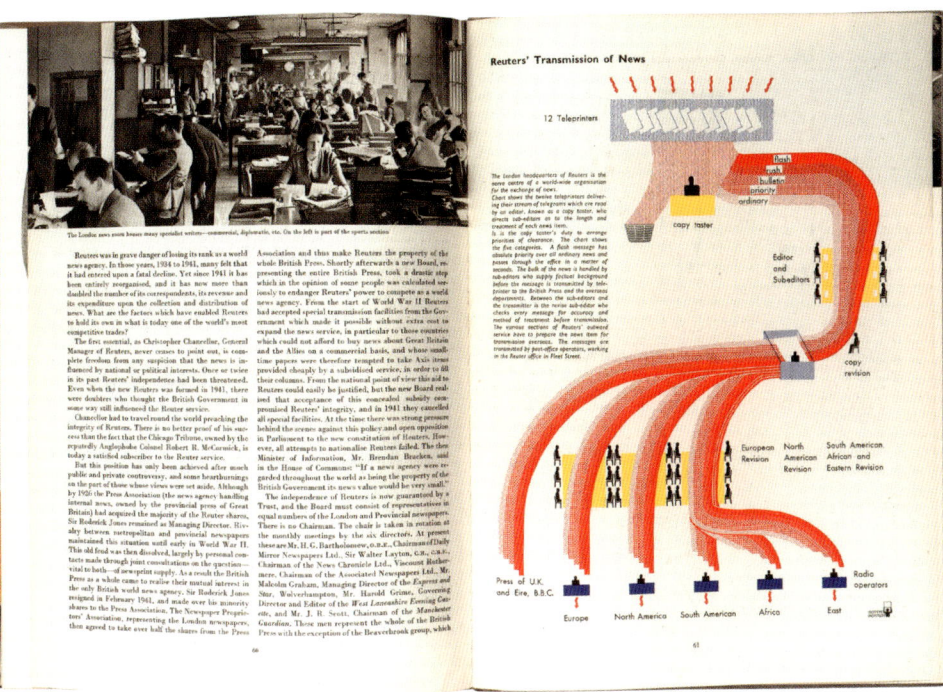

6.2 (top) *Future Books*, vol. 4: *Transformation*, 1946. From the article 'Reuters'. 295 × 215 mm. (bottom) *Future* magazine, [vol. 2,] no. 3, 1947. From the article 'Canadian diagnosis'.

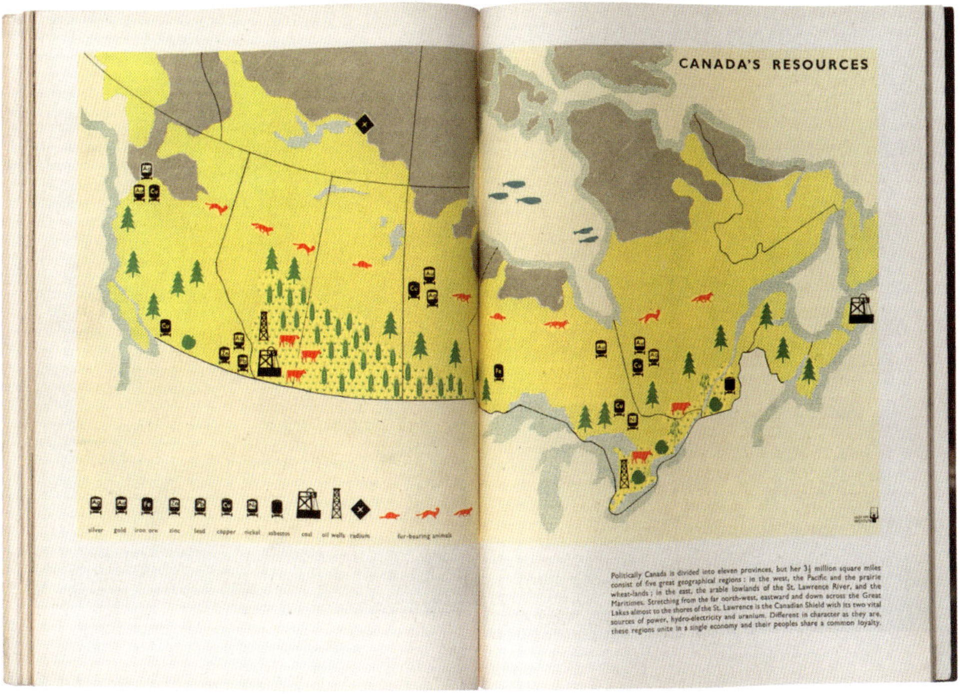

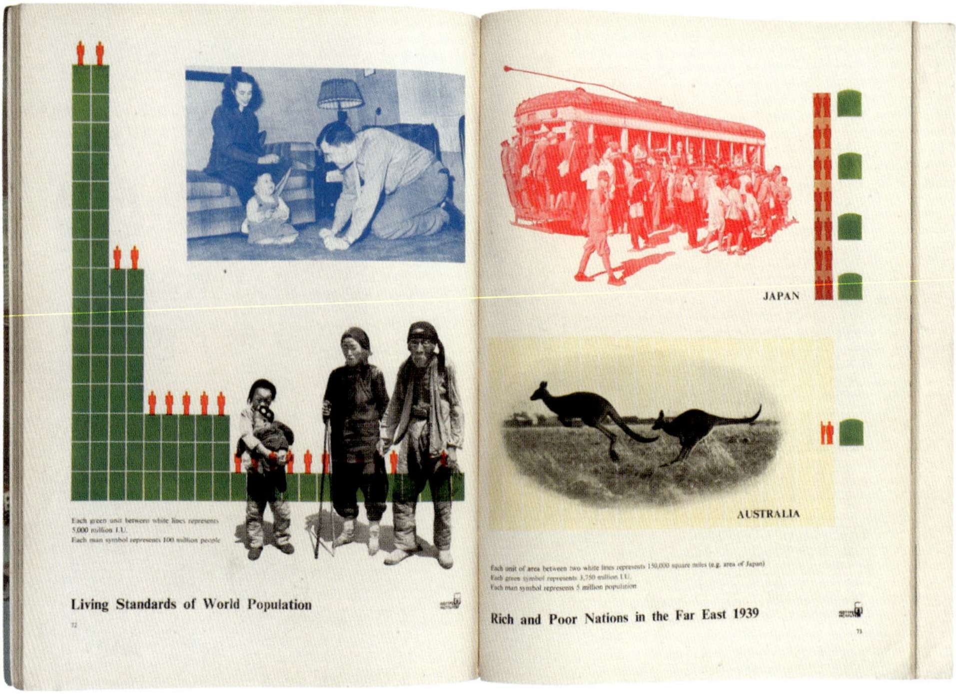

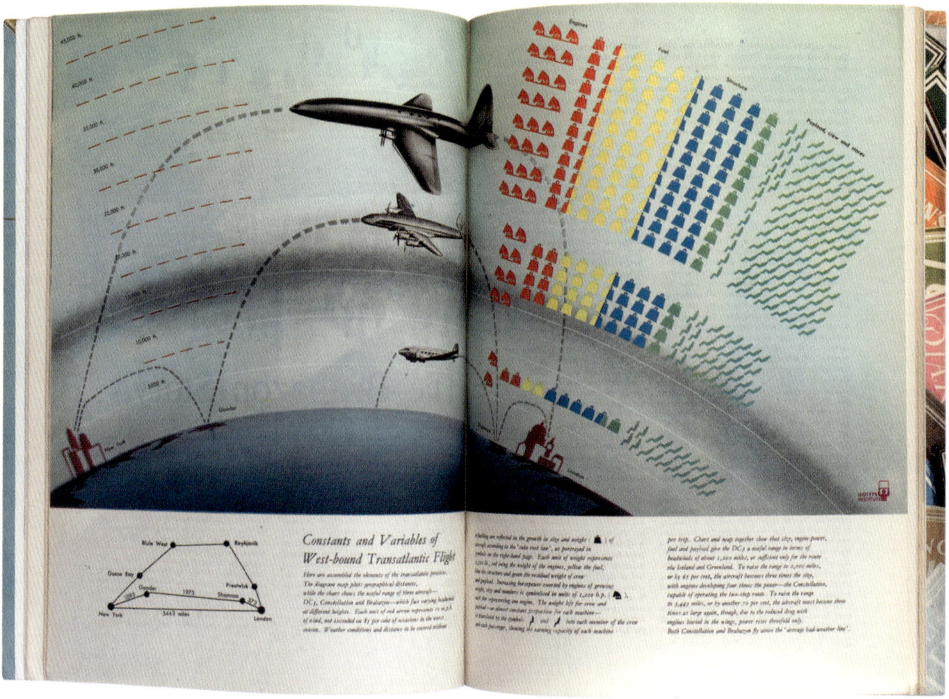

6.3 (top) *Future* magazine, vol. 3, no. 2, 1948. From the article 'Rich man, poor man …'. (bottom) *Future* magazine, vol. 4, no. 2, 1949. From the article 'The Brabazon story'.

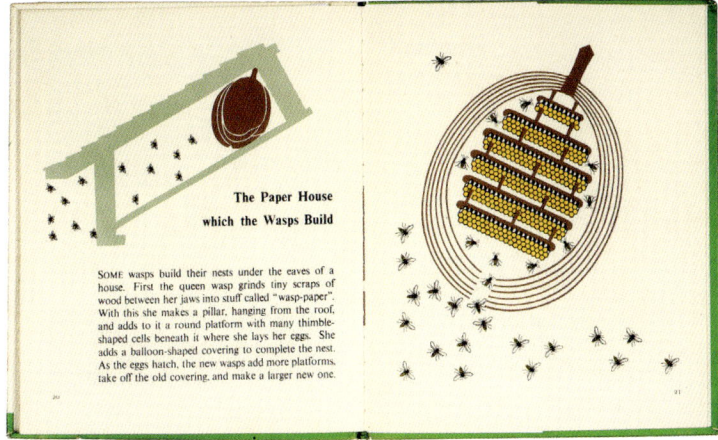

6.4 Books written and designed by Marie Neurath, 1948. 220 × 190 mm.

If You Could See Inside.

Railways Under London.

Two areas stand out from Marie Neurath's work at the Isotype Institute during the following two decades: writing and designing of educational books for young readers, and educational projects in West African countries.[24] She had already begun her work on children's books together with Otto Neurath for the series 'Visual History of Mankind' (published in 1948), but she came into her own with books on science and technology, drawing on her early education in physics. Two of the first titles that she both wrote and designed are delightful examinations beneath the surface of things: *If You Could See Inside* and *Railways Under London* (both 1948; fig. 6.4). The second of these, aimed at readers aged 9–12, treats the workings of the London Underground in serious and complex detail, and it set a pattern of rigorous research and consultation with experts in order to ensure accuracy. This was always a characteristic of Isotype and it persists here in books that contain diagrammatic illustrations instead of pictorial statistics.[25] For example, the book *Inside the Atom* (1956) benefited from Marie Neurath's exchange with nuclear physicist Otto Frisch (fig. 6.5).

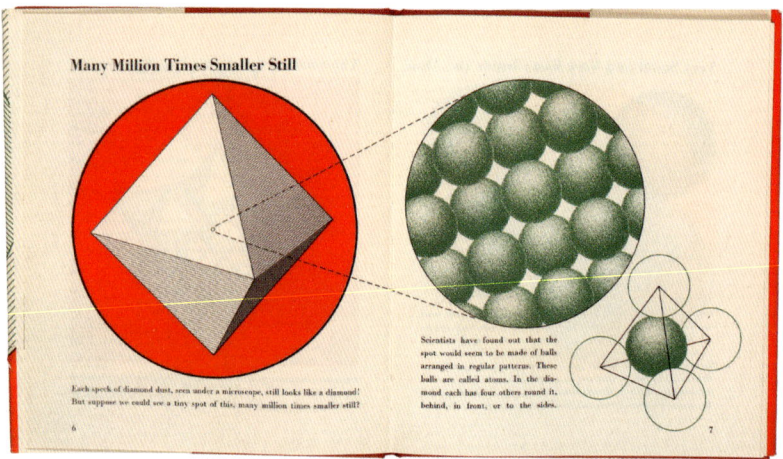

6.5 More books written and designed by Marie Neurath.

Inside the Atom, 1956.

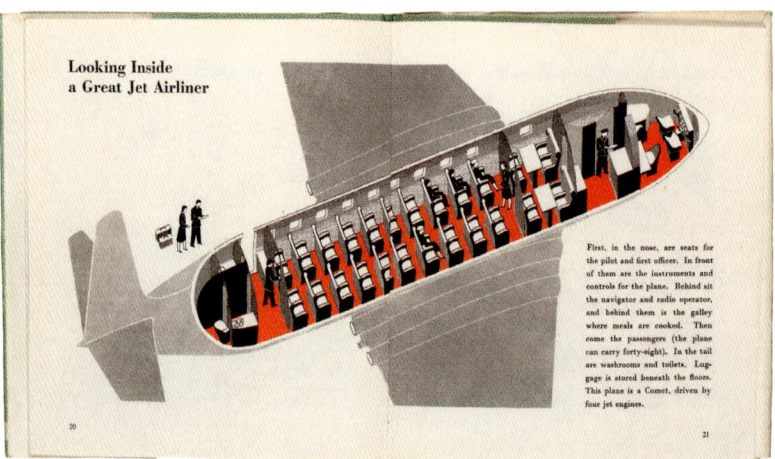

Rockets and jets, 1951.

On the title-pages of these books, a new symbol for Isotype appeared (right), as if to mark a specialization in book design.

The series 'Visual Science' (1950–2) was developed by Marie Neurath with Joseph Lauwerys to introduce schoolchildren to science in an engaging way (continuing the early efforts in Viennese schools; see chapter 1); and for the series 'Wonders of the Modern World', she worked on books with titles such as *Building Big Things*, *Machines Which Seem to Think* and *Speeding into Space*. These all render complex subjects in a deceptively simple way, with colourful, instructive images dominating short explanatory texts – very much in the tradition of Isotype (figs 6.6 & 6.7). Marie Neurath's books for children were translated into many other languages, including Danish, Dutch, French, German, Italian, Japanese, Portuguese and Swedish.[26]

6.6 Covers from the series 'Wonders of the Modern World': *Speeding into Space* (1954) and *Building Big Things* (1958). (Below) Pages from *Speeding into Space*.

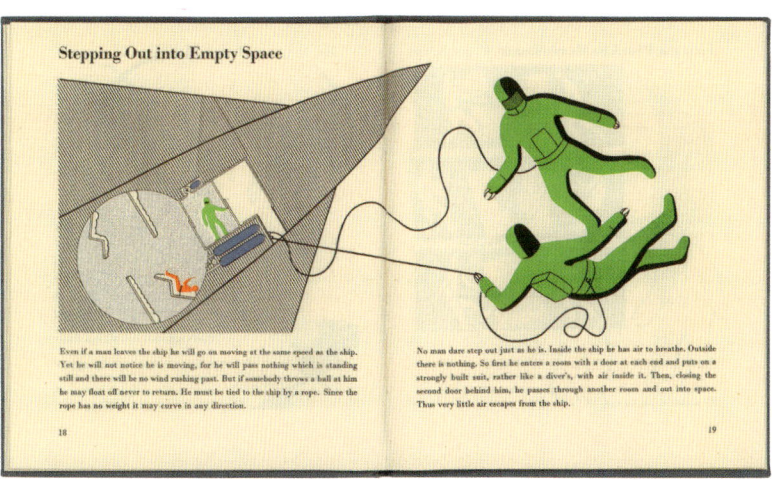

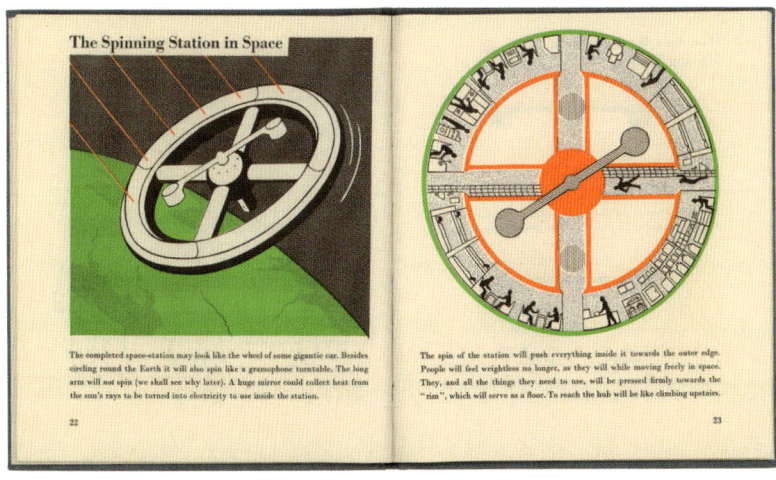

The space station shown here is an uncanny pre-figuration of that featured in the film *2001: A Space Odyssey* (1968).

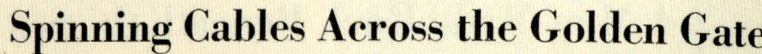

The bridge begins with tall, strong towers, built near the water's edge. First, a rope, slung over a wheel on one tower, is pulled across by a small boat.

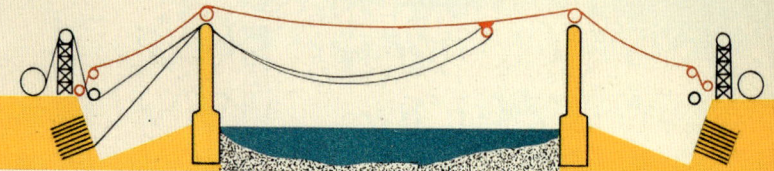

Then a loop of wire from a reel is pulled across by the rope.

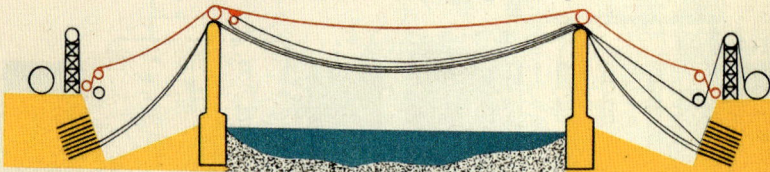

As the rope goes back, it pulls across a loop from a second reel.

To and fro goes the rope, until thousands of wires stretch across.

6.7 Pages from *Building Big Things*, 1958. 220 × 190 mm. Comparison was always an important element of Isotype, here serving to show the progress of construction in sequential images.

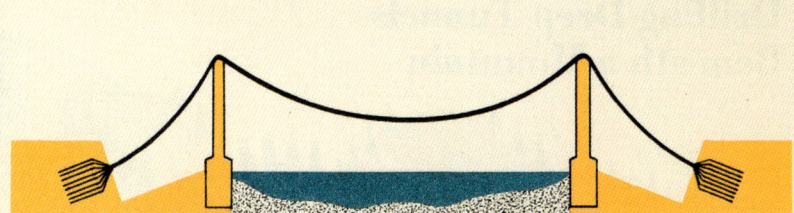

The wires are banded into one strong cable, their ends spread firmly into strong concrete. On the other side of the roadway a second cable is spun.

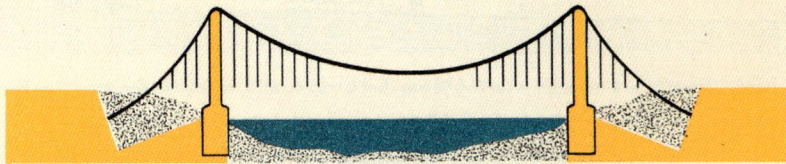

From these cables, many more thinner cables are hung, to carry the road.

Cranes lift girders into place, and soon a road rests on the cables.

The Golden Gate Bridge is complete. Ships could pass almost all the time.

15

And the woman who helped to invent the system, our

Woman

of the Month

MARIE NEURATH

MRS. MARIE NEURATH has just returned from six months in Africa. She has been working on the initial research for a series of Isotype booklets and posters to assist the West Nigerian and Gold Coast governments in their educational programme.

Mrs. Neurath was born in Brunswick, Germany, and in her youth studied art, physics and mathematics, intending to become a teacher. In Vienna, however, she met her future husband, Otto Neurath, who asked her to assist him in building up a new museum of social sciences. During 1925 to 1934 they were engaged with a team of workers on the production of charts for this museum and for exhibitions, using the method of representation known at the time as the "Vienna Method" and, later, "Isotype."

Soon after war broke out, they escaped to this country, crossing the Channel in a lifeboat. In 1942, they founded the Isotype Institute at Oxford, engaging artists and research workers to assist them. Since the death of her husband in 1945, Mrs. Neurath has continued to organise the work of the Institute on her own and has her headquarters in London.

6.8 Feature about Marie Neurath in children's educational magazine *Look and Learn*, 1956.

Otto Neurath had remarked that Isotype was being created 'not, finally, for the Viennese, but rather for the Africans', reflecting his ambitions for it to be an international picture language.[27] In his projected book 'Visual Education', he set out precisely the issues that Marie Neurath addressed in her work for African governments after his death:

> The main bulk of adult education caters to people who are able to read and write without difficulty. But no one takes proper care of the masses who do not reach this standard. This counts not only for Europe, but also in the colonies where the education of illiterates is needed as the very basis of health education, agricultural education, not to mention education in citizenship.

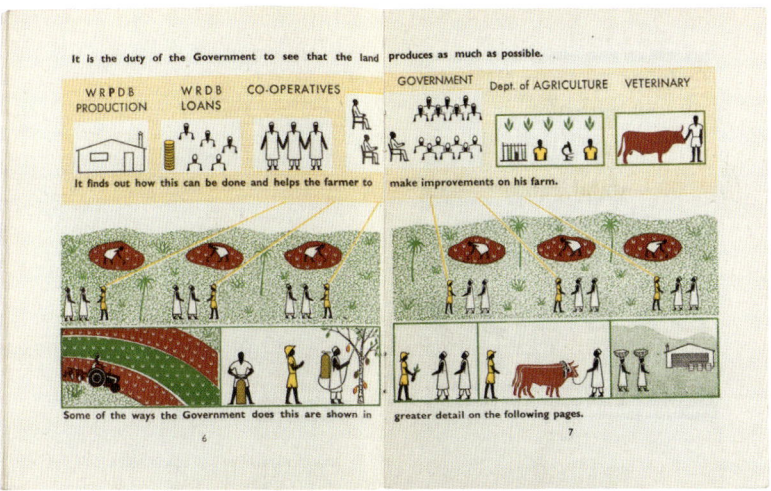

6.9 Two booklets produced for Nigeria: *Education for All in the Western Region* and *Better Farming for Better Living in the Western Region*, 1955. 204 × 163 mm.

> Colonial peoples who do not understand one of the languages which can transfer scientific knowledge like English or Chinese, Basic or Interglossa, are badly off in the educational field.[28]

During the 1950s, Marie Neurath designed educational material for the Western Region of Nigeria and (to a lesser extent) for the Gold Coast (now part of Ghana) and Sierra Leone. These territories were progressing towards independence from British colonial rule, and Marie Neurath met Obafemi Awolowo, leader of Nigeria's ruling party the Action Group, while he was in London at a congress in 1953. She made some quick sketches for him of his

6.10 Poster made for the Western Region of Nigeria, 'Vote Early at your Polling Station', 1955–6. 510 × 765 mm.

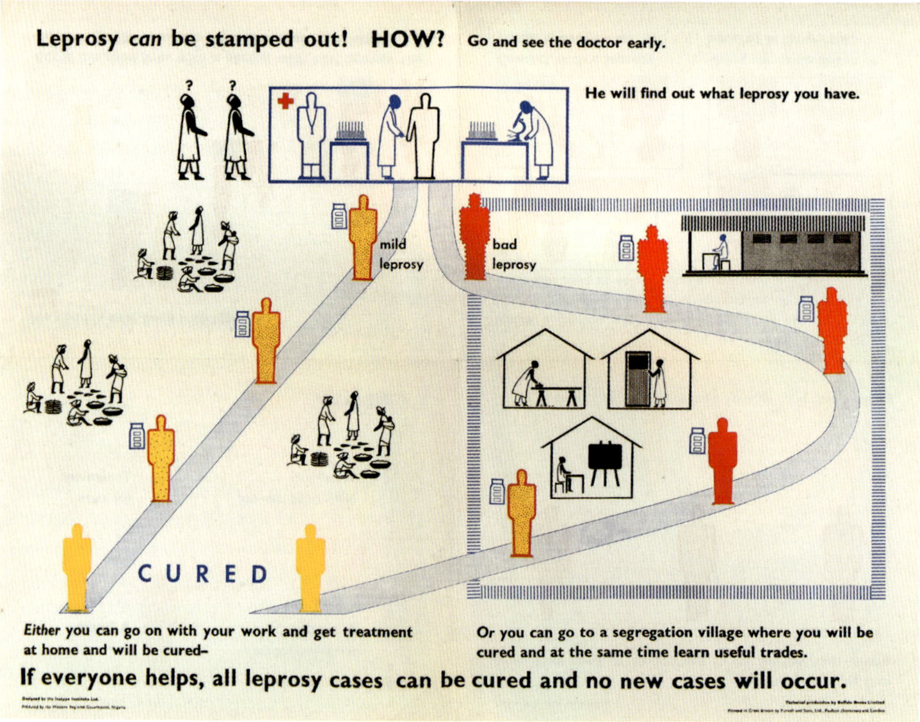

6.11 Poster-leaflet, 'Leprosy', 1955. Fold-out, 380 × 508 mm. As Eric Kindel has observed, a subtle distinction was made between Africans and the generic human pictogram in this chart on health (see Kindel, 'Isotype in Africa', p.469).

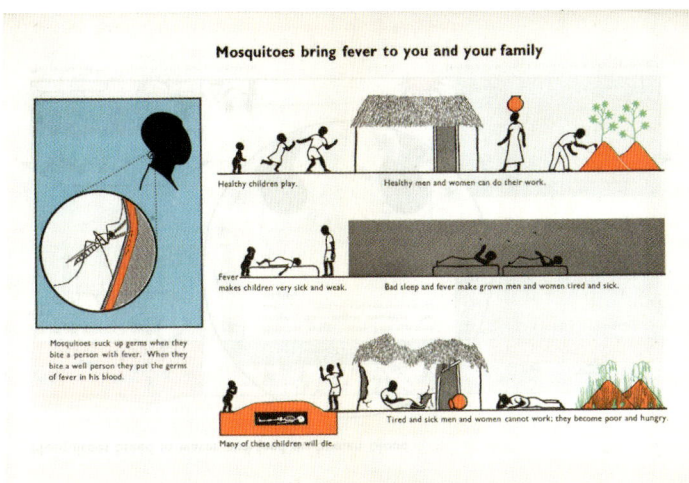

6.12 Poster-leaflet for the London-based Central Council for Health Education, 'How to save your children from sickness – malaria', 1958. 252 × 188 mm.

group's ideas and was gratified that he and his colleagues grasped the potential of Isotype very quickly from her sketches. There followed a major publication campaign of information booklets and posters to improve the level of education, farming methods and health awareness (figs 6.9–6.12). The 'style' of Isotype in these publications was more illustrative (like the children's books) than previous picture-statistical work: African traditions of attire were depicted and human figures were not strictly pictograms. In Marie Neurath's view, it was not the objective of Isotype to design a definitive set of pictograms that could represent, undifferentiated, all people and things in the world. Instead, material was designed to fulfil specific purposes in certain contexts:

> The number of symbols cannot be foreseen: new tasks and subject matters often require new symbols. The method and the approach are, I think, more universal than the symbols are. I had to discover this when I worked for Africans for some time. I had to make things clear to them, and I could not force our 'international symbols' on them. Many symbols, of man, woman, house, tree, field, etc. had to be specially designed for them. When things are equal all over the world the symbols can be the same.[29]

Marie Neurath travelled to Africa for lengthy research visits – the first aeroplane journeys of her life. There she discussed her ideas with intended users and visited schools to assess the effectiveness of visual aids in education. She described later how the experience of being in Africa led her to discard the first, rough visualizations she had made beforehand and to start again.[30]

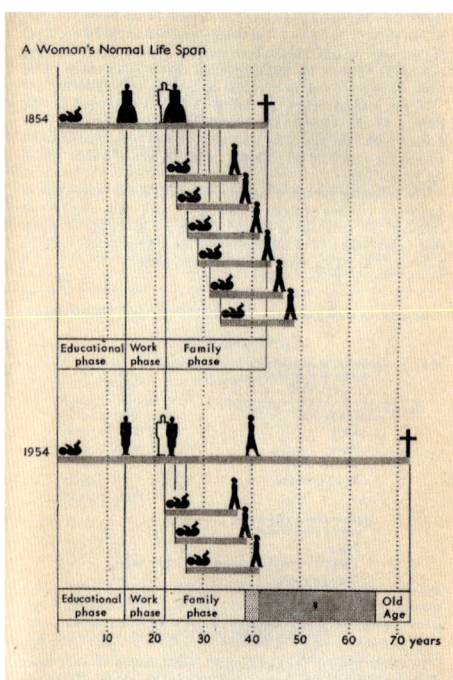

6.13 Charts by Marie Neurath for Alva Myrdal and Viola Klein, *Women's Two Roles: Home and Work* (London: Routledge, 1956). Some of the lettering in these examples is drawn by hand.

An intriguing project that Marie Neurath seems to have fitted in around her work in Africa was to design charts for the book *Women's Two Roles: Home and Work* (1956) by Alva Myrdal and Viola Klein. Myrdal was a Swedish sociologist and politician, and Klein was a Czech sociologist exiled in Britain. Myrdal visited Marie Neurath in summer 1952 to discuss her visualizing statistics for the book, but it seems that the work had to be done rather quickly after the manuscript was ready in late 1954. One sign that it did not follow the usual procedure is that the customary credit to the Isotype Institute is lacking from the charts, which also do not feature the standard Futura typeface used in Isotype (fig. 6.13). But the designing hand of Marie Neurath is evident, and these charts bring to mind those she helped to design for a pioneering feminist study during the Vienna period: the Social and Economic Museum provided charts for Käthe Leichter's book *So leben wir ...* (So We Live, 1932), subtitled '1,320 industrial working women report on their lives'.

One project that did not fit into the established series of Marie Neurath's books for young readers was *Living With One Another* (1965), a small book that she wrote as an introduction to social studies, which was then establishing itself as a school subject. She described it to Arntz as covering similar ground to *Modern Man in the Making*, although it is a far more modest production: it features no colour printing, but many monochrome charts and diagrams integrated with the text (fig. 6.14).

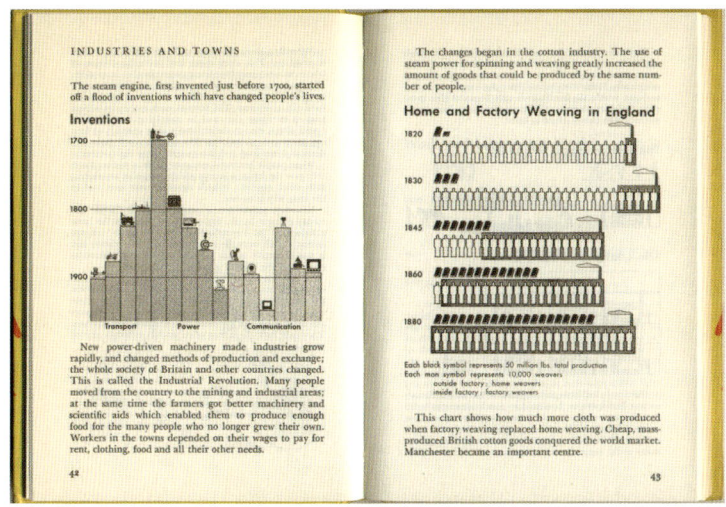

6.14 Pages from Marie Neurath, *Living With One Another*, 1965. 182 × 133 mm. The chart on the right is adapted from *Modern Man in the Making* (1939); indeed many charts in this book are reworked from earlier publications.

Failure to reunite

Arntz may have had a more traumatic experience during the war than the Neuraths. Their escape was perilous but, through their own decisive action combined with good luck, they arrived to safety, and were treated decently in internment. Arntz was forced into combat, fighting for a regime he despised, and he no doubt witnessed atrocious events. He had served in the First World War, too, and his son Peter also had to fight in the Second (while still in his late teenage years). 'In my anti-militaristic life', he reflected, 'I have worn about twelve different uniforms.'[31]

Arntz and Marie Neurath re-established contact in summer 1946. The tone of his letters was melancholy, and the instability of his situation after the war led him to remark that he was 'still living as if under occupation and the war has not yet ended for me'. She recognized that he was in a difficult position and had to remain at the NSS initially, but she asked him, in October 1946: 'I should like to know whether you would like the idea to join our institute one day.' It was a tentative enquiry, given that 'the whole situation [was] a bit delicate' at that time; yet it was a sincere question that she returned to again and again over the course of the next five years.[32] It became clear, however, that Arntz was reluctant to move to England. Understandably, he did not want to relinquish his position at NSS, which was akin to a civil service job; and his family responsibilities tied him to the Netherlands. Additionally, he may have thought that – as a German who had fought in the war (albeit unwillingly) – he would not be welcome in Britain. (The situation may not have been very pleasant for him in the Netherlands, either.)

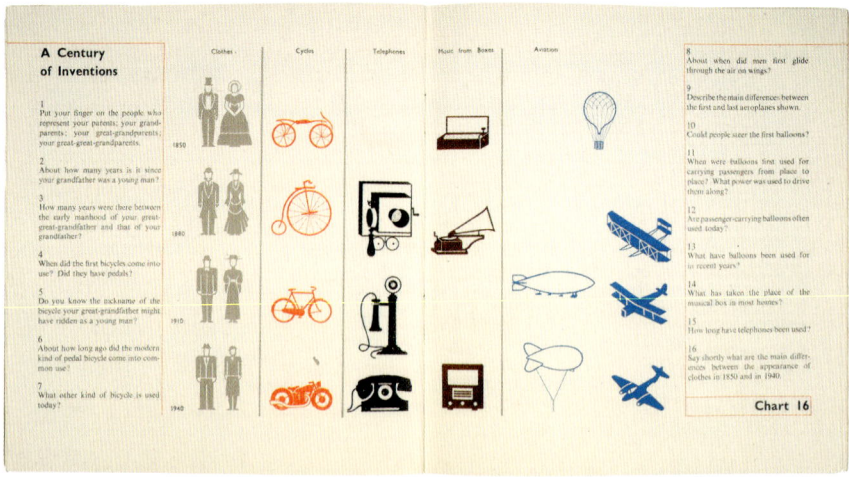

6.15 Pages from *Living in the World*, 1948. 220 × 190 mm.

Marie Neurath attempted to elicit a more definite response from Arntz:

> As you are of the opinion, like me, that good work can only be achieved by a group in co-operation … everybody here knows how much Isotype owes to you, but I see no other worthwhile solution than for us to work together again, and I also believe that this is possible. You seem to take this possibility into account less than I would like; maybe that is general pessimism: or perhaps your desire for this is not so strong. I would like to know if that is the case.[33]

Once the Isotype Institute had agreed a new three-year contract with Adprint in 1948, Marie Neurath was optimistic about her planned publishing programme and renewed her efforts to acquire Arntz's collaboration. She proposed that he could go to England for short periods to work on the Isotype Institute's projects, or at least they could collaborate by post. She even suggested that she could visit him now and again to work together, given that she had more freedom to travel after becoming a British citizen. Arntz accepted her proposal 'in theory' but, in practice, he saw little chance of it happening: 'I continue to regret that we have so drifted apart, when we could certainly do decent things together, but since I didn't know any other way (and still don't), I suppose we'll have to accept the situation.'[34]

Marie Neurath visited Arntz in The Hague and they kept each other supplied with copies of their work. While he considered the work of transformation in her children's books 'excellent', he criticized aspects of the graphic execution: 'The human figures disturb me. They seem to me often to remain too primitive and too little redrawn, even when accepting schematization as a system.' He perceived the same lack of refinement in her book *Living in the World* (fig. 6.15):

> It pleases me as much as the others, except for the occasionally unripe drawing and all too mechanical application of standard symbols. I admire the whole conception very much, but a little more aesthetic care could not hurt, since the form given to a picture language is also very important.[35]

Marie Neurath was not upset by this criticism; quite the opposite. She evidently valued Arntz's skill and opinion so much that it spurred her to renew her request that they work together: 'Now that you yourself have complained about the big, boring human figures, something really must be done!'[36] In 1951, she wrote to him:

> Indeed, I recognize the weaknesses of our work and share your opinion! I know why I want to work with you again. My conviction goes so far that it even occurred to me that I could serve our British clients from Holland, and that I will come to you if you do not want to come here! Now that I am free to move again – after the expiry of our contract of many years – all possibilities are open![37]

No such reunion took place, however, and they continued to pursue their different paths. Arntz's work at NSS became increasingly less interesting for him, involving much routine graphic design of annual reports for banks and other corporations. By 1960, Arntz rarely had the opportunity to work on pictograms, and pictorial statistics featured less frequently in his work. He had designed some new pictograms during the 1950s, which now seem dated and less 'timeless' than those he had designed in the 1930s under the critical eye of Otto Neurath. In 1960, the NSS began to publish a periodical called *Cijfers en commentaar* (Figures and commentary), which illustrated statistics in a jokey, cartoonish way that was the opposite of Isotype. The remit of the NSS included market research and business consultancy, and so it was quite a different kind of organization to the Isotype Institute, which always retained a focus on education. Marie Neurath guarded her independence and was determined to conceive and define Isotype projects herself: consequently she had more freedom, although this meant that the institute rarely made a profit.

Arntz retired from the NSS in 1966, and afterwards enjoyed some recognition of his 'free' artwork, with exhibitions in Germany and the Netherlands. Marie Neurath congratulated him on this success: 'I appreciated you from the earliest days, so I can only say: well, now they see it.' She occasionally gave lectures about Isotype and reported to him: 'I always speak about you as the most important designer of pictograms; the history can easily be divided into pre-Arntz and Arntz.'[38]

Marie Neurath's final series of books, 'They Lived Like This' – about ancient cultures – was her most extensive, comprising twenty titles, the last of which appeared in 1971. After this, she continued to document the history of Isotype and to edit the writings of Otto Neurath for publication, both activities which she had begun in the 1960s. She also sought an archival home for the work material of Isotype, settling on the University of Reading, where Professor Michael Twyman of the Department of Typography & Graphic Communication was particularly appreciative of its legacy. The gift of material was honoured with an exhibition at the university in 1975, which then travelled to Vienna in 1977 (see chapter 5).

Arntz continued to be celebrated as a fine artist, but he reassured his old friend: 'Neurath and you naturally figure in any discussions about my "applied" art.'[39] Yet, sadly, their mutual appreciation soured in their final years. Marie Neurath reacted with disproportionate anger to a published collection of the pictograms from the files of the NSS (which had been given to Gemeentemuseum Den Haag).[40] She and Arntz had discussed a joint publication of this kind over a decade before, but this does not seem to have been the reason for her chagrin; instead she took exception to the historical introduction by art historian Kees Broos, imputing the opinions in it to Arntz. In his own (very brief) foreword, Arntz pointed out that the pictograms were intended for use in pictorial statistics, and not to stand alone – an observation she would no doubt have approved. Broos's text was also a solid historical account, giving due credit to Otto and Marie Neurath, but she perceived deep resentment against Otto Neurath in it. 'But look at the symbols of this lexicon', she protested, 'it cannot be that you do not notice that the best ones are those that were created under his wing.' She concluded on a note of exasperation: 'Better that we leave each other in peace, now that we are both over eighty.'[41]

6.16 Marie Neurath at home in Hampstead, London, c. 1980. On the mantelpiece are two photographs of Otto Neurath, taken shortly before his death in 1945.

7 Rudolf Modley in America

Rudolf Modley was among the many employees of the Social and Economic Museum. Born in Vienna in 1906, his mother was active in the Social Democratic Party as a district councillor, and his father worked for an electrical company. The Modleys were a Jewish, social-democratic family that could not remain unaffected by fascism and increasing anti-Semitism. Modley's father died in December 1937, shortly before the National Socialists came to power in Austria, and his mother fled to the USA, where her son had already been living for several years.[1]

Rudolf Modley began studying law at the University of Vienna in 1924, graduating in 1929. Together with his friend Fritz Jahnel, he became politically involved in social democracy as a young man. Both were also interested in the Vienna Method of Pictorial Statistics and they began to work in the Social and Economic Museum: Jahnel as a draughtsman and economic statistician; Modley in administration and guided tours.[2] Modley also wrote an article on the importance of the Vienna Method for socialism in the struggle for liberation of the proletariat. He suggested that visual education was effective in reaching workers exhausted by wage labour.[3] However, Modley's position at the Vienna Museum also opened up the opportunity for him to leave Austria.

The American science journalist Waldemar Kaempffert (a cousin of Otto Neurath) had taken on the task of setting up a scientific and technical museum in Chicago.[4] He undertook trips to Europe in 1928 and 1929 to look at possible models for this project. In the process, he visited Otto Neurath at the Social and Economic Museum in Vienna. This visit was to be one of the most important stops on the European tour, which ultimately resulted in a cooperation between the museums in Vienna and Chicago. In 1930, Rudolf Modley was sent to Chicago to help set up the Museum of Science and Industry (MSI) and to organize the cooperation with Vienna as a liaison. He became the curator for social sciences in Chicago and a separate department was set up for this

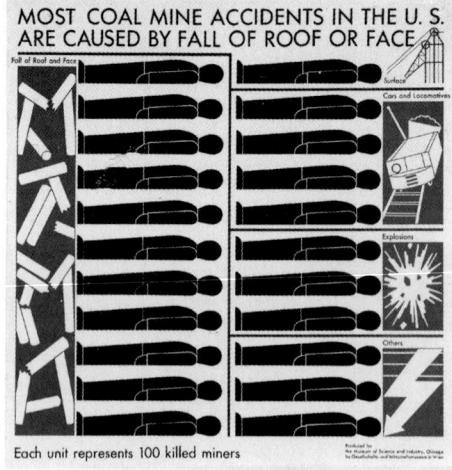

7.1 Charts produced by the Gesellschafts- und Wirtschaftsmuseum for the Museum of Science and Industry, Chicago, under the direction of Rudolf Modley, 1931–2 (IC T543, 546).

subject area at the emergent museum. Modley also began postgraduate studies at the University of Chicago in sociology and political economy.

The opening of the MSI was planned for 1932, but actually took place a year later. Modley corresponded regularly with Neurath and other staff in Vienna to seek advice and order exhibition charts. Neurath also offered animated films, magnetic charts, accident prevention pictures, and he made thematic suggestions. By 1932, the Social and Economic Museum had already completed thirty-four exhibition panels and sent them to Chicago (fig. 7.1).[5]

In this cooperation, however, differences of opinion between Neurath and Modley were already apparent, and became increasingly prominent in the following years. Their disagreement concerned concrete questions of visualization, such as the design of pictograms, but it was also about the work process and the responsibilities associated with it. Neurath wanted to control the entire production process according to his ideas of interdisciplinary teamwork; exhibition charts sent to Chicago were not to undergo any significant changes there. Modley, on the other hand, criticized some of the work from Vienna, complaining about the slowness with which, in his view, commissions were processed.[6] He also demanded the right to intervene in terms of content: he wanted to adapt charts and pictograms to the conditions in the USA, which he thought he knew better, and where he also had more direct access to figures and data. Cooperation was further complicated by the fact that Kaempffert resigned from his post as museum director at the end of February 1931 and returned to his former job as Science Editor of the *New York Times*.

In any case, in the light of the Great Depression, the general conditions for the Chicago Museum project were anything but favourable. In the summer of 1932, Modley's department was dissolved and he lost his job.[7] He decided to continue his work in the USA independently of the connection to Otto Neurath. He moved to New York and soon found opportunities to work on numerous government projects under the New Deal policy (1933–8). Introduced by president Franklin D. Roosevelt, the New Deal was supported by a broad coalition in US society, including farmers, industrial workers, women, ethnic minorities and liberal intellectuals.[8] State-funded programmes initiated and supported infrastructure projects: dams were built and schools and hospitals were constructed; social benefits were also introduced, such as unemployment benefit and old-age pensions.[9] Moreover, within the framework of the New Deal, there were numerous cultural, artistic and scientific initiatives. Politically speaking, the USA clearly moved to the left during these years.[10]

Modley founded Pictorial Statistics, Inc. in 1934 as a non-profit corporation, and a commercial offshoot, Pictograph Corporation, was added in 1940.[11] Modley himself had a talent for drawing, but he worked with different draughtsmen, graphic designers and specialists, depending on the job at hand. Public commissions were central to the work of Pictorial Statistics, Inc. for the New Deal, and themes of social welfare and health education provided common ground with the Vienna Method. Yet Modley now moved in an environment that, despite some similarities, was different to that in Vienna: in the USA, there were already several organizations active in the field of information design which produced similar pictorial representations to Modley's agency.[12] Competition thus also played a role, which did not always have a positive effect on the quality of the work; cost reduction and time pressure could sometimes result in the opposite.

The first extensive job carried out by Pictorial Statistics, Inc. was a series of charts for the Mississippi Valley Committee of the Public Works Administration. Its chairman, Morris L. Cooke, considered commissioning graphic material from Otto Neurath, who was attempting to set up an Institute for Visual Education in the USA with help from colleagues at the Russell Sage Foundation of New York. In fact, Modley had been engaged to assist the organizing committee for this project – partly, it seems, to prevent him from striking out on his own. In the end, Cooke baulked at employing Neurath, who was based outside the USA and had affiliations with the Soviet regime.[13] This left Modley ideally placed to take over, and his company contributed pictorial charts on subjects such as hydroelectric power to the committee's published report, along with other agencies such as Sociographics. Modley also received

 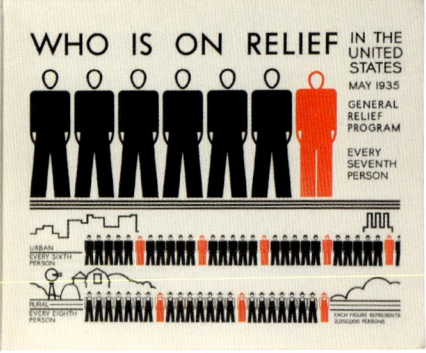

7.2 Cover and chart from *On Relief: General Relief Program, May 1935*. Prepared by the Graphic Unit of the Social Research Division of the Federal Emergency Relief Administration (later Works Progress Administration) under the direction of Calvin Banwell and Rudolf Modley, 1935. 200 × 265 mm.

further commissions from Cooke in his role as administrator of the Rural Electrification Administration. An important collaboration also developed between Pictorial Statistics, Inc. and the Works Progress Administration (WPA). The WPA had established a 'Graphic Unit' in its Division of Social Research to make charts for publications, and Modley helped direct the unit's work (fig. 7.2).[14]

1937 was a good year for Modley: he became an American citizen, and married the New Jersey-born photographer Helen Post, who had Viennese experience herself, having learned photography there from Trude Fleischmann.[15] In the same year, his instructional manual *How to Use Pictorial Statistics* was published, which also provides a historical overview that acknowledges the significance of the Vienna Method (fig. 7.3); and *The United States: a Graphic History* appeared, listing Modley as one of its authors due to the pictorial statistics interwoven with its text (fig. 7.4).

In his *How to ...* book, Modley announced a syndicated newspaper feature called 'Telefact', which was intended to bring 'pictographs' (as he called pictographic charts) to the attention of a wide readership. Around 1000 small charts were produced between 1938 and 1945, appearing in daily newspapers all over the USA. Considering how quickly these had to be designed and produced, they are mostly very effective nuggets of graphic design in black and white.[16] (They have a similar graphic impact to the charts made by the Izostat Institute for *Izvestia* a few years earlier.)[17] Projects such as 'Telefact' are perhaps what led Helen Post to remark later: 'No literate American, and quite a few who were not literate, could escape frequent exposure to the Modley group's charts during the Thirties and Forties.'[18]

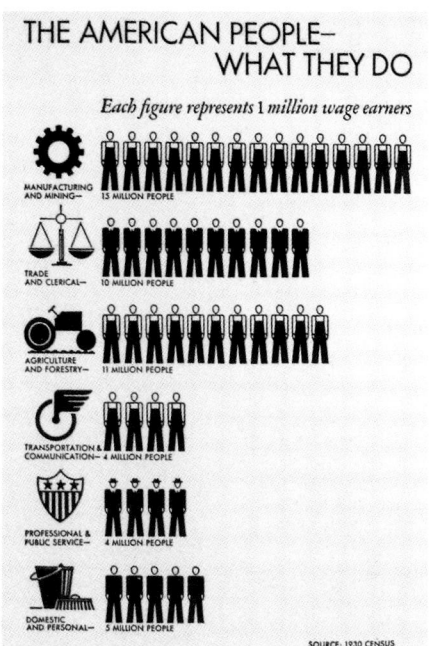
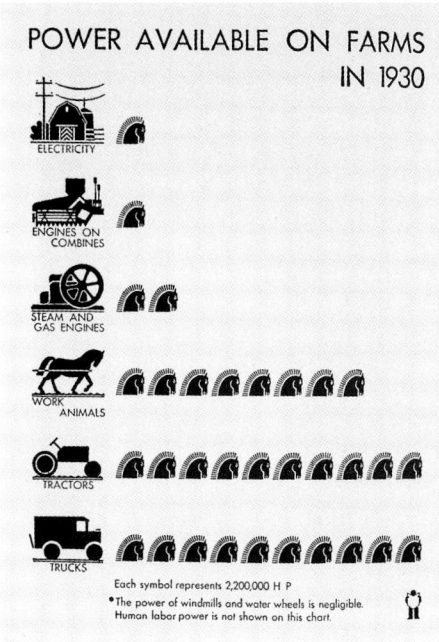

7.3 Representative examples from Rudolf Modley's *How to Use Pictorial Statistics*, 1937.

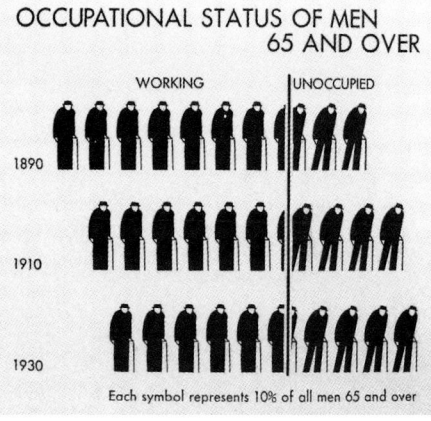

Examples from the chapter on 'Symbol arrangement' in Modley's *How to Use Pictorial Statistics*. In the caption to the chart above, he explained: 'Here the axis cuts through a full symbol so that parts of it fall on either side. The pictorial quality remains intact even if smaller fractions than halves are used. This system should be used only where greater exactness is demanded.' (p.65)

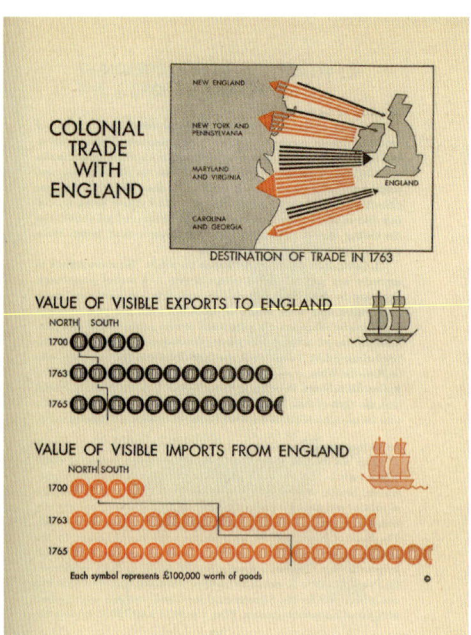

7.4 Charts from Louis M. Hacker, Rudolf Modley and George R. Taylor, *The United States: a Graphic History*, 1937.

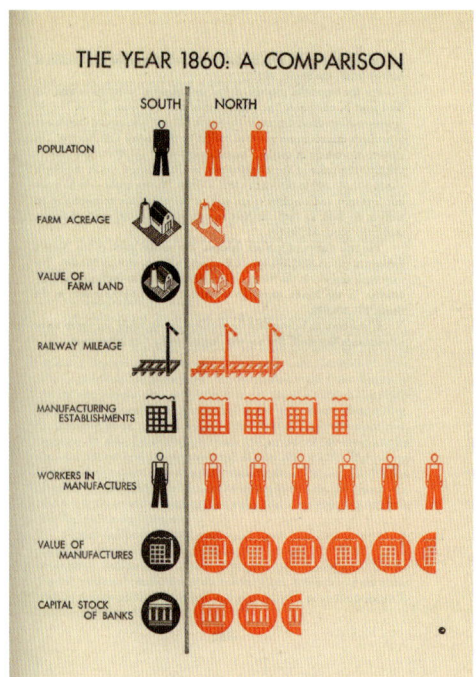

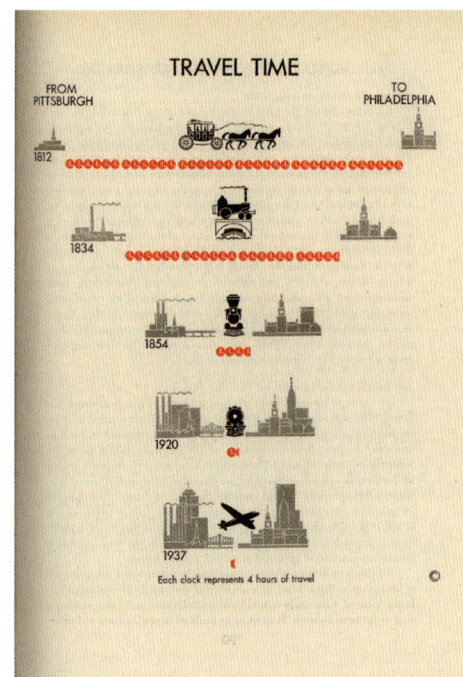

Note the similarity of configuration in this chart with fig. 2.11.

7.5 Charts from *The New York Primer*, 1939.

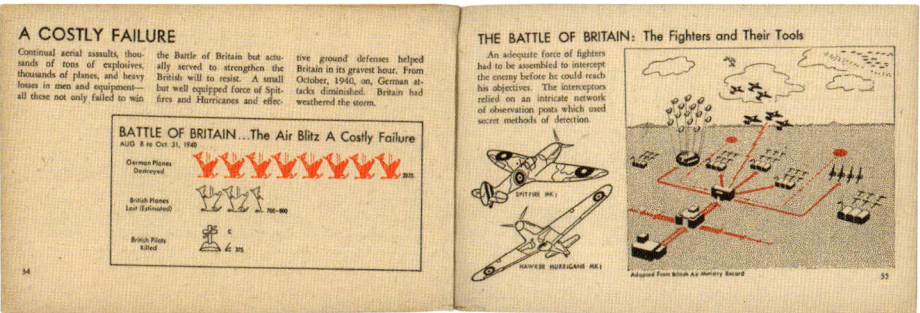

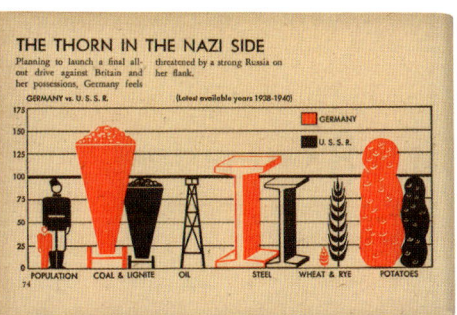
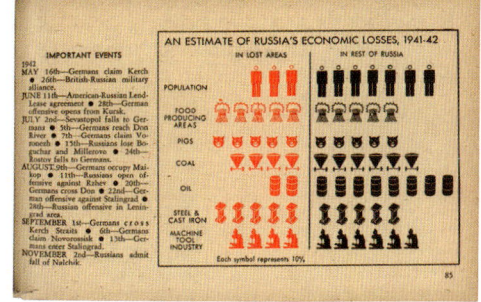

7.6 Pages from *A History of the War*, 1942. 109 × 178 mm.

Examples of work by Modley and his agency, which were elaborate, well thought-out and sophisticated in their design, were the annual report of the Museum of Modern Art for 1939/40, *The New York Primer* (1939), a survey of that state's schooling by Modley and the social scientist Luther Gullick (fig. 7.5), and Modley's book *A History of the War* (1942), produced after the USA entered the Second World War (fig. 7.6). From the latter's preface, we learn that some 40,000 copies of its predecessor publication, *A Graphic History of the War*, were distributed to Army units in the summer of 1942.

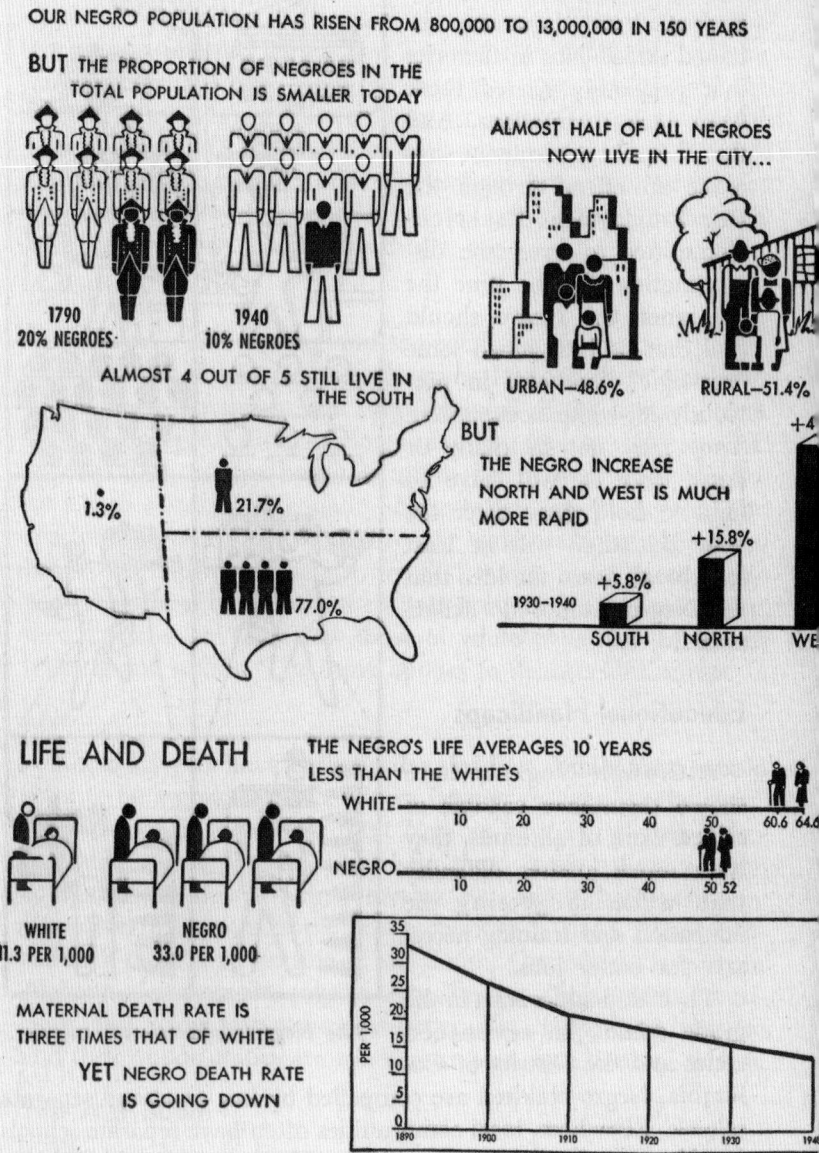

7.7 Pages from the booklet *The Negro in America* by Maxwell S. Stewart, published by the Public Affairs Committee, New York, 1944. Charts originally made by Modley's Pictograph Corporation for *Survey Graphic*. Shown at actual size.

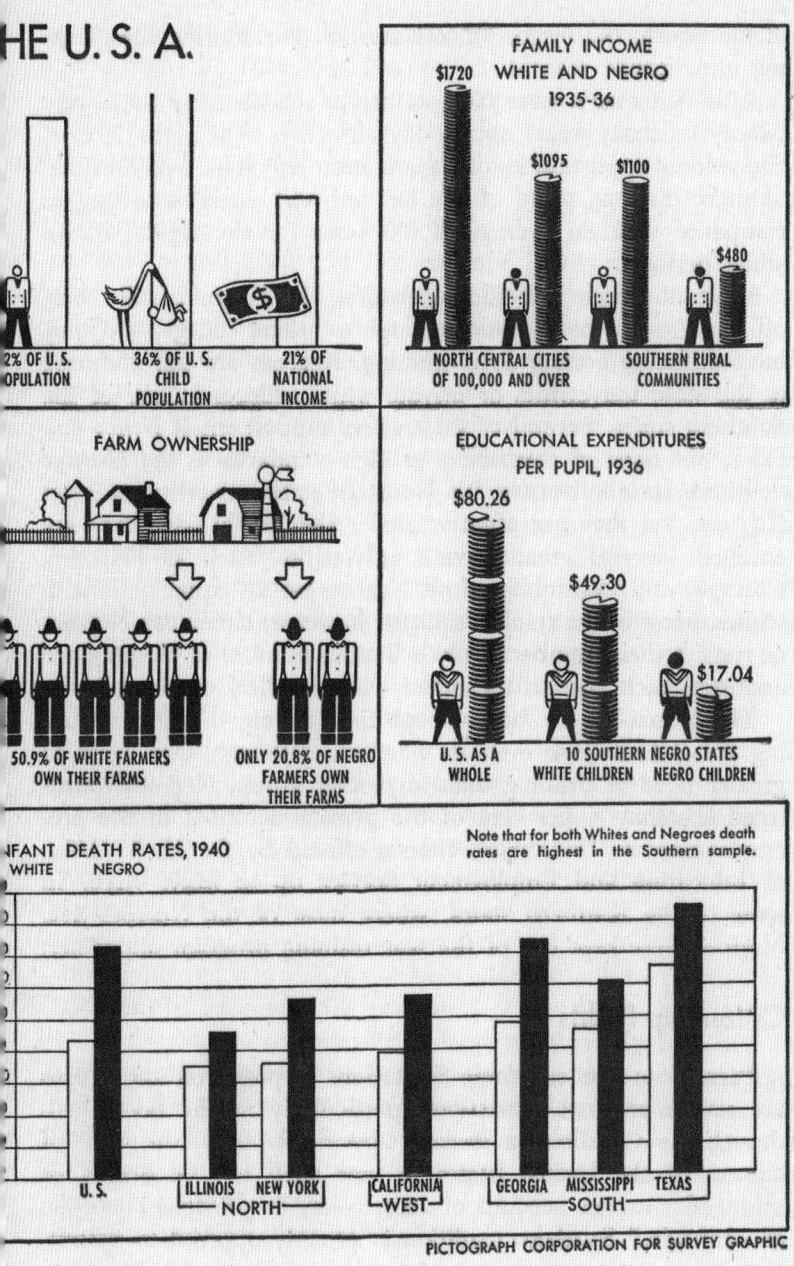

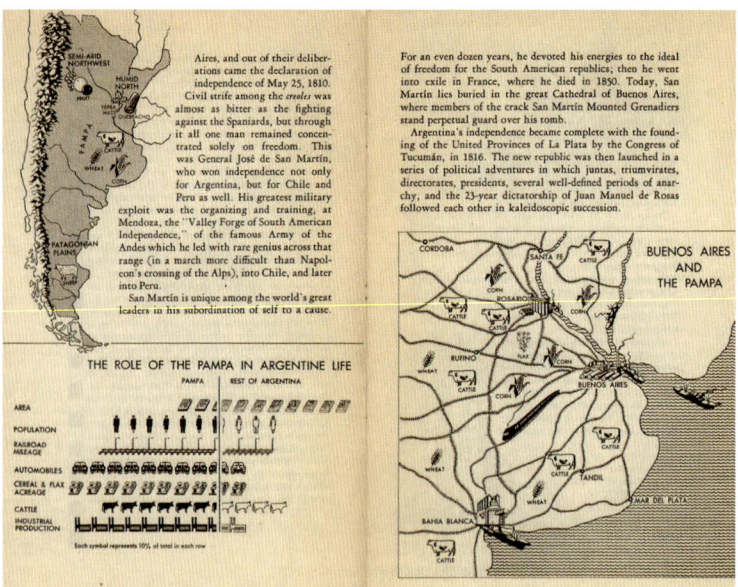

7.8 Pages from *Argentina: Profile of a Nation*, 1944. One of a series of books on Latin American countries published by the Office of the Coordinator of Inter-American Affairs.

During the war, Modley worked for the Office of the Coordinator of Information (COI), the forerunner of the Office of Strategic Services (OSS), which later became the CIA. The Pictograph Corporation under Modley also produced numerous brochures about Latin American countries for the Office of the Coordinator of Inter-American Affairs, which sought to minimize the influence of the fascist Axis powers on the development of this region (fig. 7.8).[19]

After the war, Rudolf Modley and Helen Post moved to Kent (Connecticut), and Modley sold the Pictograph Corporation to his friend Fritz Jahnel in 1946. When Jahnel died in 1952, the agency was taken over by Dyno Lowenstein, with whom Modley co-wrote the book *Pictographs and Graphs: How to Make Use of Them* (1952). Lowenstein, who had also worked for the OSS during the war, continued the pictorial work for many years. Modley worked in management consulting, was active in organizations concerned with standardization, and prepared reports for government agencies. He also emerged as the founder and, for over twenty years, the editor of a credit union's magazine.

The New Deal era coincided with a brief period of American internationalism, and the USA and USSR were even allies for the latter part of the war. But as the chill of the Cold War settled in, with Senator Joseph McCarthy's committee to weed out 'un-American activities' in the 1950s, the political climate turned against the kind of projects that Modley had worked on in the 1930s – and this may account for his change of professional direction, to some extent. As the

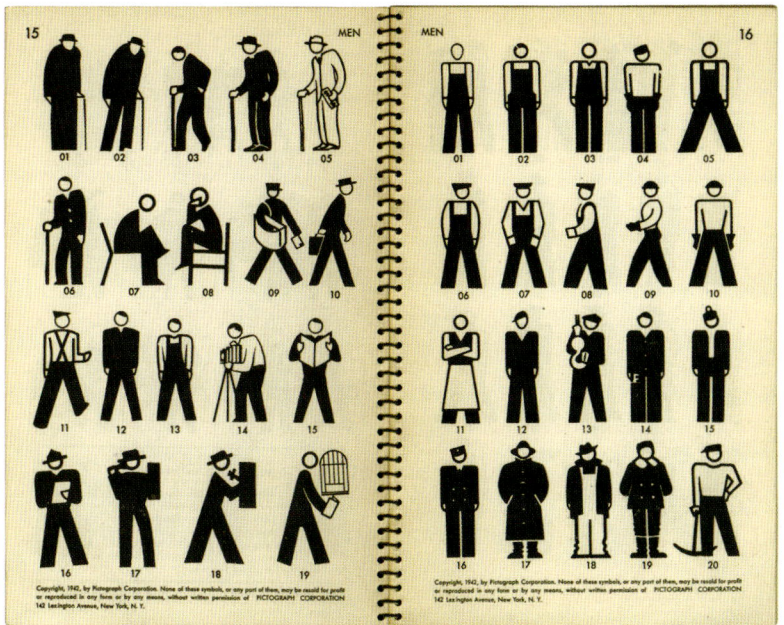

7.9 Pages from *1000 Pictorial Symbols* (Pictograph Corporation, 1942). 217 × 140 mm.

American historian Jill Lepore put it, politics and society in the USA became 'small-minded, vulgar and confused'.[20]

Modley's work in the USA never had the political character that the work of the Social and Economic Museum had in Red Vienna; indeed, Modley's professional career would probably have been affected if his attitudes of the Viennese years had become known. In contrast to his youth in Austria, Modley was hardly active in party politics in the United States, although he was a member of the rather left-liberal Union for Democratic Action.[21] On a more personal level, he and his wife were active in helping emigrants from Nazi Germany, whom they took in at their home.[22]

Glyphs

The last of Modley's projects in the USA had a long history. Its precursors date back to 1940, when he and the political scientist Harold Lasswell unsuccessfully sought funding from the Carnegie Foundation to create and publish a 'Dictionary of Graphic Symbols' currently used in America.[23] Instead, Pictograph Corporation published *1000 Pictorial Symbols* (1942), a catalogue of all the pictograms it had developed (fig. 7.9). Modley offered to make them available to 'schools and colleges and social agencies' at minimal cost, and freely extended the right to use them 'in experiments' (the book's title-page declared that they were 'designed and copyrighted by Pictograph Corporation'). In the

1950s, Modley again planned a symbol project under the title 'Communication through Symbols', which he had formulated at the request of the industrial designer Henry Dreyfuss. After support for a preliminary study was secured from the Fund for the Advancement of Education (established by the Ford Foundation), Marie Neurath was employed for a few months in 1958 to collect and classify existing signs and symbols, with a view to compiling a dictionary of them.[24] But financial support for the complete project was not approved.

Yet it seemed to be a favourable time for universal language projects. After the Second World War, efforts to standardize international symbols intensified, with an important role being played by the International Organization for Standardization (ISO), which had existed since 1947. The 1960s appeared to be a time of 'design universalism' in general.[25] The economic background for this was the rapid increase in tourist travel and international trade, especially in the Western world. Widely understandable pictures and symbols, independent of national languages, became an important form of communication.[26] Organizations such as the International Committee for the Breaking of Language Barriers (ICBLB) or the International Council of Graphic Design Associations (ICOGRADA) were founded in the early 1960s with the aim of developing models for cross-national and cross-cultural communication. ICOGRADA cooperated with German designer Martin Krampen (of the Hochschule für Gestaltung Ulm) in a large-scale research project to develop international symbols in the late 1960s. The intention was to submit proposals to a newly formed International Commission on Travel Signs and Symbols (ICTSS), but no documented standards resulted from this initiative.[27]

The Olympic Games provided a recurrent impetus for the development of language-independent pictograms, and continue to do so, accompanied by an element of national branding. In particular, the events in Tokyo (1964) and Mexico (1968) resulted in influential designs, and the pictograms designed by Otl Aicher for the 1972 Munich Olympics still have cult status today.[28]

In 1965, the United Nations declared its twentieth anniversary to be 'International Cooperation Year' (ICY) and, from a competition to design a symbol for it, a motif of intertwined hands was chosen. In the course of preparations for the anniversary, anthropologist Margaret Mead submitted a proposal to develop a system of universal symbols under the title 'Glyphs', with the help of the Canadian UN delegation. Mead had been a best-selling author since her books *Coming of Age in Samoa* (1928) and *Growing Up in New Guinea* (1930), and she had a high profile in the media and politics.[29] Glyphs was also explicitly mentioned in a memorandum of the ICY Preparatory Committee in 1964: 'One of the useful tasks which could be encouraged during the International Cooperation Year would be the development of a new kind of symbol technically known as a glyph. A glyph is a symbol which has meaning which is separable and independent from names given to the symbol in different languages.'[30] However, it was explicitly left to the member states to decide which symbols they chose, rather contradicting the idea of a universal language.

Rudolf Modley was also involved in the Glyphs project from the beginning and he was to become its main organizer. He developed a basic differentiation of glyphs, which was referred to repeatedly during the project. According to Modley, there were three types of glyphs: image-related, concept-related or arbitrary. Respectively (in semiotic terms), these were icons (pictograms), indexes (e.g. wavy lines for water), and symbols such as numbers, letters or other abstract signs. He remarked that image-related glyphs could lead to misunderstandings: for example, the pictogram of an old steam locomotive could no longer be interpreted as an index for a level crossing but as a reference to a railway museum.[31] (A counter-example of pictogram survival is the old telephone handset, which remains in use, despite the changing shape of telephones.)

Glyphs, Inc. was founded in 1966. In addition to Modley and Mead, the central figures of this NGO were psychologist Lawrence K. Frank, political scientist Harold Lasswell and the UN official Curtis Roosevelt. In the following years, however, it was mainly Modley who made numerous requests and applications for financial support, corresponded, organized meetings and established networks. He wrote internal reports and also published articles on Glyphs.

The working plan was to collect, test and systematize existing symbols, and to determine which glyphs would be suitable for the areas most in need of them. For this, not only experts from different fields would be required, but also political support and funding from both philanthropic and commercial organizations. The hope was to organize cooperation with eight major companies, each of which would provide $10,000 per year. However, it was mainly funds from Mead and Modley themselves that made up the bulk of Glyphs, Inc.'s modest income.[32]

A detailed concept was developed for a travelling exhibition, 'Glyphs for World Communications', but attempts to develop it were unsuccessful. An archive of symbols was also planned but, again, never materialized, despite intensive negotiations with various institutions. An interesting newsletter named *Glyphs* did appear regularly from 1966 until Modley's death in 1976. It was written mainly by him and was published in cooperation with the Japanese magazine *Graphic Design* (founded by Katsumi Masaru, design coordinator of the 1964 Tokyo Olympics). In addition to reporting on new initiatives, Modley paid tribute to the lasting influence of Otto Neurath and Isotype (fig. 7.10).[33]

The plans for Glyphs were far-reaching – one might even say over-ambitious. In 1968, the article 'Communication Among All People, Everywhere' by Mead

7.10 *Glyphs Newsletter* no.15 (1973/4). The illustration in the middle of the right column is an example of an industrial safety warning designed at the Social and Economic Museum of Vienna, c. 1927.

7.11 Pages from Rudolf Modley's *Handbook of Pictorial Symbols*, 1976.

and Modley was published in the periodical *Natural History*.[34] Mead had been a frequent contributor for decades to this magazine, which reached a broad public. In their article, Mead and Modley outlined three steps in the construction of new universal language communication. Firstly, they wanted to establish a limited number of glyphs for worldwide, basic orientation in international travel and trade, and also in hazard prevention. Secondly, an existing, natural language would be chosen as an auxiliary to enable basic communication, although they did not specify which one. They felt that, 'in the present climate of opinion' (in 1968), a European language would be unacceptable politically; it should be a language that privileged no large, existing community of speakers. (Mysteriously, Armenian was at least once envisaged, which may have been the result of a suggestion by Mead's daughter.)[35] And thirdly, an 'invented' written language was to be developed for 'high-level philosophical, political, and scientific communication'. 'With all three', wrote Mead and Modley, 'we could take full advantage of our new mobility and share in the kind of relationship once available only on "the village green"; and educated men and women, whatever their mother tongue, could exchange – efficiently and unimpeded by historical nuances – the highest developments of human thought.'[36]

These were idealistic aims and, unsurprisingly, none of this ever came to pass. The main, concrete outcomes that were at least indirectly related to the Glyphs project were the *Symbol Sourcebook* (1972) by Henry Dreyfuss, and the *Handbook of Pictorial Symbols* (1976) by Rudolf Modley (fig. 7.11). By classifying and illustrating existing symbols according to certain criteria, both books could only serve as the beginning of a universal language project.

Mead and Modley's Glyphs project eventually failed for several reasons.[37] First and foremost, it suffered from a lack of resources. Neither public nor private funds could be obtained on a sufficient scale. As a result, it also lacked the staffing that would have been necessary, both in terms of experts and administrative personnel.[38] Modley obviously only wanted to work in the background, but in the end, he had to do most of the work alone. Margaret Mead was also fully occupied with other work and only participated sporadically in the efforts to establish Glyphs. As Modley himself once remarked, the creation of a universal language was not just about a good idea, but above all was about politics and organization, and this was lacking at both a national and international level.[39] It was not possible to resolve a common project that was acceptable to all of the different people and organizations who were committed to the idea a universal language. There were repeated polemical disputes with the director of the ICBLB, Soichi Kato, but also with Charles Bliss, the inventor of the symbol script 'Semantography', later renamed Blissymbolics.[40] Bliss (originally Karl Blitz, an Austrian exiled in Australia) felt that his system, published in 1949, was unjustly neglected and pounced on any opportunity to put it into use. Modley wrote to Mead that 'Bliss, in his way is going to be as much of a nuisance as Kato'.[41]

In a late essay, 'World Language Without Words', Modley reiterated the requirements for achieving the goals of Glyphs: collection, classification and testing of all existing symbols; an international, interdisciplinary group of experts to determine which symbols are most necessary; and leading designers to develop new symbols on this basis, which in turn would need to be tested, revised and finally evaluated. Most importantly (but unrealistically), 'a single worldwide organization' with globally recognized authority had to introduce the standard designs: 'Only government co-operation with private institutions on a national and international basis can assure that universal graphic symbols can become a reality.' Modley recognized that the 'working group' of ISO on public symbols had potential to implement these aims, but that it 'still lacks the financial resources and authority to take all of the essential steps required'.[42] ISO published its standard 7001 on 'Public Information Symbols' in 1980, which was approved by some national standardization institutes. It is a useful benchmark, but nobody is obliged to accept it – the same question of how to establish normative usage remains.

The multi-faceted ideals for 'universal' communication in the Glyphs project were far more extensive than the aims of Isotype, which Otto Neurath always wisely defined as an auxiliary form of communication with great possibilities but also many limitations. In a sense, the ambitions of Glyphs placed it in the longer, utopian tradition of defining a new language that would dissolve the barriers to mutual understanding.

Isotype and Modley in the USA

Otto and Marie Neurath had themselves been active in the USA until they fled to England. Notable examples of their work for US clients were the health campaign 'Fighting Tuberculosis' – a travelling exhibition and brochures in the late 1930s and early 1940s (fig. 4.6) – and the book *Modern Man in the Making* (1939), which Marie Neurath referred to, in retrospect, as a highpoint of Isotype work. Yet (as mentioned earlier) the plan to establish an Institute for Visual Education as an institutional basis for their work in the USA foundered, leaving Modley ideally placed to fill the gap.[43] Otto Neurath considered this a kind of betrayal: 'We experienced the most unpleasant "competition" in the USA, where the secretary paid by us realized that he could easily swim off with the people who had been interested.'[44]

The name of Neurath was used by American journalists as synonymous with pictorial statistics, even in cases that did not involve him (nor even Modley). For example, the book *Rich Man, Poor Man: Pictures of a Paradox* (1935) was

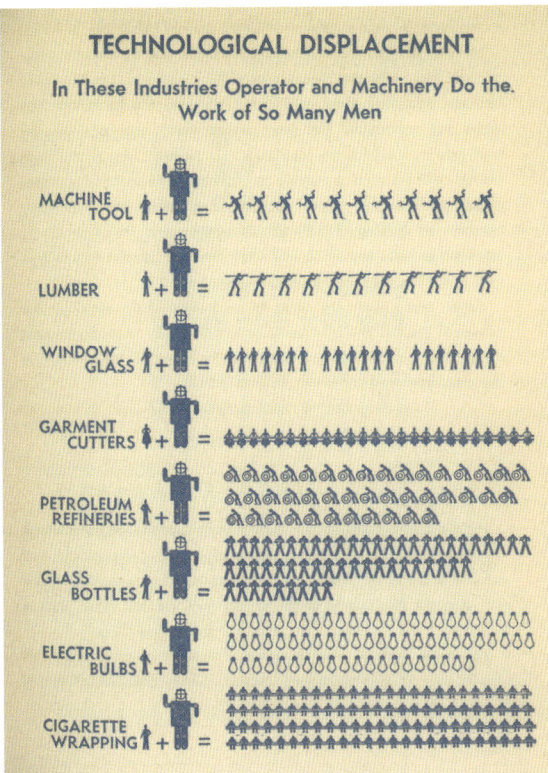

7.12 Chart from R. A. & O. P. Goslin, *Rich Man, Poor Man: Pictures of a Paradox*, 1935. Modley illustrated this example in his book, *How to Use Pictorial Statistics*, making the following criticism (p. 57): 'This chart contains numerous incorrect usages. The symbols are not equally spaced, the first row showing eleven, the third twenty, the fourth twenty-five symbols covering almost the same length. The change from a linear treatment in the first four rows to an irregular area treatment in the following four is confusing. The symbols differ too much and show too much detail. Light bulbs are used to represent workers. The chart does not actually show displacement but an equation between operator plus machine and workers employed before.'

advertised in *Survey Graphic* magazine as 'Neurath's method Americanized' (fig. 7.12). Modley, too, was credited for doing an 'effective job of Americanisation' on the Vienna Method by one reviewer of his book *How to Use Pictorial Statistics*.[45] In the preface to this book, Modley recognized the founding work of Neurath and the team at the Vienna Museum, but he also insisted on being able to pursue a modified version of Isotype independently of Neurath's influence:

> Any book which attempts to deal with the method of pictographs must acknowledge its indebtedness to the genius of Otto Neurath. He more than any one man created that method and made it into a significant tool of communication. This makes it more regrettable that Dr. Neurath has not found it possible to follow what seems to me the inevitable trend in the development of pictographs. I hope the success of our American experiments will convince him that the restrictions he has set up are not fundamental implications of the method.[46]

In discussing a project that Modley submitted to the Rockefeller Foundation, Lawrence Frank spoke of a visual method that Neurath had developed and Modley had improved.[47]

The strength with which Neurath rejected Modley's work becomes clear from his correspondence with his son, Paul Neurath, who went on to become a distinguished sociologist. Soon after settling in the USA, he wrote to his father explaining that he was using Modley's instructional book to teach pictorial statistics in university courses, mainly because Otto Neurath had (deliberately) not written such a book. Neurath senior replied curtly: 'We hope that you are more sincere in your other scientific and educational activities than you are in the field of Visual Education, based partly on material which you may find in our files under the heading COUNTEREXAMPLES.'[48]

Nevertheless, after Otto Neurath's death, Rudolf and Marie Neurath remained in friendly contact, and also collaborated briefly but substantially on the precursor to the Glyphs project, for which Marie Neurath collected and classified graphic symbols. During the course of this work, she gently but firmly reminded Modley of Otto Neurath's legacy:

> I thought it should not be left unmentioned that some first steps in a scientific treatment of the question of symbols had been made by Otto Neurath[,] without which probably neither you nor I would be in this project. Also many of the designers who are now actually designing symbols have been under his influence as most of them acknowledge.[49]

As she did to Gerd Arntz, Marie Neurath emphasized to Modley the central role of her deceased husband, which in her view was not adequately considered and valued by them. In the same year that Marie Neurath wrote this to him, Modley looked back on his time with Otto Neurath in Vienna: 'When I was still in high school, I became acquainted with Otto Neurath's isotypes. I went all out for them. Through high school and university years, I spent all my spare time working for him and with him.'[50]

The interdisciplinary working process of a stable team, as practised in Vienna and on a smaller scale in The Hague and Oxford, did not underpin Rudolf Modley's work to the same extent. The information graphics that his agency produced consequently showed a greater fluctuation in quality. The social commitment, reflection and creativity, which Neurath demanded of himself and his team, was not always evident in Modley's work. No continuous team of collaborators seemed to form around Modley in the USA (perhaps with the exception of Fritz Jahnel) and there emerged no distinctive personalities comparable to Marie Neurath or Gerd Arntz. Otto Neurath wrote of a 'living community' in connection with his team: 'transformation', the cooperation between science and graphics within a group tradition, could not happen according to fixed rules, but would emerge from the experience of several years of cooperation.[51]

In the year before his death, Modley wrote about his last major project: 'It is in the direction of a limited number of self-explanatory symbols that Glyphs is trying to continue Neurath's vision.'[52] Yet Glyphs – at least in the first of its three largely unconnected parts – was much more narrowly defined than Isotype, by concentrating on establishing a set of fixed symbols. This was never an end in itself for Otto Neurath: while he acknowledged the importance and quality of Gerd Arntz's work in designing Isotype pictograms, he viewed their function as constituent elements of larger 'visual arguments'.

Epilogue

In examining the history and legacy of Isotype, the question of what constitutes Isotype continually arises. Strictly speaking, this name applied only to work done after 1935, when Marie Reidemeister coined the term.[1] Yet both Otto and Marie Neurath retrospectively referred to work in the Vienna Method of Pictorial Statistics as Isotype, too, and this book has followed that usage occasionally. When the name first came into use, with the establishment of the IFVE in the Netherlands, it was proposed as a kind of brand, not only (and perhaps not principally) for commercial protection, but to safeguard the integrity of the method.

However, Isotype did not fulfil the promise contained in its acronymic name of an 'international system' because firm guidelines and procedures for it were never published. The original makers of Isotype never documented a comprehensive set of rules, and this was undoubtedly deliberate.[2] Otto Neurath's book *International Picture Language* (1936) is not a manual for practice, and the title's claim that it was a 'language' is misleading. The subtitle was 'the First Rules of Isotype', and these basic principles are clear. The most important one is that pictogram units should not be increased in size to indicate an increase in quantity, but should instead be repeated at the same size in greater numbers.

Although there was a certain amount of theory behind Isotype, it was worked out as a pragmatic activity of design. Some systematic elements were crucial, but Otto Neurath was sceptical of all-encompassing systems. In the same year that the Isotype name was invented, he wrote the following: '"The" system is the great scientific lie. Not even as an anticipated goal is it a useful guiding thought … Multiplicity and uncertainty are essential.'[3] This view was reflected in some statements he made about the Isotype design process: 'Up to now there is no Isotype curriculum in existence which would enable people to learn this new technique properly from the start. It is more or less routine work, based on a great many rules, the application of which depends upon a highly skilled judgement.'[4] While Isotype should be easily understood by everybody, it could only be created by those with special training and graphic imagination. In Neurath's view, this involved habitual, collaborative teamwork, in which the central activity was the 'transformation' of verbal/numerical data into pictures.

There was always a fine balance between creativity and standardization in Isotype. Consistency was important, but so was variety. Neurath resisted codifying Isotype because he wanted it to be versatile and creative – and ideally colourful: vivid and attractive graphic qualities were an aid to effective communication. However, he did not want Isotype to be entertaining at the cost of educational value. It would be difficult to make guidelines for such a nuanced approach.

Otto Neurath thought there should be a central institute to control Isotype work produced by subsidiary offices, which might be established in different countries. This would entail regional staff – in particular, transformers – being taught at the central institute. After the Second World War, Marie Neurath felt that the British Isotype Institute should perform this function, given that she was the only transformer from the original team then active as such, and consequently the person best qualified to teach prospective Isotype designers. But no lineage was created in this way. Otto Neurath's son Paul wrote to his father expressing doubt about 'the usefulness of any method, graphical or technical or sociological or anything, that cannot be taught in other ways than by the originator in person, and that is therefore practically doomed to die with the author'.[5]

Even if Isotype had been documented in an instructional manner, ambitions for its widespread use would have been limited by the lack of power (or desire) among its creators to impose it as a global norm. Perhaps the strongest possibility for this was the central Soviet declaration of 1931 that the Vienna Method should be made official in the USSR; the extent to which this happened, however, is questionable. An even more unsettling idea is that examples of the Method modified for the purposes of Nazi propaganda may have encountered an enormous audience: millions saw exhibitions such as the 'The Soviet Paradise' (1942; see chapter 3).

Otto Neurath lamented the misguided imitations of Isotype but neither he nor Marie Neurath were inclined to pursue the legal protection of it. For them, Isotype did not solely consist in using the pictograms designed by Gerd Arntz and colleagues in Vienna and The Hague. In response to a request to use these pictograms independently, Otto Neurath explained:

> we feel very strongly that the effect of our method depends not only on the characters, but very largely on the way how they are used [sic], on the selection of representations, on the simplifications, and many other

measures. [...] Therefore we cannot allow the use of the symbols if we have no influence on the entire layouts.⁶

Nevertheless, this reflects a view that the elements of Isotype were indivisible, to some extent. The pictograms were significant identifiers, and were rejected by some in order to distance their work from the originators. For example, Rudolf Modley made a point of using different pictograms as a way of rebranding pictorial statistics in the USA. Yet many examples of his work were designed for social welfare purposes similar to those favoured by Isotype, and generally follow the same principles. The work of Gerd Arntz for the Dutch Foundation for Statistics from 1940 bears an even closer family resemblance to Isotype, and was (at least initially) very much a continuation of it.

Can work be considered as Isotype if it does not employ pictograms that originated in Vienna but adheres to Isotype principles in all other respects? Perhaps not entirely, but if so, then what makes it Isotype? It would need to reflect a scientific attitude, with rigorous analysis of data and maximum possible objectivity; this includes the cardinal rules for consistent use of pictograms and colour. Above all, it should be educational, employing graphic means to create a memorable information-picture. Neurath liked to call these 'visual arguments'. It seems incorrect to name the use of pictograms in directional signs as Isotype, not only because Isotype pictograms were never used for this purpose, but because there is no 'visual argument': pictograms function merely as labels in this context. Yet, if Isotype pictograms had been used in this way, as Neurath proposed, he may well have let it be known as Isotype, given that he was open to modified usage of the term – for example, not only to refer to the method but to specific examples of it (even in the plural as 'Isotypes').⁷

An additional characteristic of Isotype was surely its political standpoint. Although Otto Neurath often mentioned neutrality as an aim, the uses and purposes that defined Isotype were initially socialist and always democratic: this is clear in what Neurath stated about its suitability for enlightenment in the field of social progress (see p. 78). It was designed to inform citizens for participation in democracy. A complex question arises, therefore, in considering the work produced in the 1930s at the Soviet Izostat institute, where the Viennese team acted as consultants. Social progress was a theme there, but industrial progress took priority in depicting the Five-Year Plans. Indeed, many Izostat charts followed the basic rules of the Vienna Method quite strictly, and are effective statistically but tend to be monotonous – a pitfall that Isotype tried to avoid. However, some material produced by Izostat contradicted a central principle of Isotype – to be based on empirical data. In propaganda for the Five-Year Plans, projected figures were given, and misleading statistics masked the brutal reality of Soviet oppression.

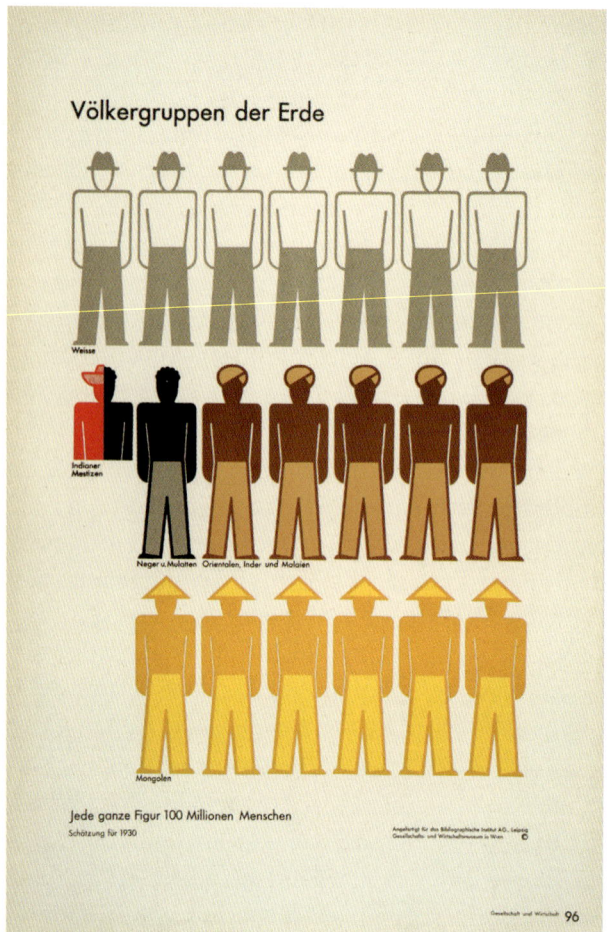

8.1 Chart 96 from *Gesellschaft und Wirtschaft*: 'Human groups of the world', 1930.

A clearer case is presented by some examples of pictorial statistics made by the institutes that usurped the Social and Economic Museum in Austria during the fascist regimes. The newspaper infographic on 'The Jewification of Vienna' (1938; fig. 3.5) was a travesty of Isotype for both graphic and ideological reasons. In graphic terms, the pictograms are not impersonal figures of a standard design, repeated as modular units; each is different, and the mannerisms depicted in the Jewish figures tend towards caricature. Moreover, this racially biased representation aligned with Nazi attitudes on the 'Jewish question' and would never have been addressed by the team led by Otto Neurath (who was partly Jewish). Some work produced for the Third Reich by the Institute for Exhibition Technology and Pictorial Statistics follows the Vienna Method more closely – largely due to the continued involvement of Alois Fischer – but its right-wing political motives mean that describing it as Isotype would be a distortion.

For a full appreciation of Isotype and its future potential, it must be understood in context of the period and places in which it developed. Ideas about universality were naturally different in the 1920s and 1930s than they are today. Some might consider Isotype's aspirations to international validity as an example of Western arrogance. Yet Otto Neurath was able to step back from his own society and view it anthropologically, to some extent, and he was clearly no advocate of Western hegemony. In 1928 he remarked: 'Roughly speaking, the whites are above all carriers of capitalism and imperialism. They are the "masters", with battleships and poison gas at their disposal.'[8] Indeed, an iconic chart from *Gesellschaft und Wirtschaft* was designed to counter Western prejudices about the 'yellow peril' by making clear that (in 1930) white people still formed the majority of the world's population (fig. 8.1). When Marie Neurath was able to realize her late husband's dream of applying Isotype beyond the West in the 1950s, her work was geared to education and enfranchisement of Africans during liberation from British colonial rule. The Isotype mission in Africa was not ideological in the way that other kinds of missionary expeditions to Africa were.

Given that Isotype was so closely connected with the educational objectives and attitudes of its initiators, one could argue that the term Isotype should only be used to refer to work involving its central figures, Otto Neurath, Marie Reidemeister/Neurath and Gerd Arntz.[9] Conversely, one may question that such a restriction is justifiable or useful in considering the influence of Isotype on information design today. An alternative term (favoured by Otto Neurath) would be 'visual education', but that could encompass many things. 'Data visualization' has become a common term in recent years, but it does not necessarily imply an educational intention, which should be a decisive factor for work inheriting the spirit of Isotype today. Renewed scholarship about Isotype has led to revaluation and revival of its ideas and approaches. Traces of it appear frequently in serious infographics, although sometimes in a semi-conscious and inconsistent way.[10] The legacy of Isotype can partly be recognized in some features of current work, although Otto Neurath had qualms about such a piecemeal effect.

One recurrent theme in Isotype charts that connects with today's concerns, and stems from Neurath's background in economics, is the exploitation of the Earth's resources and energy production. Education about human-induced climate change would be a perfect subject for Isotype, and some steps in this direction have been made in the series of books by Esther Gonstalla.[11] Health education was a consistent priority for Isotype, and some recent studies have made reference to its example in this field – in particular on the subject of combating microbial diseases.[12] Inspiration has also been drawn from Marie Neurath's science books for a recent project in visualizing atomic physics.[13]

The impersonality of Isotype, in which people are represented generically and not as individuals, seemed at odds with the era of postmodern individualism. Yet this kind of visualization became relevant again in the context of the COVID-19 pandemic. This disease is a levelling force, emphasizing our common humanity, and requires information that reflects this. Television news graphics, in particular, tended to show the potential effect of COVID-19 using quantities of human pictograms, as an effective way of indicating the mass of people who would be affected. On a basic level, this reflects Otto Neurath's proposal to 'humanize' knowledge by using such visual means.[14] One issue that often arises today in depicting quantities of people statistically is the requirement for a gender-neutral pictogram for 'person'. It has been suggested that pictograms of people should change perceptions of gender, but this was not part of the agenda for Isotype, in which pictograms sometimes relied on traditional stereotypes in the interest of being instantly recognizable.[15]

A mode of pictorial communication that is increasingly familiar to all of us on personal electronic devices is emoji (Japanese, meaning pictorial character or pictogram).[16] Emoji and Isotype differ in some important respects. The human pictograms of Isotype are usually silhouettes and literally faceless, expressing no emotion. The most frequently used emojis are precisely the opposite: faces expressing varied emotions. Emojis are often used jokingly; Isotype was intended to be as scientific as possible, and it was never used to make jokes. People choose emojis to express themselves; Isotype designers tried to avoid personal expression. Isotype is an example of graphic design from the pre-digital age: making Isotype charts was laborious work done by a trained team of experts, and the choices of depiction were made by them. While they were very interested in feedback from viewers, Isotype was not democratic in the sense that social media is. Communication only went one way, essentially. One could imagine interactive, digital examples of Isotype, which reconfigure dynamically according to user control of certain parameters. However, remembering Neurath's warning against mechanistic design that precludes creativity, such tools would need to contain adaptable intelligence to manage fluid graphic arrays in a controlled way that maintains clarity.

Digitalization brings great variety, but also insidious standardization. Even emojis are now included in the Unicode standard for cross-platform compatibility in digital communication, giving them a global reach that the creators of Isotype could only have dreamed about.

Reference notes

Prologue

1. O. Neurath, 'Bildliche Darstellung sozialer Tatbestände' (1926), pp. 61–2.
2. M. Neurath, 'Isotype' (1974), p. 136.

1 The Vienna Method in school

1. O. Neurath to Deutsch, 21 August 1924 (VGA).
2. 'Denkschrift über die Schaffung eines Gesellschafts- und Wirtschaftsmuseums in Wien', 7 August 1924 (VGA), p. 1.
3. O. Neurath, *Bildstatistik nach Wiener Methode in der Schule*, p. 294.
4. M. Neurath, 'Isotype' (1974), p. 143. It is likely that Otto Neurath was aware of Greek precedents for the museum as a centre of philosophy and science.
5. Reidemeister, 'Bildpädagogik', p. 314.
6. Reidemeister, 'Die bunte Welt', p. 142.
7. O. Neurath, 'Bildstatistik und Arbeiterbildung', p. 139.
8. O. Neurath and Reidemeister, 'Das Gesellschafts- und Wirtschaftsmuseum im neuen Rathause'; 'Wie organisiert man eine Führung ins Gesellschafts- und Wirtschaftsmuseum', *Das Bild* 5, H. 1 (January 1928), p. 23.
9. O. Neurath and Reidemeister, 'Bildstatistik im Unterricht', p. 215.
10. O. Neurath, 'Bildhafte Pädagogik im Gesellschafts- und Wirtschaftsmuseum in Wien', p. 205.
11. O. Neurath, *From Hieroglyphics to Isotype*, p. 114.
12. Norah Davis to O. Neurath, 22 September 1943, and O. Neurath to Davis, 27 September 1943 (IC 1/2).
13. Occasional contributions do credit an author, including Museum staff such as Friedrich Bauermeister and Alois Fischer, implying that the others were written by Neurath and Reidemeister. There are similarities in phrasing and tone of voice with their other writings of that period. One of the essays that was uncredited in *Das Bild* – 'Kurven in der statistischen Darstellung' – had been previously published under Reidemeister's name in *Österreichische Gemeinde-Zeitung* (see note 27 on the next page).
14. O. Neurath and Reidemeister, 'Das Gesellschafts- und Wirtschaftsmuseum und die Schule', p. 57. The same sentiment is expressed in other words at the beginning of Otto Neurath's essay 'Gesellschaft und Wirtschaft im Lehrbild' (1927), p. 93.
15. See also 'Handzettel für den Unterricht', *Das Bild* 5, H. 11 (November 1928), pp. 213–5; and 'Bildstatistische Lehrmittel', *Das Bild* 5, H. 12 (December 1928), pp. 233–6.
16. O. Neurath and Reidemeister, 'Das Gesellschafts- und Wirtschaftsmuseum und die Schule', p. 58.
17. O. Neurath (with Rudolf Carnap & Hans Hahn), 'The Scientific Conception of the World: the Vienna Circle', p. 305. See Burke & Sandner, 'Isotype, Logical Empiricism, and the Scientific World-Conception'.
18. O. Neurath and Reidemeister, 'Bildstatistik für Kinder', p. 82. The Vienna Circle rejected 'unfathomable depths': 'In science there are no "depths"; there is surface everywhere' (O. Neurath *et al*, 'The Scientific Conception of the World', p. 306).
19. O. Neurath, 'Unified Science and Psychology', p. 9.
20. O. Neurath and Reidemeister, 'Schulbesuch im Gesellschafts- und Wirtschaftsmuseum', pp. 117–19.
21. 'Statistik in der ersten Volksschulklasse', *Das Bild* 4, H. 7/8 (July/August 1927), pp. 145–7. Examples of such early experiments in encouraging pupils to make their own pictorial statistics were exhibited in a special display at the Vienna School Board building on the occasion of the exhibition 'Wien und die Wiener'. *Das Bild* 4, H. 5 (May 1927), p. 97.
22. O. Neurath and Reidemeister, 'Der Kreis'.
23. O. Neurath and Reidemeister, 'Orientierendes Diagramm und sprechendes Merkbild', p. 187.
24. Ibid., p. 188.
25. O. Neurath and Reidemeister, 'Abrunden und Weglassen in der Bildstatistik', p. 194. This pre-empts later criticism that Isotype was not a proper language: for example, by Karl Müller in 'Neurath's Theory of Pictorial-Statistical Representation'. See also Burke, 'The Linguistic Status of Isotype'.

26. O. Neurath, 'Bildstatistik nach Wiener Methode', p. 185.
27. Reidemeister, 'Kurven in der statistischen Darstellung', p. 44. A similar criticism of line graphs appears in Otto Neurath, *International Picture Language* (1936), p. 100.
28. O. Neurath and Reidemeister, 'Bildstatistik für Kinder', p. 81.
29. 'Mengenbild und Kartogramm im gewerblichen Unterricht', *Das Bild* 6, H. 2 (February 1929), p. 40.
30. [Gesellschafts- und Wirtschaftsmuseum in Wien], *Entwicklung von Landwirtschaft und Gewerbe in Deutschland*.
31. 'Mengenbild und Kartogramm im gewerblichen Unterricht', p. 38.
32. O. Neurath, 'Schwarzweißgrafik', p. 55.
33. 'Grundsätzliches zur Methode' (Principles of the Method; IC 3.1/4).
34. In the foreword to *Bildstatistik nach Wiener Methode in der Schule* (p. 265), Neurath names the teachers and states that the contribution of the School Board 'will be acknowledged in a separate publication on the Vienna school experiments', which never appeared.
35. O. Neurath, *Bildstatistik nach Wiener Methode in der Schule*, p. 267.
36. Glöckel's aims summarized by Helmut Gruber in *Red Vienna: Experiment in Working-Class Culture, 1919–1934*, p. 76.
37. O. Neurath, 'Bildstatistik nach Wiener Methode', p. 188.
38. Ibid., p. 188.
39. O. Neurath and Reidemeister, 'Bildstatistik für Kinder', p. 83.
40. O. Neurath, 'Bildstatistik nach Wiener Methode', p. 187.
41. O. Neurath and Reidemeister, 'Magnettafeln des Gesellschafts- und Wirtschaftsmuseums in Wien', pp. 206–7. See also 'Magnetkarten für Schulen', *Das Bild* 4, H. 9 (September 1927); and 'Die Magnet-Tafel auf der untersten Schulstufe', *Das Bild* 5, H. 5, May 1928.
42. Hans Pemmer, 'Versuche über die Verwendung von Mengenbildern im Unterricht', *Die Quelle* H. 4 & 5 (1933), pp. 5–6 (typescript English translation by Marie Neurath, IC 8.2 Pem). This article includes reports by several teachers involved in the experiment.
43. Details of these efforts in German schools are documented by O. Neurath in *Bildstatistik nach Wiener Methode in der Schule*, pp. 267–8.
44. O. Neurath, *From Hieroglyphics to Isotype*, p. 116.
45. O. Neurath, 'Bildstatistik nach Wiener Methode', p. 190.
46. O. Neurath, *Bildstatistik nach Wiener Methode in der Schule*, p. 306.
47. See O. Neurath, *International Picture Language*, p. 27.
48. O. Neurath, *Bildstatistik nach Wiener Methode in der Schule*, p. 270.
49. Ibid., pp. 297, 269, 279.
50. Ibid., pp. 301–2. These results are also discussed by O. Neurath in *From Hieroglyphics to Isotype*, p. 117.
51. O. Neurath, *Bildstatistik nach Wiener Methode in der Schule*, pp. 303–6.
52. Uebel, 'Otto Neurath, the Vienna Circle and the Austrian Tradition', in *German Philosophy since Kant*, ed. Anthony O'Hear (Cambridge University Press, 1999), p. 253; and Uebel, 'Intersubjective Accountability: Politics and Philosophy in the Left Vienna Circle', in *Perspectives on Science* 28, no. 1 (2020), p. 45.
53. O. Neurath, *Bildstatistik nach Wiener Methode in der Schule*, pp. 280–2.
54. Ibid., pp. 284–5. Here a distinction is made between the 'transformer' [*Transformator*], who was the conceptual designer (typically Marie Reidemeister), and the 'graphic artist' [*entwerfenden Grafiker*] who renders the final form (typically Gerd Arntz).
55. Ibid., p. 286.

2 Branching out

1. M. Neurath, 'Social and Economic Museum of Vienna, 1925–1934', in Burke, Kindel, Walker (ed.), *Isotype*, pp. 527–31; Burke, 'The Gesellschafts- und Wirtschaftsmuseum in Wien', p. 62.
2. O. Neurath, 'Museums of the Future', pp. 462–3.
3. Leichter, 'Vom Versammlungssaal zum Museum', *Arbeiter-Zeitung*, 7 December 1927, p. 8. In this article there are also pictorial statistics on the development of the municipal children's outdoor swimming pools.
4. O. Neurath and Reidemeister, 'Das Gesellschafts- und Wirtschaftsmuseum im neuen Rathause', pp. 227–8. See also the partial reconstruction of the Volkshalle exhibition in Burke, Kindel, Walker (ed.), *Isotype*, pp. 51–61.

5. M. Neurath, 'Otto Neurath, Wiener Methode, Isotype – ein Bericht', p. 27.
6. 'Ausstellung „Die Weltwirtschaft"', *Wiener Zeitung*, 10 October 1930, p. 4. Vienna's mayor Karl Seitz spoke at the opening.
7. Otto Neurath wrote a review essay of Ichheiser's book *Kritik des Erfolges. Eine soziologische Untersuchung* (1930). In O. Neurath, *Gesammelte philosophische und methodologische Schriften* (vol. 1), 363–7.
8. Hualla, 'Was wollen die Massen in den Tuchlauben'; and 'Rundfunk, Kartoffelbau und Nervenprobe', *Kleine Volkszeitung*, 25 September 1933, p. 8.
9. O. Neurath, 'The Isotype Work', p. 118. Here Neurath translated *Zeitschau* as 'March of Time', alluding to the well-known American newsreel.
10. Ichheiser, 'Intelligenz, Begabung und Tüchtigkeit', *Arbeiter-Zeitung*, 23 November 1933, p. 10; Pointer 'Die Zeitschau – ein modernes Bildungsmittel', *Der Abend*, 13 September 1933, p. 2.
11. M. Jahoda, 'Statistik und Alltag', *Arbeiter-Zeitung*, 22 October 1933, p. 15.
12. *Der Wiener Tag*, 11 February 1934, p. 8.
13. David Clay Large, *Berlin: Biographie einer Stadt* (Munich: Beck, 2002), p. 113. Christian Engeli, *Gustav Böß. Oberbürgermeister von Berlin 1921–1930* (Stuttgart: Kohlhammer, 1971).
14. Large, *Berlin*, p. 197.
15. Otto Neurath also attended the opening in 1926 of Walter Gropius's Bauhaus building at Dessau, which he wrote an essay about: 'Das Neue Bauhaus in Dessau', in O. Neurath, *Gesammelte Schriften: Ergänzungsband*, 214–17.
16. Günther Sandner and Christian Pape, 'From "Late Enlightenment" to Logical Empiricism: The Berlin Society of Empirical/Scientific Philosophy and the Ernst Mach Association in Vienna', in *Logical Empiricism and Pragmatism*, ed. Sami Pihlström, Friedrich Stadler, Niels Weidtmann (Cham: Springer, 2017), p. 221.
17. *Vorwärts*, 19 June 1928, p. 6.
18. M. Neurath, 'Social and Economic Museum of Vienna, 1925–1934', p. 530.
19. Sandner, *Otto Neurath*, pp. 170–6.
20. *Vorwärts*, 3 March 1929, p. 10.
21. *Arbeiter-Zeitung*, 9 March 1929, p. 7.
22. Carl Herz, 'Wien im Bild', *Die Kunstgemeinde: Mitteilungsblatt der Kunstgemeinde des Bezirks Kreuzberg* 5, Nr. 4 (March 1929).
23. Examples of exhibition panels from Berlin are shown in Burke, Kindel, Walker (ed.), *Isotype*, pp. 95, 152–3, 156–7, 160, 170–2, and in Stadler (ed.), *Arbeiterbildung in der Zwischenkriegszeit*, p. 274.
24. *Vorwärts*, 16 March 1929, p. 6.
25. *Vorwärts*, 20 November 1930, p. 3.
26. Richard Junge, 'Wissen als Volksgut', *Vorwärts*, 21 May 1931, p. 5.
27. *Vorwärts*, 26 October 1932, p. 5.
28. O. Neurath to Frank, 20 November 1944 (ÖNB 1219-5).
29. Today, a stele in front of the Kreuzberg district office in Berlin also commemorates this.
30. O. Neurath to Herz, 21 November 1944 (IISH, Herz Papers). After the war, Carl Herz moved to Palestine, where he died in Haifa (Israel) in 1951.
31. 'Mitteilungen des österreichischen Werkbundes', *Die Form* 7, H. 11 (November 1932).
32. Statutes of the 'Novus Orbis Pictus' cited in Vossoughian, *Otto Neurath*, p. 104; see also Vossoughian, 'The Language Of The World Museum: Otto Neurath, Paul Otlet, Le Corbusier'.
33. O. Neurath, 'Das Gesellschafts- und Wirtschaftsmuseum in Wien', p. 193.
34. See the introduction to *Gesellschaft und Wirtschaft* in O. Neurath, *GbS*, p. 145. In 'Bildstatistiken des Gesellschafts- und Wirtschaftsmuseums in Wien', Neurath remarks that it had founded the 'International Orbis-Institut' with the Palais Mondial. See also *Bildstatistik nach Wiener Methode in der Schule*, p. 268.
35. Vossoughian, *Otto Neurath*, p. 110.
36. M. Neurath, 'What I remember', p. 54. See also her recollections, '26 September 1924 and after', p. 62.
37. See Voysey, 'The Vienna Method of Pictorial Statistics', *The Labour Magazine* (May 1933).
38. O. Neurath to Shand, 27 December 1933 and 22 March 1934 (Shand Collection, University of Dundee).
39. The full title of Izostat in Russian is: Всесоюзный институт изобразительной статистики советского строительства и хозяйства (Vsesoiuznyi institut izobrazitel'noi statistiki sovetskogo stroitel'stva i khoziaistva).
40. 'Gerd Arntz', interview in *Pulchri*, p. 4.

41. O. Neurath to Martha Tausk, Easter Monday (undated: 1932/33; IISH Tausk Papers).
42. Decree of 12 September 1931, cited by O. Neurath in 'Die pädagogische Weltbedeutung der Bildstatistik nach Wiener Methode', p. 241.
43. See Laptev, *Русская инфографика*, p. 218.
44. *Dognat' i peregnat' v tekhniko-ekonomicheskom otnoshenii peredovye kapitalisticheskie strany v 10 let.*
45. 'Ot izdatel'stva' (Publisher's preface), *Dognat' i peregnat'*, p. 6.
46. Ivanitskii, *Izobrazitel'naia statistika i venskii metod* (Pictorial Statistics and the Vienna Method, 1932), p. 43.
47. M. Neurath, 'What I remember', p. 49.
48. Sophie Lissitzky-Küppers, *El Lissitzky: Life, Letters, Texts*, p. 86. Lissitzky seemed to have been out of official favour at that time, but he designed some notable examples of pictorial statistics after 1934, working with one of the best linocut artists from Izostat, Aleksandr Grigorovich. (Arntz, '3.7.'72', p. 3.)
49. See Benus and Jansen, 'The Vienna Method in Amsterdam: Peter Alma's Office for Pictorial Statistics', p. 20.
50. M. Neurath, 'What I remember', p. 49.
51. Minns, 'Picturing Soviet progress: Izostat, 1931–4', pp. 262–3; Rudolf Carnap, *Tagebücher*, ed. Christian Damböck (Hamburg: Meiner, 2022) vol. 2, p. 612.
52. O. Neurath, 'Bildstatistik nach Wiener Methode in der Sowjetunion', p. 208.
53. M. Neurath, 'Gesellschafts- und Wirtschaftsmuseum in Wien en Mundaneum'.
54. Arntz, '3.7.'72', p. 4.
55. 'Grundsätzliches zur Methode' (Principles of the Method; IC 3.1/4).
56. See Minns, 'Picturing Soviet progress', p. 270.
57. Karl Schlögel, *The Soviet Century: Archaeology of a Lost World* (Princeton/Oxford: Princeton University Press, 2023), pp. 473–4.
58. Snyder, *Bloodlands: Europe Between Hitler and Stalin* (London: Bodley Head, 2010), p. 53.
59. See Gruber, *Red Vienna: experiment in working-class culture, 1919–1934*.
60. M. Neurath, 'Otto Neurath and Isotype', p. 13. Gerd Arntz recalled: 'There was nothing that we were forced to do, and moreover [we] could refuse, we were entitled to do so.' ('Gerd Arntz', interview in *Pulchri*, p. 4.)
61. O. Neurath to Herz, 25 October 1942 (IISH Herz papers 60/7).
62. Schlögel, *The Soviet Century*, p. 475.
63. Chizlett, 'Damned lies and statistics: Otto Neurath and Soviet propaganda in the 1930s', p. 305.
64. Otto Neurath was once taken – 'rather against his will' – to meet former Pravda editor Nikolai Bukharin by an early Russian Director of Izostat, Erik Asmus. Bukharin was an opponent of Stalin but was 'then still tolerated'. (M. Neurath, 'What I remember', p. 49.)
65. O. Neurath, 'The Current Growth in Global Productive Capacity', p. 482. A stronger statement in favour of Soviet planning is contained in the Vienna Museum periodical, *Bildstatistik* (no. 10, 1931, p. 2), but it is not credited to Neurath (or indeed any individual): 'The only region that is crisis-free is the USSR, where the means of production are fully exploited and are in continual development. We see here, despite the incompleteness of the production apparatus, decisive considerations for a methodical economy oriented to standard of living. While unemployment is in continual growth in the rest of the world, there are no unemployed in the Soviet Union.'
66. Chizlett, 'Damned Lies and Statistics', p. 301.
67. Kinross, 'Blind Eyes, Innuendo and the Politics of Design', p. 77.
68. Conquest, *The Harvest of Sorrow: Soviet Collectivization and the Terror-Famine* (London: Hutchinson, 1986), p. 7.
69. Arntz, *Zeit unterm Messer*, pp. 31–3. Marie Reidemeister also witnessed 'starving people who came to the trains' ('What I remember', p. 50). Ukrainians have a special name for the famine of 1932–3, Holodomor, which they consider a genocide.
70. 'Gerd Arntz', interview in *Pulchri*, p. 6.
71. *Arbeiter-Zeitung*, 29 June 1932, p. 1.
72. O. Neurath to Carnap, 1 October 1932, quoted in Galison, 'Aufbau/Bauhaus', p. 741.
73. See Sandner, 'Friendship and Estrangement: Margarete Schütte-Lihotzky and Otto Neurath'.
74. Arntz, *Zeit unterm Messer*, pp. 35–7.

3 Pictorial statistics in times of dictatorship

1. O. Neurath, *Bildstatistik nach Wiener Methode in der Schule*, p. 281.
2. Heiko Zielke, '"Die große Masse des Volkes wirtschaftlich denken lehren". Zur Geschichte des Düsseldorfer Reichs- und Landesmuseums für Wirtschaft 1926 bis 1958', *Geschichte im Westen* 15 (2000), pp. 65-94.
3. 'Auflösung Verein Gesellschafts- und Wirtschaftsmuseum' (GZ 169608-G.D.2 aus 1934), Bundeskanzleramt (Generaldirektion für die öffentliche Sicherheit), 18 May 1934 (OeStA, AdR).
4. 'Verein Gesellschafts- und Wirtschaftsmuseum in Wien, Auflösung' (M. Abt. 49/3272/34), Sicherheits-Kommissär des Bundes für Wien, 5 April 1934 (OeStA, AdR).
5. Letter Drexel to Hellwig, 8 May 1934 (OeStA, AdR).
6. www.architektenlexikon.at/de/470.htm (accessed 1 February 2024).
7. 'Schreiben an das Bundeskanzleramt, Gesellschafts- und Wirtschaftsmuseum in Wien' (L.St. II – 751/12/34), Bundes-Polizeidirektion in Wien, 29 May 1934 (OeStA, AdR).
8. 'Verein Gesellschafts- und Wirtschaftsmuseum in Wien, behördliche Auflösung Widerruf' (M. Abt. 49/9161/34), Sicherheit-Kommissär des Bundes für Wien, 27 November 1934 (OeStA, AdR).
9. 'Bescheid Dr. Skrubel', Bundespolizeidirektion für Wien, 4 December 1934 (ÖGWM, Folder 'Gelöschte Vereine').
10. Gerard Botz, *Nationalsozialismus in Wien: Machtübernahme, Herrschaftssicherung, Radikalisierung, Kriegsvorbereitung* (Vienna/Berlin: Mandelbaum 2018), pp. 75-80.
11. Franz Rauscher, 'Nach Otto Neurath: Österreich von 1934 bis 1972', in Stadler (ed.), *Arbeiterbildung*, p. 198.
12. *Salzburger Volksblatt*, 2 April 1935, p. 4.
13. *Neue Freie Presse*, 2 April 1935, p. 7.
14. *Arbeiter-Zeitung*, 7 April 1935, p. 7.
15. The reprographic quality of *Arbeitsschlacht* was impressive: it was printed by the former official printing house of the Social Democratic Party, Vorwärts.
16. See Detlev Humann: *»Arbeitsschlacht«. Arbeitsbeschaffung und Propaganda in der NS-Zeit 1933-1939* (Göttingen: Wallstein, 2011).
17. Gesellschafts- und Wirtschaftsmuseum in Wien to Sicherheitskommissär des Bundes für Wien, 21 January 1937 (ÖGWM, Folder 'Gelöschte Vereine').
18. According to Arntz, the exhibition material of the Museum was destroyed in a warehouse fire (Arntz, *Zeit unterm Messer*, p. 35).
19. *Innsbrucker Nachrichten*, 12 October 1935, p. 7.
20. *Das interessante Blatt*, 19 August 1937, p. 2.
21. Fabian Kalleitner went into detail about Fischer's role in 'Arbeiterbildung und Propaganda: Bildstatistik als janusköpfige Methode zur Volksbildung' (seminar paper: University of Vienna, 2016).
22. Österreichisches Institut für Bildstatistik, *Industrie und Wohlstand: bildstatistisches Tafelwerk* (Vienna: Deutscher Verlag für Jugend und Volk 1938).
23. Fischer referred to his own two-part essay of 1925: 'Zur Frage der Tragfähigkeit des Lebensraumes', *Zeitschrift für Geopolitik* 1, H. 10 (1925), 762-79, and H. 11 (1925), 842-58.
24. Alois Fischer, 'Sozialpolitik und Sozialbelastung', in *Industrie und Wohlstand*.
25. *Arbeiter-Zeitung*: 14 April 1937, pp. 9-10; 12 May 1937, p. 9; and 23 June 1937, p. 7. See also Christian Fleck, 'Politische Emigration und sozialwissenschaftlicher Wissenstransfer: Das Beispiel Marie Jahoda', in *Arbeitslose bei der Arbeit: die Nachfolgestudie zu „Marienthal"*, ed. Christian Fleck and Marie Jahoda (Frankfurt/New York, Campus, 1989), p. LIV.
26. These publications sometimes appeared under variations of his name: Fischer von der Eger or Fischer-Egerbrück. The publisher of the *Historisch-statistisches Handbüchlein*, Verlag für Jugend und Volk, had been formed as a schoolbook publisher with help from the Vienna municipality in 1921. The publisher of the *Taschen-Atlas*, Freytag und Berndt of Vienna, had also published editions of *Prof Hickmann's Geographisch-Statistischer Universal Atlas* expanded by Fischer since 1921. The pictorial statistics in that atlas were a counter-example for the definition of the Vienna Method, but Fischer's work on it may nevertheless have led to his initial employment at the Social and Economic Museum. See Burke, Kindel, Walker (ed.), *Isotype*, pp. 13 & 194.

27. See the file on Trautenegg in the archive of the Sigmund Freud Museum (Vienna), as well as Indes Rieder and Diana Voigt, *Die Geschichte der Sidonie C. Sigmund Freud's berühmte Patientin* (Vienna: Zaglossus, 2012).
28. Franz Rauscher to M. Neurath, 20 August 1948 (IC 1/22).
29. Otto Jahn personal file, Künstlerhausarchiv (WStLA).
30. Christoph Kivelitz, *Die Propagandaausstellung in europäischen Diktaturen: Konfrontation und Vergleich: Nationalsozialismus in Deutschland, Faschismus in Italien und die UdSSR der Stalinzeit* (Bochum: Winkler, 1999), pp. 222-227.
31. Rosemarie Burgstaller, *Inszenierung des Hasses: Feindbildausstellungen im Nationalsozialismus*, pp. 325–30; on Trautenegg, pp. 329–30.
32. *Neues Wiener Tagblatt*, 20 May 1939, p. 8. The exhibition was also praised – specifically for its design by the Institut für Ausstellungstechnik und Bildstatistik – in *Das Kleine Volksblatt*, 21 April 1939, p. 11.
33. *Kleine Volkszeitung*, 15 May 1938, p. 22.
34. *Volks-Zeitung*, 13 August 1938, p. 4.
35. *Das Sowjetparadies: Ausstellung der Reichspropagandaleitung der NSDAP* (Berlin: Zentralverlag der NSDAP 1942), p. 2. According to the entry on Baszel at www.geschichtewiki.wien.gv.at, he had been involved in exhibitions designed by the Social and Economic Museum during the 1920s – the Hygiene exhibition (1925), 'Wien und die Wiener' (1927) and 'Frau und Kind' (1928) – as well as in the exhibition 'Niemals Vergessen!' (1946). But he is not mentioned in accounts by Otto or Marie Neurath, who named important collaborators at various points, or in publications and documents of the Museum.
36. An intriguing exception was Italy, where a kind of Futurist modernism continued in favour, no doubt due to the close ties of Futurism to Italian fascism.
37. Burgstaller, *Inszenierung des Hasses*, p. 416.
38. Cited ibid., p. 415.
39. Ibid., pp. 417–18.
40. Ibid., pp. 457–63.
41. Hugo Keller, *Zur Psychologie des volkstümlichen Zahlenbildes* (Leipzig: Barth, 1941), p. IV. The booklet was issued as a supplement to the journal *Zeitschrift für Angewandte Psychologie und Charakterkunde*, and was subtitled 'Two studies on the nature, forms and effectiveness of the pictorial representation of comparisons of magnitude'.
42. Ibid., p. 8.

4 Isotype in exile

1. O. Neurath, 'The Isotype work', p. 122.
2. M. Neurath, 'What I remember', p. 57.
3. O. Neurath to Josef Frank 8 July 1939 (ÖNB 1219/3-3).
4. O. Neurath to Arntz, Bernath, Reidemeister, and Scheer, 31 July 1935 (ÖNB Ser.n.878).
5. Ogden and Richards, *The Meaning of Meaning*, p. XIII. See also McElvenny, 'International Language and the Everyday: Contact and Collaboration Between C. K. Ogden, Rudolf Carnap and Otto Neurath'.
6. M. Neurath, 'What I remember', p. 58.
7. O. Neurath, 'Visual aids and arguing', p. 52n; M. Neurath, 'Isotype' (1955), p. 28. She also stated that Isotype could indicate 'uniformity of symbolism' (in 'The origin and theory of Isotype', p. 112).
8. O. Neurath, 'Isotype und die Graphik', pp. 342–8.
9. *Wereldverkeer* is included in the bibliography of Otto Neurath's writings compiled by Marie Neurath for *Empiricism and Sociology*, although he is not credited as the author in the publication itself.
10. M. Neurath and Kinross, *The Transformer*, p. 49; See also McElvenny, 'International Language and the Everyday' on the centrality of Lockhart's contribution to Basic.
11. O. Neurath, *International Picture Language*, p. 29.
12. Ibid., pp. 20–2.
13. Ibid., pp. 33–7. The traffic signs shown accorded with the standards proposed in 1931 by the Geneva conference of the League of Nations on traffic signs, which were subsequently ratified by several countries including Austria and the Netherlands.
14. Ibid., p. 106.
15. Ibid., pp. 18 & 20.
16. Ogden and Richards, *The Meaning of Meaning*, p. VIII.

17. O. Neurath, 'Isotype und die Graphik', pp. 342–3.
18. Former Bauhaus teacher Herbert Bayer designed that exhibition, and later the *World Geo-Graphic Atlas*, which borrowed from Isotype.
19. Neurath's trip was also (surprisingly) supported by his rival Rudolf Modley's company Pictorial Statistics, Inc. See Ihara, 'Isotype in America: Otto Neurath and Rudolf Modley, 1930–9', p. 319.
20. M. Neurath and Kinross, *The Transformer*, pp. 51–4.
21. The series of posters (1938) is illustrated in full in Burke, Kindel, Walker (ed.), *Isotype*, pp. 342–8.
22. Kaempffert, 'Week in science: language of Isotypes', *New York Times*, 17 January 1937. Kaempffert stated that 'the isotypes themselves' (consistently but unusually spelling the term without an initial capital) were 'the individual signs', which was not a usage of the word employed by Otto Neurath (see Epilogue).
23. O. Neurath to Carnap, 24 January 1937; no. 338 in *Rudolf Carnap / Otto Neurath: Briefwechsel*.
24. Ihara, 'Isotype in America', p. 325. Ideas for *Modern Man in the Making* were developed in lectures that Neurath gave in 1935 at the Peace House in The Hague.
25. O. Neurath to Carnap, 24 January 1937.
26. M. Neurath, 'Isotype' (1974), p. 147. For the connections of Isotype to ancient Latin American culture, see María del Mar Navarro, 'Isotype of the conquest: pictographic numeracy in sixteenth-century colonial México', *Information Design Journal* 27, no. 1 (2022): 35–51.
27. O. Neurath to Arntz, 17 December 1946 (ÖNB 1226/8).
28. Otto Neurath had acted as consultant to the Fair's committee until 1936, in which capacity he gave a lecture at the Empire State Building. See Ihara, 'Isotype in America', p. 320.
29. M. Neurath and Kinross, *The Transformer*, p. 57.
30. Cited in Benjamin Benus, 'Otto Neurath's social history of art', p. 143.
31. Memorandum titled 'Information on Isotype plan, dealing with comprehensive education, museums and exhibitions, wall posters, illustrations, picture-text-style books, Isotype films', sent to Julian Huxley, December 1942 (IC 1/35).
32. O. Neurath to Carnap, 22 April 1940; no. 542 in *Rudolf Carnap / Otto Neurath: Briefwechsel*.
33. O. Neurath to Mr Coppock, 2 September 1943 (IC 1/2).
34. M. Neurath, 'What I remember', pp. 68–9.
35. O. Neurath to Fleddérus, 18 March 1941 (IC 1/3).
36. Rotha to O. Neurath, 7 April 1941 (IC 1/42).
37. Reported by H. Swaffer in 'The Mickey Mouse of Social Fact', *Daily Herald*, 17 November 1933. See also Burke, 'Animated Isotype on film, 1941–7', p. 367. No prints of the Vienna films seem to have survived.
38. O. Neurath to Rotha, 11 April 1944 (IC 1/44).
39. Mayer had written the screenplays for *Das Cabinet des Dr. Caligari* and F. W. Murnau's *Sunrise*; Wilhelm had been working in Britain since the mid-1930s and wrote wartime spy thrillers concurrent with his work for Rotha.
40. Rotha to Oxford Labour Exchange, 3 June 1941 (IC 1/42).
41. For more detailed discussion of *A Few Ounces a Day*, see Burke, 'Animated Isotype on film'.
42. Elton to Rotha, 19 December 1941 (IC 1/42).
43. Knight was tragically killed in an air crash before *World of Plenty* was completed, and before the film of his book *Lassie Come Home* was released.
44. Rotha to C. K. Lynton-Harris (MOI Film Division), 17 February 1944 (INF 1/214).
45. O. Neurath to Rotha, 11 January 1943 (IC 1/44).
46. O. Neurath to Rotha, 7 October 1943 (IC 1/44).
47. Rotha to O. Neurath, 8 October 1943 (IC 1/44).
48. This echoes comments from the Mass-Observation report about *A Few Ounces a Day*, in which some viewers considered that a serious subject matter should not be treated with animation due to its popular association with Disney.
49. Rotha to Elton, 21 October 1942; Elton to Calder-Marshall, 29 October 1942 (INF 1/214).
50. Calder-Marshall to Jack Beddington 4 February 1942 (INF 1/214).

51. Rotha to Calder-Marshall, 27 October 1942 (INF 1/214).
52. Elton to Arthur Calder-Marshall, cited by Farmer in 'Exploiting a Universal Nostalgia for Steak and Onions', p. 172.
53. Rotha, *The Film Till Now*, p. 60 (preface to 2nd edition, dated August 1948).
54. O. Neurath to Rotha, 4 June 1942 (IC 1/43).
55. F. J. H. Corbyn to Shelton Smith (Director of Public Relations, Ministry of Food), 6 April 1943 (INF 1/214).
56. Alexander Schwinghammer, '„Food Matters" – Isotype in Paul Rothas Dokumentarfilm World of Plenty', in Hartmann (ed.), *Sachbild und Gesellschaftstechnik*, p. 129.
57. *New Statesman*, 12 June 1943.
58. Farmer, 'Exploiting a Universal Nostalgia for Steak and Onions', p. 170.
59. O. Neurath to Rotha, 8 December 1943 (IC 1/44).
60. Neurath recommended that a pioneer of electronic sound whom he had met in internment, Wolja Saraga, should create the voice.
61. *News Chronicle*, 27 April 1946; *The Times*, 26 April 1946
62. Rotha to O. Neurath, 14 September 1945 (IC 1/45).
63. O. Neurath to Walter Neurath, 4 July 1942 & 28 August 1942 (IC 1/30). For detailed analysis of the design and production of these books, See Burke and Jansen, *Soft Propaganda, Special Relationships, and a New Democracy: Adprint and Isotype, 1942–1948*, pp. 59–92.
64. Smollett was in fact the Austrian Hans Peter Smolka, who had been a friend and colleague of Wolfgang Foges in Vienna, and who was later revealed to have been a Soviet spy. See Burke & Jansen, *Soft Propaganda*, pp. 96–7.
65. O. Neurath to Foges, 26 September 1944 (IC 1/32).
66. Henrion to O. Neurath, 23 July 1943 (IC 1/40).
67. O. Neurath to Cadbury, 4 June 1943 (IC 1/2). As a result, Paul Redmayne, who worked on graphics for Cadbury, came to Oxford to consult with Neurath, and Neurath was invited to consult for the West Midland Group on Post-War Reconstruction and Planning. Redmayne went on to write a series of books featuring Isotype-like graphics, including *Transport by Land* (1948), *Transport by Sea* (1950) and *Britain's Food* (1963).

5 The Austrian Social and Economic Museum after 1945

1. 'Letter Magistrat Abteilung 7', 20 November 1946 (ÖGWM, Folder 'Gelöschte Vereine').
2. See the very revealing letter from Edith Matzalik to M. Neurath, 1 March 1946 (IC 1/17).
3. Hertha Wohlrab, 'Das Gesellschafts- und Wirtschaftsmuseum in Wien', *Wiener Geschichtsblätter* 25, no. 2, 1970, p. 34; Gerhard Halusa, 'Das Museum nach der Ära Otto Neurath', pp. 103–4.
4. 'Österreichisches Institut für Gesellschafts- und Wirtschafts-Statistik' (Protokoll), 17 July 1948 (ÖGWM, Folder 'Rauscher 1948–1972').
5. Rauscher to M. Neurath, 20 August 1948 (IC 1/22).
6. '1945 – heute', Typescript (ÖGWM, 'Folder Prof. Franz Rauscher'). This paper also states that the restitution of the property was obtained in court.
7. Rauscher to M. Neurath, 20 August 1948 (IC 1/22).
8. Newspaper clipping (without publication details), 1 July 1949; and letter from Sicherheitsdirektion Wien to Österreichisches Institut für Bildstatistik, 20 August 1949 (ÖGWM, Folder 'Gelöschte Vereine').
9. Viktor Matejka, 'Unangenehme Notizen – Otto Neurath – dreimal mißbraucht', in *Der Abend*, no. 188, 13 August 1949.
10. Rauscher, 'Das Österreichische Gesellschafts- und Wirtschaftsmuseum' (1964) (AAK, Franz Rauscher Papers, Folder 10).
11. Rauscher to M. Neurath, 7 April 1951 (IC 1/48).
12. The announcement of the dissolution of the Association on 3 March 1952 was signed by Julius Raab. The actual dissolution then dragged on into the summer of 1952 for formal reasons (ÖGWM, Folder 'Gelöschte Vereine').
13. Halusa, 'Das Museum nach der Ära Otto Neurath', p. 104.
14. According to Edith Matzalik, it supplied 'the majority of the panels'. Matzalik to M. Neurath, 22 December 1946 (IC 1/17).

15. Rochowanski, 'Bilder und Statistiken klagen an', *Wiener Kurier*, 14 September 1946. See also the letter from Matzalik to M. Neurath, 22 December 1946 (IC 1/17). In *Vergessen? Niemals! Die antifaschistische Ausstellung im Wiener Künstlerhaus 1946*, Heidrun-Ulrike Wenzel writes that the 'Institute for Pictorial Statistics' was responsible for providing the 'data material for the visualization of the statistics' (p. 86) and identifies Günter von Baszel as the liaison and key figure in this cooperation.
16. Wenzel, *Vergessen? Niemals!*, p. 84.
17. Victor Matejka quoted in *Wiener Zeitung*, 17 December 1946, p. 3.
18. 'The sadness of Vienna: taint and innocence in the Austrian capital; ashes and the phoenix', *The Times* (London), 16 November 1946, p. 5.
19. M. Neurath, 'Otto Neurath and Isotype', pp. 11–18.
20. M. Neurath to Gerd Arntz, 17 December 1946 (ÖNB 1226/8).
21. Rauscher, 'Mein Lehrer Otto Neurath', in Stadler (ed.), *Arbeiterbildung*, p. 46.
22. Otto Neurath, 'The current growth in global productive capacity', p. 487; 'World planning and the USA', p. 626.
23. 'Thanks are due to all scientific specialists, of whom Robert Bleichsteiner, Alois Fischer and Karl Peucker are still permanently involved today', wrote Neurath in *Bildstatistik nach Wiener Methode in der Schule*, p. 3.
24. Alois Fischer, 'Zur Frage der Tragfähigkeit des Lebensraumes', *Zeitschrift für Geopolitik* 1, H. 11 (1925), p. 858.
25. Alois Fischer-Egerbrück, 'Erdumfassender Bericht über die Bevölkerungsentwicklung 1937–1941', *Zeitschrift für Geopolitik* 18, H. 8 (1941): 448–61.
26. Alois Fischer von der Eger, *Quo vadis, Europa?* (Graz, Vienna, Leipzig, Berlin: Bergland Buch, 1933), pp. 29–32.
27. Matzalik to M. Neurath, 22 December 1946 (IC 1/17). It is unclear, however, to what extent they were aware of Fischer's role in Austrofascism and National Socialism.
28. Remember Austria Committee, *Vienna – The town and its buildings* (Vienna: Österreichische Kulturvereinigung, 1946).
29. www.friedhoefewien.at (accessed 16 April 2023).
30. Manfred Marschalek, *Untergrund und Exil: Österreichs Sozialisten zwischen 1934 und 1945*, pp. 38 & 107.
31. Manfred Marschalek, 'Der Wiener Sozialistenprozess 1936', in *Sozialistenprozesse. Politische Justiz in Österreich 1870–1936*, edited by Karl R. Stadler (Vienna/Munich/Zurich: Europaverlag 1986), p. 482.
32. Marschalek, *Untergrund und Exil*, p. 249.
33. CV Franz Rauscher (ÖGWM, Folder 'Prof. Franz Rauscher').
34. See also the interviews by Erika Thurner (8 June 1985) and Ingrid Bauer (9 November 1982) with Franz Rauscher (tape recordings, Österreichische Mediathek).
35. CV Franz Rauscher (ÖGWM, Folder 'Prof. Franz Rauscher').
36. Dyno Lowenstein to Franz Rauscher, 9 April 1947 and 15 April (n.d.) (VGA, Franz Rauscher, Lade 23, Folder 2). See also Sandner, 'Rudolf Modley and the Americanization of Isotype', p. 48.
37. Franz Rauscher, 'Wirkliche Verstaatlichung', *Arbeiter-Zeitung*, 22 June 1946, pp. 1–2; 'Fragen der Verstaatlichung', *Arbeiter-Zeitung*, 3 October 1946, pp. 1–2; 'Verstaatlichung allein genügt nicht', *Arbeiter-Zeitung*, 19 May 1945, pp. 1–2.
38. CV Franz Rauscher (ÖGWM, Folder 'Prof. Franz Rauscher').
39. Gérard Kasemir, 'Spätes Ende für „wissenschaftlich" vorgetragenen Rassismus: die Borodajkewycz-Affäre 1965', in *Politische Skandale und Affären in Österreich: Von Mayerling bis Waldheim*, edited by Michael Gehler and Hubert Sickinger (Innsbruck, Wien, Bozen: Studienverlag, 2007), 486–501.
40. Franz Rauscher, *Darstellungsmethoden der Statistik* (Vienna: Österreichisches Gesellschafts- und Wirtschaftsmuseum, 1959), p. 4.
41. Franz Rauscher, 'Museum und Schule' (offprint marked 'NTW 5', 1964; AAK, Rauscher Papers, Folder 10), p. 125.
42. See Otto Neurath, 'Museums of the Future'.
43. Franz Rauscher to M. Neurath, 7 August 1969 (ÖNB 1237/8-9).
44. Fred Duval, 'Bild eines Bildners – Franz Rauscher', *Die Solidarität* (1967), p. 13 (ÖGWM, Folder 'Prof. Franz Rauscher').
45. Rauscher to M. Neurath, 7 August 1969 (ÖNB 1237/8-9).

46. Ibid.
47. Österreichische Liga der Vereinten Nationen, *Die Vereinten Nationen und ihre Bedeutung für Österreich* (Vienna: UN, 1947).
48. *100 Jahre Aufstieg einer Klasse: Ausstellung in der AK 1951*, volume 1 (ÖGWM).
49. 'Protokoll Generalversammlung', 15 February 1968 (ÖGWM, Folder 'Rauscher 1948–1972').
50. Walter Pfitzner, 'Photographieren! Wie's gemacht wird und wie es gemacht werden soll!', *Photo-Börse* 34, no. 4 (1932): 101–4; 'Andere „Gesichtspunkte"', *Photo-Börse* 34, no. 6, (1932): 169–71.
51. 'NS-Registrierungslisten der Bezirkshauptmannschaft St. Johann im Pongau' (NS-SOKO A 58.358), Bestand Entnazifizierungssonderkommission (SLA).
52. Otto Neurath to Franz Roh, 1 June 1929 (OeStA, AdR, Neurath Papers, 1433-1-22).
53. Walter Pfitzner to M. Neurath, 21 September 1961 (ÖNB 1236/38).
54. Kurt Willvonseder, Egon Lendl, Walter Pfitzner (ed.), *Salzburg-Atlas: Bundesland Salzburg in 66 Kartenblättern* (Salzburg: Otto Müller Verlag, 1955).
55. Walter Pfitzner, 'Zur Methodik der Darstellung,' in *Salzburg-Atlas*, p. 2.
56. M. Neurath to Franz Rauscher, 23 November 1956 (IC 1/48). She asked Rauscher and his Museum to foot her bill for a copy of it, and he obliged.
57. Robert Obermair, *Kurt Willvonseder: vom SS Ahnenerbe zum Salzburger Museum Carolinum Augusteum* (Salzburg: Otto Müller, 2016); Alexander Pinwinkler, *Die „Gründergeneration" der Universität Salzburg: Biographien, Netzwerke, Berufungspolitik 1960–1975* (Vienna, Cologne, Weimar: Böhlau, 2020), pp. 86-91.
58. Hans Schreckeis, 'Die biologische Kraft der Heimatvertriebenen', in *Flüchtlingsland Österreich*, edited by Adalbert Gauss, (Salzburg: Donauschwäbische Verlags-Gesellschaft, 1957), p. 87.
59. Karl Hartl, *Wie? Wann? Wo? Wie das Alltägliche zum Alltäglichen wurde* (Vienna: Globus-Verlag, several editions, including 1948 and 1950).
60. Arntz to M. Neurath, 17 November 1963 (ÖNB 1226/6).
61. M. Neurath to Arntz, 17 December 1946 (ÖNB 1226/8).
62. Rauscher to M. Neurath, 20 August 1948 (IC 1/22).
63. Ibid.
64. M. Neurath to Rauscher, 17 March 1949 (IC 1/22).
65. Rauscher to M. Neurath, 26 September 1950 and M. Neurath to Rauscher, 16 October 1950 (IC 1/28).
66. M. Neurath to Rauscher, 8 December 1950 (IC 1/28).
67. M. Neurath to Arntz, 25 March 1952 (ÖNB 1226/8-19).
68. M. Neurath to Rauscher, 19 July 1955 (IC 1/48). The tone between the two was always friendly and Rauscher, as a stamp collector, was always pleased to receive stamps that Marie Neurath sent to him, including some from the West African countries where she worked in the 1950s.
69. M. Neurath to Rauscher, 23 May 1957 (IC 1/48).
70. Aims of Cooperation, handwritten paper by Philipp Rieger (IC 1/48).
71. Rauscher to M. Neurath, undated [1951] (IC 1/28).
72. See also Otto and Marie Neurath Papers (ÖNB 31.896).
73. M. Neurath to Arntz, 12 November 1961 (ÖNB 1226/8).
74. M. Neurath, 'Otto Neurath and Isotype', p. 18.
75. Otto and Marie Neurath papers (ÖNB 31.980).
76. Halusa, 'Das Museum nach der Ära Otto Neurath', p. 106.
77. Interview with Josef Docekal by Günther Sandner and Nora Walch, 13 April 2021.
78. Rauscher to M. Neurath, 10 November 1975 (ÖNB 1237/9).
79. Rauscher to M. Neurath, 1 June 1975 (ÖNB 1237/9-3).
80. Josef Docekal, 'Das Österreichische Gesellschafts- und Wirtschaftsmuseum von 1972 bis 1982', in Stadler (ed.), *Arbeiterbildung*, pp. 201–2.
81. Interview with Josef Docekal, 13 April 2021.
82. Docekal, 'Das Österreichische Gesellschafts- und Wirtschaftsmuseum', pp. 203–4.
83. See O. Neurath, 'Visual Education: Humanisation Versus Popularisation', p. 252.
84. Friedrich Stadler, 'Arbeiterbildung in der Zwischenkriegszeit: persönliche Erinnerungen und Reflexionen', in Waldner (ed.), *Die Konturen der Welt*, 115–30.

85. Correspondence between Friedrich Stadler and Marie Neurath (Private archive Friedrich Stadler).
86. Both authors were present at the event.

6 Following Otto Neurath: Marie Neurath and Gerd Arntz on separate paths

1. O. Neurath to Gerd Arntz, undated [September 1945] (IC 1/13). Neurath referred here to Julian Huxley, Bertrand Russell and Susan Stebbing.
2. Testimony by Neurath to the American POW administration in France, 10 July 1945 (IC 1/13).
3. Neurath to Agnes Arntz, 10 July 1945 (ÖNB 1217/10).
4. 'Gerd Arntz', interview in *Pulchri* 8 [part 2], no. 4 (1980), p. 2.
5. De Kanter to Neurath, 18 July 1945 (ÖNB 1220/48).
6. Arntz to M. Neurath, 15 January 1947 (ÖNB 1226/4).
7. Testimony by Neurath, 10 July 1945 (IC 1/13).
8. Idenburg's introduction to *Volkswohlstand und Industrie in den Niederlanden* (NSS, 1941).
9. 'Gerd Arntz', interview in *Pulchri* [part 2], pp. 2–3.
10. Arntz, *Zeit unterm Messer*, p. 40; 'Gerd Arntz', interview in *Pulchri* [part 2]; Arntz to M. Neurath, 1 December 1946 (ÖNB 1226/4).
11. Martin Ledermann to M. Neurath, 20 May 1946 (IC 1/16).
12. Neurath to Agnes Arntz, 10 July 1945 (ÖNB 1217/10).
13. De Kanter to Neurath, 18 July 1945 (ÖNB 1220/48).
14. De Kanter to Neurath, 8 July and 17 October 1945 (ÖNB 1220/48). The three board members of IFVE that met to agree this were Peter De Kanter, Anneke de Kanter and Jan Tinbergen. The constitution of the IFVE required that its director, Otto Neurath, should approve and sign any such resolution.
15. Neurath to Fleddérus, 18 December 1946 (IC 1/15).
16. See the examples in part two of Robin Kinross's clear examination, 'Copyright in Isotype work', at www.hyphenpress.co.uk (viewed 9 March 2023).
17. M. Neurath, 'What I remember', pp. 92–3, and M. Neurath to Martin Ledermann (lawyer), 14 April 1947 (IC 1/15). See also Eve, 'Isotype in Trouble, 1946–1948'.
18. M. Neurath to Arntz, 27 August 1969 (ÖNB 1226/8). She added: 'The preferred solution for us would be if the IFVE could be revived and could handle trusteeship of the material. But our efforts to get financial support have foundered'.
19. M. Neurath to Kaempffert, 18 June 1954 (IC 1/47).
20. M. Neurath to Container Corporation of America, 26 November 1957 (ÖNB 1232/14). See also Benjamin Benus, *Herbert Bayer, the World Geo-Graphic Atlas, and Information Design at Mid-Century* (Rochester: RIT Press, 2023).
21. M. Neurath to Ledermann, 14 April 1947 (IC 1/16).
22. Kindel 'Future Books & Future Magazine, 1946–52' in Burke, Kindel, Walker (ed.), *Isotype*, p. 438. See also Kindel, '*Future*, *Fortune*, and the graphic design of information'.
23. George Orwell criticized *Contact* and *Future Books* in the *Partisan Review* (Summer 1946), describing them as 'streamlined, high-powered, slickly got-up, semi-intellectual' magazines. In his view, the visual emphasis gave 'the average reader the feeling of being "advanced" without actually forcing him to think'. Cited by Alan Powers in 'Contact books', *Parenthesis* 30 (Spring 2016). There seems to have been a Dutch equivalent to these magazines, with contributions by Gerd Arntz and the NSS, named *The Way Ahead*: 'a Quarterly Economic Review'.
24. These aspects of Isotype work have been thoroughly documented and analysed by Sue Walker and Eric Kindel respectively. See their essays in Burke, Kindel, Walker (ed.), *Isotype*.
25. M. Neurath, 'Report on the last years of Isotype work'.
26. See the listing in [University of Reading], *Graphic Communication Through Isotype*, pp. 38–9.
27. M. Neurath, 'Otto Neurath, Wiener Methode, Isotype – ein Bericht', pp. 29–30.
28. O. Neurath, 'Visual Education: ', p. 256.
29. M. Neurath, 'Otto Neurath and Isotype', p. 19.
30. M. Neurath, 'What I remember', p. 96.
31. Arntz, *Zeit unterm Messer*, p. 40.

32. M. Neurath to Arntz, 26 October 1946; and Arntz to M. Neurath, 15 January 1947 (ÖNB 1226/4 & 1226/8).
33. M. Neurath to Arntz, 29 January 1947 (ÖNB 1226/8).
34. Arntz to M. Neurath, 8 February 1948 (ÖNB 1226/4).
35. Arntz to M. Neurath, 5 January and 26 April 1949 (ÖNB 1226/5).
36. M. Neurath to Arntz, 25 January 1949 (ÖNB 1226/8).
37. M. Neurath to Arntz, 20 March 1951 (ÖNB 1226/8).
38. M. Neurath to Arntz, 28 June and 17 February 1975 (ÖNB 1226/8).
39. Arntz to M. Neurath, 11 May 1975 (ÖNB 1226/7).
40. G. Arntz, F. Bool and K. Broos, *Symbolen voor Onderwijs en Staistiek: Wenen-Moskou-Den Haag / Symbols for education and statistics: Vienna-Moscow-The Hague* (Amsterdam: Spruijt, 1979).
41. M. Neurath to Arntz, 9 February 1981 (Private Archive Friedrich Stadler).

7 Rudolf Modley in America

1. Sandner, 'Rudolf Modley and the Americanization of Isotype', p. 35.
2. M. Neurath, 'Social and Economic Museum of Vienna, 1925–1934', in Burke, Kindel, Walker (ed.), *Isotype*, p. 530.
3. Rudolf Modley 'Das Gesellschafts- und Wirtschaftsmuseum', *Arbeit und Wirtschaft*, 6 (January 15, 1928), p. 59. Otto Neurath had made similar suggestions in 'Statistik und Proletariat' (1927).
4. On the early history of the MSI, see Sandner, 'Rudolf Modley and the Americanization of Isotype', pp. 39–40.
5. Ihara, 'Isotype in America', p. 304.
6. Sandner, 'Rudolf Modley and the Americanization of Isotype', p. 40.
7. Ibid., p. 306.
8. Jill Lepore, *These Truths: a History of the United States* (New York: Norton & Company, 2018), p. 525.
9. Kiran Klaus Patel, 'Improvisierend durch die Krise: Der New Deal', *Aus Politik und Zeitgeschichte* 72, nos. 3–4 (2022,) pp. 13-15.
10. Eric Hobsbawm, *The Age of Extremes: the Short Twentieth Century, 1914–1991* (London: Abacus, 1995), p. 105.
11. Ihara, 'Isotype in America', pp. 313 & 339. Evidently the idea was for Pictorial Statistics, Inc. to continue operating as a parent organization concerned more with research. This reflected the similar division of responsibilities between the Social and Economic Museum and the Mundaneum in Vienna, and between the IFVE and the Mundaneum (plus the putative Isotype Ltd) in The Hague (see chapter 4).
12. Hisayasu Ihara lists five of them in 'Rigor and Relevance in the International Picture Language: Rudolf Modley's Criticism against Otto Neurath and his Activity in the Context of the Rise of the "Americanization of Neurath's Method"' (2009), https://api.lib.kyushu-u.ac.jp/opac_download_md/20302/Hisayasu_ihara_IASDR2009.pdf (accessed 12 May 2023).
13. See Ihara, 'Isotype in America', pp. 308–14.
14. Modley, 'Facts Told Pictorially', *The New York Times*, 15 September 1935, p. 6.
15. Mick Gidley, *The Grass Shall Grow: Helen Post; Photographs the Native American West* (Lincoln: University of Nebraska Press, 2020), pp. 5–6.
16. Jason Forest, 'The Telefacts of Life: Rudolf Modley's Isotypes in American Newspapers 1938–1945' (2023), online at www.nightingaledvs.com (accessed 10 May 2023).
17. A series of these had been reproduced in the article 'Otto Neurath visits Russia', *Survey Graphic* 21, no. 8, (1932), pp. 538–9.
18. Helen Post, Speech at the Conference of the Council on Social Graphics in Leesburg, Virginia, 22 October 1978 (PAM).
19. For example, *Argentina: Profile of a Nation*; *Chile: Land of Contrasts*; *Cuba: Island Neighbour*; *Ecuador: Snow on the Equator* (Washington D.C: Coordinator of Inter-American Affairs, all 1944). See also Sandner, 'Rudolf Modley and the Americanization of Isotype', pp. 44–6.
20. Lepore, *These Truths*, p. 678.
21. 'Rudolf Modley', (RG 226, Entry 224, Box 531, OSS Archives: NARA).
22. Gidley, *The Grass Shall Grow* (see note 15), pp. 5–6, 31.
23. Sandner, 'Rudolf Modley and the Americanization of Isotype', p. 49.
24. Burke, 'Pictogram design: Vienna and beyond', in Burke, Kindel and Walker (ed.), *Isotype*, p. 514; Sandner, *Weltsprache ohne Worte: Rudolf Modley*,

Margaret Mead und das Glyphs-Projekt, p. 48 & pp. 100–2.

25. Jilly Traganou, *Designing the Olympics: Representation, Participation, Contestation* (New York: Routledge, 2016).
26. Otto Neurath had hinted at this usage for Isotype pictograms in *International Picture Language*, and also tried to have signs produced with them during the war, but they were never used in signage. See chapter 4.
27. Wibo Bakker, 'Icograda and the Development of Pictogram Standards: 1963–1986', *Iridescent* 2, no. 2 (2013): 38–48.
28. See Markus Rathgeb, *Otl Aicher* (London: Phaidon, 2006).
29. Peter Mandler, *Return from the Natives: How Margaret Mead Won the Second World War and Lost the Cold War* (New Haven, London: Yale University Press, 2013). Mandler describes Mead as 'the most famous anthropologist who ever lived' (p. xi). She would eventually publish forty-four books (eighteen of which she co-authored) plus hundreds of essays and articles.
30. 'United Nations Memorandum from the I.C.Y. Committee to the General Assembly of March 19, 1964', quoted from Rudolf Modley and Mary C. Bateson, 'Symbols, Inc. for Intercultural Communications' (Preliminary Draft) (Box K 62, Folder 8, Margaret Mead Papers; LOC). Bateson (Mead's daughter) wrote a memorandum on Glyphs that was an important point of reference: 'Some Theoretical Comments on Glyphs: Memorandum Prepared for International Cooperation Year, 1964' (Box 63, Folder 3, Margaret Mead Papers; LOC).
31. Rudolf Modley, 'Memorandum: Guidelines on Designing Universally Usable Graphic Symbols (Glyphs)', 23 June 1965 (Box 63, Folder 3, Margaret Mead Papers; LOC).
32. Sandner, *Weltsprache ohne Worte*, pp. 72–4.
33. *Glyphs Newsletter* 4 (March 1971), and *Glyphs Newsletter* 26 (Autumn 1976).
34. Margaret Mead and Rudolf Modley: 'Communication Among All People, Everywhere', *Natural History* LXXVII, no. 7 (August–September 1968): 56–63.
35. Mary Catherine Bateson, *With a Daughter's Eye: a Memoir of Margaret Mead and Gregory Bateson* (New York: Washington Square Press, 1985) p. 98.
36. Mead and Modley: 'Communication Among All People, Everywhere', p. 63.
37. For a more detailed discussion of the failure of Glyphs, see Sandner, *Weltsprache ohne Worte*, pp. 119–31.
38. For example, Marie Neurath reported to Gerd Arntz (27 August 1969) that Modley had asked her if she knew of anyone to head the Glyphs project (ÖNB 1226/8).
39. Rudolf Modley, 'Universal Symbols and Cartography', paper presented at Queen's University, Ontario, 9 September 1970, p. 6.
40. Charles Bliss, *International Semantography: a Non-Alphabetical Symbol Writing Readable in All Languages* (Sydney: Institute of Semantography, 1949).
41. Modley to Mead, 13 January 1967 (Box 63, Folder 1, Margaret Mead Papers; LOC). For another example of Bliss making a nuisance of himself to promote his system, see Arika Okrent, *In the Land of Invented Languages* (New York: Random House, 2010), pp. 173–7.
42. Rudolf Modley, 'World Language Without Words', *Journal of Communication* 24, no. 4 (1974), pp. 64–6.
43. Ihara, 'Isotype in America', pp. 309–13.
44. O. Neurath to Josef Frank, 8 July 1939 (ÖNB 1219/3).
45. Evart G. Routzahn, review of *How to Use Pictorial Statistics* by Rudolf Modley, *American Journal of Public Health* 6 (June 1938), pp. 785–6.
46. Modley, *How to Use Pictorial Statistics*, p. XIII.
47. 'LK F. (= Larry K. Frank), interview with Mr. Modley' (Series 1.2 B226 F2167), Gen. Education Board, 2 April 1935 (RAC).
48. Otto to Paul Neurath, 27 February 1944 (ÖNB 1222/55-8).
49. M. Neurath to Modley, 19 June 1959 (IC 1/49).
50. Rudolf Modley, *The Challenge of Symbology* (New York: Fund for the Advancement of Education, 1959).
51. O. Neurath, 'Remarks made by the director of the Gesellschafts- und Wirtschaftsmuseum in Vienna in connection with the charts prepared for the Museum of Science and Industry', 13 February 1932 (MSI).
52. Rudolf Modley, 'Signs and Symbols in Review', in *Glyphs Newsletter* 22 (Autumn 1975), p. 80.

Epilogue

1. A similar naming problem pertains to Marie Neurath herself, who was Marie Reidemeister until 1941.
2. The closest they came to this were guideline notes written for internal use at the Vienna Museum; see Kinross, 'The Graphic Formation of Isotype'.
3. O. Neurath, 'The Unity of Science as a task', in Neurath, *Philosophical papers 1913–1946*, p. 116.
4. O. Neurath, *From Hieroglyphics to Isotype*, p. 102.
5. Paul to Otto Neurath, 21 December 1945 (ÖNB 1222/54-2). This was the day before Otto Neurath died, so he did not receive the letter.
6. O. Neurath to Mr James (Calcium Chloride Association, Detroit), 26 November 1941 (IC 1/4).
7. O. Neurath, 'Isotype Institute and Adult Education', p. 13.
8. O. Neurath, 'Kolonialpolitische Aufklärung durch Bildstatistik', p. 130.
9. This is broadly the definition adopted in Burke, Kindel, Walker (ed.), *Isotype*.
10. For example, data graphics in *The Guardian* newspaper and the Viennese weekly *Falter*.
11. For example, *Das Klimabuch* (2019) and *Das Wald-Buch* (2021). See also M. Moretti, 'Design for Graphicacy: The Case of Glocal Climate Change', in *Proceedings of the 3rd International and Interdisciplinary Conference on Image and Imagination; IMG 2021* (Lecture Notes in Networks and Systems, vol. 631), edited by D. Villa and F. Zuccoli (Cham: Springer, 2023), 733–41.
12. Sue Walker, 'Effective Antimicrobial Resistance Communication: the Role of Information Design', *Palgrave Communcations* 5, no. 24 (2019); and Walker *et al*, 'Beat Bad Microbes: Raising Public Awareness Of Antibiotic Resistance in Rwanda', *Information Design Journal* 26, no. 1 (2021): 17–32. See also McCrorie et al, 'Infographics: Healthcare Communication for the Digital Age', *Ulster Med J* 85, no.2 (2016): 71–75.
13. See the essay by Gökhan Ersan *et al* in Waldner (ed.), *Die Konturen der Welt*, 263–96.
14. O. Neurath, 'Visual Education', p. 257. See also Jeremy Boy *et al*, 'Showing People Behind Data: Does Anthropomorphizing Visualizations Elicit More Empathy For Human Rights Data?' in *CHI '17: Proceedings of the 2017 CHI Conference On Human Factors In Computing Systems* (New York: Association for Computing Machinery, 2017), pp. 5462–74.
15. See Pedro Bessa, 'Skittish Skirts and Scanty Silhouettes: The Tribulations of Gender in Modern Signage', *Visible Language* 42, no. 2 (2008), pp. 119–41.
16. Vyvyan Evans, *The Emoji Code: the Linguistics Behind Smiley Faces and Scaredy Cats* (London: Michael O'Mara, 2017).

Select bibliography

Note: Otto Neurath's writings about visual education have been collected in the German-language edition, *Gesammelte bildpädagogische Schriften*. Wherever possible, for writings by Neurath originally in German, details of inclusion in that volume (abbreviated as *GbS*) are given in the following bibliography.

Annink, Ed, and Max Bruinsma (ed.), *Gerd Arntz: Graphic Designer*. Rotterdam: 010, 2010.

Arntz, Gerd, '3.7.'72'. Typescript memoir. Manuscript English translation by Robin Kinross, IC 8.4.

[Arntz, Gerd] 'Gerd Arntz', interview in *Pulchri* 8, nos. 3 & 4 (1980). Typescript English translation by Marie Neurath, IC 8.4.

–. *Zeit unterm Messer: Holz- & Linolschnitte 1920–1970*. Cologne: Informationspresse Leske, 1988.

Benus, Benjamin, 'Otto Neurath's Social History of Art'. In *Creative Collaboration in Art, Practice, Research and Pedagogy*, edited by M. Kathryn Shields and Sunny Spillane, 135–62. Newcastle upon Tyne: Cambridge Scholars Publishing, 2018.

Benus, Benjamin and Wim Jansen, 'The Vienna Method in Amsterdam: Peter Alma's Office for Pictorial Statistics'. *Design Issues* 32, no. 2 (2016): 19–35.

Blau, Eve, 'Isotype and Architecture in Red Vienna: the Modern Projects of Otto Neurath and Josef Frank'. *Austrian Studies* 14 (2006) *Culture and Politics in Red Vienna*: 227–59.

Bool, Flip and Kees Broos, *Gerd Arntz: kritische Grafik und Bildstatistik*. The Hague: Haags Gemeentemuseum, 1976.

Brinton, Willard C., *Graphic Methods for Presenting Facts*. New York: The Engineering Magazine Company, 1914.

Burgstaller, Rosemarie, *Inszenierung des Hasses: Feindbildausstellungen im Nationalsozialismus*. Frankfurt/New York: Campus, 2022.

Burke, Christopher, 'Animated Isotype on film, 1941–7'. In Burke, Kindel, Walker (ed.), *Isotype*, 366–89.

–. 'The Gesellschafts- und Wirtschaftsmuseum in Wien (Social and Economic Museum of Vienna) 1925–34' In Burke, Kindel, Walker (ed.), *Isotype*, 21–102.

–. 'The Linguistic Status of Isotype'. In *Image and Imaging in Philosophy, Science and the Arts*, vol. 2 (Proceedings of the 33rd International Ludwig Wittgenstein-Symposium in Kirchberg, 2010), edited by Richard Heinrich, Elisabeth Nemeth, Wolfram Pichler, David Wagner, 31–57. Frankfurt: Ontos Verlag, 2011.

Burke, Christopher and Wim Jansen, *Soft Propaganda, Special Relationships, and a New Democracy: Adprint and Isotype, 1942–1948*. Amsterdam: De Buitenkant, 2022.

Burke, Christopher, Eric Kindel, and Sue Walker (ed.), *Isotype: Design And Contexts 1925–1971*. London: Hyphen Press, 2013.

Burke, Christopher and Günther Sandner, 'Marie Reidemeister and Otto Neurath: Interwoven Lives and Work'. *The European Journal of Life Writing*, 11 (2022): 103–29.

–. 'Isotype, Logical Empiricism, and the Scientific World-Conception'. In *Ways of the Scientific World-Conception: Rudolf Carnap and Otto Neurath*, edited by Christian Damböck, Johannes Friedl, and Ulf Höfer. Leiden: Brill, 2024.

Burke, Michael and Toby Haggith, 'Words Divide: Pictures Unite. Otto Neurath and British Propaganda Films of the Second World War'. *Imperial War Museum Journal* 12 (1999): 59–71.

Carnap, Rudolf and Otto Neurath, *Rudolf Carnap / Otto Neurath: Briefwechsel*, edited by Johannes Friedl und Ulf Höfer. 2022 (online at VALEP – DOI: 10.48666/872268).

Cat, Jordi and Adam Tamas Tuboly (ed.), *Neurath Reconsidered: New Sources and Perspectives*. Boston Studies in the Philosophy and History of Science Volume 336. Cham: Springer Nature, 2019.

Chizlett, Clive, 'Damned Lies and Statistics: Otto Neurath and Soviet Propaganda in the 1930s'. *Visible Language* 26, nos. 3/4 (1992): 298–321.

Dreyfuss, Henry, *Symbol Sourcebook: an Authoritative Guide to International Graphic Symbols*. New York: McGraw-Hill, 1972.

Eve, Matthew, 'Isotype in Trouble, 1946–1948'. *Typography Papers 8: Modern Typography in Britain*, edited by Paul Stiff, 129–34. London: Hyphen Press, 2009.

Farmer, Richard, 'Exploiting a Universal Nostalgia for Steak and Onions: The Ministry of Information and the Promotion of *World of Plenty* (1943)', *Historical Journal of Film, Radio and Television* 30, no.2 (2010): 169–185.

Galison, Peter, 'Aufbau / Bauhaus: Logical Positivism and Architectural Modernism'. *Critical Inquiry* 16, no.4 (1990): 709–52.

[Gesellschafts- und Wirtschaftsmuseum in Wien], *Die bunte Welt: Mengenbilder für die Jugend*. Vienna: Artur Wolf Verlag, 1929.

–. *Entwicklung von Landwirtschaft und Gewerbe in Deutschland*. Gesellschafts- und Wirtschaftsmuseum in Wien, 1928.

–. *Gesellschaft und Wirtschaft: bildstatistisches Elementarwerk*. Leipzig: Bibliographisches Institut, 1930.

–. *Die Gewerkschaften*. Gesellschafts- und Wirtschaftsmuseum in Wien, 1928.

–. *Technik und Menschheit: Bilder des Gesellschafts- und Wirtschaftsmuseum in Wien*. Vienna & Leipzig: Deutscher Verlag für Jugend und Volk, 1932.

Gruber, Helmut, *Red Vienna: Experiment in Working-Class Culture, 1919–1934*. New York & Oxford: Oxford University Press, 1991.

Halusa, Gerhard, 'Das Museum nach der Ära Otto Neurath'. In Waldner (ed.), *Die Konturen der Welt*, 101–14.

Hartmann, Frank (ed.), *Sachbild und Gesellschaftstechnik: Otto Neurath*. Hamburg: Avinus, 2015.

Hartmann, Frank, and Erwin K. Bauer, *Bildersprache: Otto Neurath, Visualisierungen*. 2nd edn; Vienna: Wiener Universitätsverlag, 2006.

Holter, Marie Christine, and Barbara Höller (ed.), *Zeit(lose) Zeichen / Timeless Signs: Contemporary Art in Reference to Otto Neurath*. Vienna: Künstlerhaus / Kerber Art, 2013.

Ihara, Hisayasu, 'Isotype in America: Otto Neurath and Rudolf Modley, 1930–9'. In Burke, Kindel, Walker (ed.), *Isotype*, 298–353.

Ivanitskii, Ivan Petrovich, *Izobrazitel'naia statistika i venskii metod*. Moscow / Leningrad: Ogiz-Izogiz, 1932.

Kindel, Eric, 'Future, Fortune, and the Graphic Design of Information'. In *Information Design: Research and Practice*, edited by Alison Black, Paul Luna, Ole Lund, and Sue Walker, 127–46. London & New York: Routledge, 2017.

–. 'Isotype in Africa, 1952–8'. In Burke, Kindel, Walker (ed.), *Isotype*, 448–97.

Kinross, Robin, 'Blind Eyes, Innuendo and the Politics of Design: a Reply to Clive Chizlett'. *Visible Language* 28, no.1 (1994): 68–79.

–. 'Émigré Graphic Designers in Britain: Around the Second World War and Afterwards'. *Journal of Design History* 3, no.1 (1990): 5–57.

–. 'The Graphic Formation of Isotype'. In Burke, Kindel, Walker (ed.), *Isotype*, 107–77.

–. 'The Lessons of Isotype for Information Design'. In *Information Design: Research and Practice*, edited by Alison Black, Paul Luna, Ole Lund, and Sue Walker, 107–116. London & New York: Routledge, 2017.

–. 'Marie Neurath 1898–1986' [obituary]. In Kinross, *Unjustified Texts: Perspectives on Typography*, 51–5. London: Hyphen Press, 2002.

–. 'On the Influence of Isotype'. *Information Design Journal* 2, no.2 (1981): 122–30.

Köstenberger, Julia, 'Otto Neurath und die Sowjetunion'. In *Update! Perspektiven der Zeitgeschichte*, edited by Linda Erker *et al*, 101–07. Innsbruck: Studienverlag, 2012.

Kraeutler, Hadwig, *Otto Neurath. Museum and Exhibition Work: Spaces Designed for Communication*. Frankfurt a.M.: Peter Lang, 2008.

Krampen, Martin, 'Signs and Symbols in Graphic Communication'. *Design Quarterly*, no.62 (1965): 1–31.

Krichevskii, Vladimir, 'Izostatistika i "Izostat"/ Pictorial Statistics and "Izostat"'. *Proekt Rossiia / Project Russia* 1 (1995): 63–7.

Laptev, Vladimir V. [В. В. Лаптев], *Русская инфографика* [*Russian Infographics*]. St Petersburg Polytechnic University, 2018.

Leonard, Robert J., '"Seeing is Believing": Otto Neurath, Graphic Art, and the Social Order'. In *Economic Engagements With Art*, edited by Neil De Marchi and Craufurd D.W. Goodwin, 453–78. Durham, NC: Duke University Press, 1999.

Lissitzky-Küppers, Sophie, *El Lissitzky: Life, Letters, Texts*. London: Thames & Hudson, 1968.

Lupton, Ellen, 'Reading Isotype'. In *Design Discourse: History, Theory, Criticism,* edited by Victor Margolin, 145–56. University of Chicago Press, 1989.

McElvenny, James, 'International Language and the Everyday: Contact and Collaboration Between C. K. Ogden, Rudolf Carnap and Otto Neurath'. *British Journal for the History of Philosophy* 21, no. 6 (2013): 1194–1218.

Marschalek, Manfred, *Untergrund und Exil: Österreichs Sozialisten zwischen 1934 und 1945*. Vienna: Löcker, 1990.

Mead, Margaret, and Rudolf Modley: 'Communication Among All People, Everywhere'. *Natural History* LXXVII, no. 7 (August–September 1968): 56–63.

Mertens, Ferdinand, *An Idealist in The Hague: Otto Neurath's Years in Exile*. Municipality of The Hague: n.d. [2007].

Minns, Emma, 'Picturing Soviet progress: Izostat, 1931–4'. In Burke, Kindel, Walker (ed.), *Isotype*, 257–81.

–. '"Unity in Difference": the Representation of Life in the Soviet Union Through Isotype'. In *A People Passing Rude: British Responses to Russian Culture*, edited by Anthony Cross, 269–84. Cambridge: Open Book, 2012.

Modley, Rudolf, *Handbook of Pictorial Symbols: 3,250 Examples from International Sources*. With the assistance of William R. Myers. New York: Dover, 1976.

–. *How to Use Pictorial Statistics*. New York & London: Harper and Brothers, 1937.

–. 'World Language without Words', *Journal of Communication* 24, no. 4 (1974): 59–66.

[Modley, Rudolf] (ed.), *1000 Pictorial Symbols*. New York: Pictograph Corporation, 1942.

Müller, Karl, 'Neurath's Theory of Pictorial-Statistical Representation'. In *Rediscovering the Forgotten Vienna Circle*, edited by Thomas E. Uebel, 223–54. Dordrecht/London: Kluwer, 1991.

Nemeth, Elisabeth, 'Visualizing Relations in Society and Economics: Otto Neurath's Isotype-Method Against the Background of his Economic Thought'. In Cat and Tuboly (ed.), *Neurath Reconsidered*, 117–40.

Nemeth, Elisabeth, and Friedrich Stadler (ed.), *Encyclopedia and Utopia: the Life and Work of Otto Neurath (1882–1945)*. Dordrecht: Kluwer, 1996.

Neurath, Marie, '26 September 1924 and After'. In Otto Neurath, *Empiricism and Sociology*, 56–64.

–. 'Gesellschafts- und Wirtschaftsmuseum in Wien en Mundaneum'. *Museumjournaal* 21, Nr. 5 (1976): 205–9. English typescript, IC 8.1a.

–. 'Isotype'. *Health Education Journal* 13, no. 1 (1955): 28–38.

–. 'Isotype'. *Instructional Science* 3, no. 2 (1974): 127–50.

–. 'Isotype: Education Through the Eye'. In Dreyfuss, *Symbol Sourcebook*, 24–5.

–. 'Isotype in films'. *Scannan: Journal of the Portlaoighise Film Society* 1, no. 3 (1946): 12, 15. Unabridged text online at www.isotyperevisited.org, under 'Texts'.

–. 'The Origin And Theory of Isotype'. *Yearbook of Education* (1960): 112–20.

–. 'Otto Neurath and Isotype'. *Graphic Design* [Tokyo] 42 (1971): 11–30.

–. 'Otto Neurath und die ›Wiener Methode der Bildstatistik‹'. *Arbeit und Wirtschaft*, Nr. 12 (1978): 3.

–. 'Otto Neurath, Wiener Methode, Isotype – ein Bericht'. In Stadler (ed.), *Arbeiterbildung in der Zwischenkriegszeit*, 24–30.

–. 'Report on the Last Years of Isotype work'. *Synthese* 8, nos. 1/2 (1950–1): 22–7.

–. 'What I remember'. Unpublished typescript memoir 'told and written down for Henk Mulder', 1980–2. English translation by Robin Kinross, approved by Marie Neurath in 1984. IC 8.1c.

–. 'Zum 40. Geburtstag des Gesellschafts- und Wirtschaftsmuseums in Wien'. *Arbeit und Wirtschaft*, Nr. 6 (1965): 24–6.

Neurath, Marie, and Robin Kinross, *The Transformer: Principles of Making Isotype Charts*. London: Hyphen Press, 2009.

Neurath, Otto, *Basic by Isotype*. Psyche miniatures, general series, no. 86. London: Kegan Paul, Trench, Trubner & Co., 1937. Reprint, London: Basic English Publishing, 1948.

–. 'Bildhafte Pädagogik im Gesellschafts- und Wirtschaftsmuseum in Wien' (1931), *GbS*, 197–206.

–. 'Bildliche Darstellung gesellschaftliche Tatbestände' (1927), *GbS*, 118–25.

–. 'Bildliche Darstellung sozialer Tatbestände' (1926), *GbS*, 57–62.

–. 'Bildstatistik: Führer durch die Ausstellung des Gesellschafts- und Wirtschaftsmuseums in Wien' (1927), *GbS*, 99–117.

–. 'Bildstatistik nach Wiener Methode' (1931), *GbS*, 180–91; translated as 'Pictorial Statistics Following the Vienna Method'. *ARTMargins* 6, no. 1 (2017): 108–18.

Neurath, Otto [cont.], *Bildstatistik nach Wiener Methode in der Schule*. Vienna & Leipzig, Deutscher Verlag für Jugend und Volk, 1933. Reprinted in *GbS*, 265–336 (page numbers given for citations are from the reprint).

–. 'Bildstatistik nach Wiener Methode in der Sowjetunion' (1932), *GbS*, 207–9.

–. 'Bildstatistik und Arbeiterbildung' (1929), *GbS*, 139–43.

–. 'Bildstatistiken des Gesellschafts- und Wirtschaftsmuseums in Wien' (1932), *GbS*, 210–13.

–. 'The Current Growth in Global Productive Capacity'. In O. Neurath, *Economic Writings*, 475–505.

–. 'Darstellungsmethoden des Gesellschafts- und Wirtschaftsmuseums' (1925), *GbS*, 18–27.

–. *Economic Writings: Selections, 1904–1945.* Edited by Thomas E. Uebel and Robert S. Cohen. Dordrecht: Kluwer, 2004.

–. *Empiricism and Sociology.* Edited by Marie Neurath and Robert S. Cohen. Dordrecht & Boston: Reidel, 1973.

–. *From Hieroglyphics to Isotype: a Visual Autobiography.* Edited by Matthew Eve and Christopher Burke. London: Hyphen Press, 2010.

–. *Gesammelte bildpädagogische Schriften.* Edited by Rudolf Haller and Robin Kinross. Vienna: Hölder-Pichler-Tempsky, 1991.

–. *Gesammelte philosophische und methodologische Schriften.* Edited by Rudolf Haller and Heiner Rutte. Vienna: Hölder-Pichler-Tempsky, 1981. 2 volumes.

–. *Gesammelte Schriften: Ergänzungsband; Varia – Verstreute Schriften.* Edited by Ulf Höfer, Christopher Burke und Günther Sandner. Vienna: LIT Verlag, 2023.

–. 'Gesellschaft und Wirtschaft im Lehrbild' (1927), *GbS*, 93–8.

–. 'Das Gesellschafts- und Wirtschaftsmuseum auf der Internationalen Städtebauausstellung in Wien' (1926), *GbS*, 63–71.

–. 'Gesellschafts- und Wirtschaftsmuseum in Wien' (1925), *GbS*, 1–17.

–. 'Das Gesellschafts- und Wirtschaftsmuseum in Wien' (1931), *GbS*, 192–6.

–. *International Picture Language: the First Rules of Isotype.* Psyche miniatures, general series, no. 83. London: Kegan Paul, Trench, Trubner & Co., 1936. Reprint, London: Basic English Publishing, 1948. Reprint of first edition (with German translation), Reading: Department of Typography & Graphic Communication, University of Reading, 1980.

–. 'Isotype Institute and Adult Education'. *Bulletin of World Association for Adult Education*, 2nd series, no. 31 (1942): 12–17.

–. 'Isotype und die Graphik' (1935), *GbS*, 342–54.

–. 'The Isotype Work'. In *Image Factories: Infographics 1920–1945: Fritz Kahn, Otto Neurath et al*, edited by Helena Doudova, Stephanie Jacobs, Patrick Rossler, 115–23. Leipzig: Spector Books, 2018.

–. 'Kolonialpolitische Aufklärung durch Bildstatistik' (1928), *GbS*, 126–32.

–. *Modern Man in the Making*, New York: Alfred A. Knopf, 1939.

–. 'Museums of the Future'. *Survey Graphic* 22, no. 9 (September 1933): 458–63, 479. Abriged version in O. Neurath, *Empiricism and Sociology*, 218–23.

–. 'Österreichs Sozialversicherung auf der „Gesolei" in Düsseldorf' (1926), *GbS*, 28–33.

–. 'Die pädagogische Weltbedeutung der Bildstatistik nach Wiener Methode' (1933), *GbS*, 240–3.

–. *Philosophical Papers 1913–1946.* Edited by Robert S. Cohen and Marie Neurath. Dordrecht & Boston: Reidel, 1983.

–. 'Pictorial statistics – an international problem'. *The Listener*, 27 September 1933, 471–2.

–. 'Das Sachbild' (1930/1), *GbS*, 153–71.

–. 'Schwarzweißgrafik' (1926), *GbS*, 51–5.

–. 'Soziale Aufklärung nach Wiener Methode' (1933), *GbS*, 231–9.

–. 'Statistik und Proletariat' (1927), *GbS*, 78–84.

–. 'Statistik und Schule' (1927), *GbS*, 85–7.

–. 'Statistische Bildertafeln zur Sozialversicherung (1926), *GbS*, 72–7.

–. 'Statistische Hieroglyphen' (1926), *GbS*, 40–50.

–. 'Unified Science and its Encyclopedia' (1937). In O. Neurath, *Philosophical Papers*, 172–82.

–. 'Unified Science and Psychology' (1933). In *Unified science*, edited by B. McGuinness, 1–23. Dordrecht: Reidel, 1987.

–. 'Universal Jargon and Terminology' (1941). In O. Neurath, *Philosophical Papers*, 213–29.

–. 'Visual Aids and Arguing'. *The New Era in Home and School* 25, no. 3 (1944): 51–61.

Neurath, Otto [cont.], 'Visual Education: a New Language'. *Survey Graphic* 26, no. 1 (January 1937): 25–8.

–. 'Visual Education: Humanisation Versus Popularisation' (1945). In Nemeth and Stadler (ed.), *Encyclopedia and Utopia*, 245–335. Abridged version in O. Neurath, *Empiricism and Sociology*, 227–47.

–. 'Visual Representation of Architectural Problems'. *Architectural Record* 82, no. 1 (July 1937): 57–61.

–. 'Ways of the Scientific World-Conception' (1930). In O. Neurath, *Philosophical Papers*, 32–47.

–. 'Der Weg des Gesellschafts- und Wirtschaftsmuseum in Wien' (1927), *GbS*, 88–92.

–. 'World Planning & the USA'. *Survey Graphic* 20, no. 6 (March 1932): 621–8.

Neurath, Otto, with Rudolf Carnap, Hans Hahn, [and Herbert Feigl], 'Wissenschaftliche Weltauffassung: der Wiener Kreis' (1929). In O. Neurath, *Empiricism and Sociology*, 299–318.

Neurath, Otto, and H. E. Kleinschmidt, *Health Education by Isotype*. New York: American Public Health Association, 1939.

Neurath, Otto, and Marie Reidemeister [uncredited], 'Abrunden und Weglassen in der Bildstatistik'. *Das Bild* 5, H. 10 (October 1928): 193–5.

–. 'Anordnung der Zeichen im Mengenbild'. *Das Bild* 5, H. 7 (July 1928): 149–52.

–. 'Bildstatistik für Kinder'. *Das Bild* 5, H. 4 (April 1928): 81–4.

–. 'Bildstatistik im Unterricht'. *Das Bild* 5, H. 11 (November 1928): 215.

–. 'Form und Farbe der Mengenbilder des Gesellschafts- und Wirtschaftsmuseums'. *Das Bild* 6, H. 10 (October 1929): 193–6.

–. 'Das Gesellschafts- und Wirtschaftsmuseum auf der Ausstellung „Wien und die Wiener"'. *Das Bild* 4, H. 5 (May 1927): 97–100.

–. 'Das Gesellschafts- und Wirtschaftsmuseum im neuen Rathause'. *Das Bild* 4, H. 12 (December 1927): 225–8.

–. 'Das Gesellschafts- und Wirtschaftsmuseum und die Schule'. *Das Bild* 4, H. 3 (March 1927): 57–9.

–. 'Der Kreis'. *Das Bild* 4, H. 9 (September 1927): 165–8.

–. 'Magnettafeln des Gesellschafts- und Wirtschaftmuseums in Wien'. *Das Bild* 4, H. 11 (November 1927): 206–7.

–. 'Orientierendes Diagramm und sprechendes Merkbild'. *Das Bild* 4, H. 10 (October 1927): 185–8.

–. 'Schulbesuch im Gesellschafts- und Wirtschaftsmuseum'. *Das Bild* 4, H. 6 (June 1927): 117–19.

Ogden, C. K., and I. A. Richards, *The Meaning Of Meaning: a Study of the Influence of Language Upon Thought and of the Science of Symbolism* [1923]. Eighth edition; London: Kegan Paul, Trench, Trubner & Co., 1946.

Reidemeister, Marie, 'Bildpädagogik'. *Die Erziehung* 7, H. 5 (1932): 313–17.

–. 'Die bunte Welt'. *Arbeit und Wirtschaft* 8, H. 4 (15 February 1930): 141–6.

–. 'Die Kunst der statistischen Darstellung'. *Kulturwille: Monatsblätter für Kultur der Arbeiterschaft* 4, Nr. 9 (September 1927): 194–5.

–. 'Kurven in der statistischen Darstellung'. *Österreichische Gemeinde-Zeitung* 4, Nr. 9 (1 May 1927): 46–9; *Das Bild* 5, H. 2 (February 1928): 41–4.

–. 'Die moderne Hieroglyphenschrift: Bildstatistik des Gesellschafts- und Wirtschaftsmuseums in Wien'. *Daheim* 65, Nr. 7 (17 November 1928): 3–4.

Rotha, Paul, *Documentary Film* [1935]. Third edition; London: Faber & Faber, 1952.

–. *The Film Till Now: a Survey of World Cinema* [1930]. Fourth edition; London: Spring Books, 1967.

Sandner, Günther, 'Bilder trennen und Bilder verbinden: Wege der Wiener Bildstatistik (1934–1945)'. In *Die Soziologie und der Nationalsozialismus in Österreich*, edited by Andreas Kranebitter and Christoph Reinprecht, 281–97. Bielefeld: Transcript, 2019.

–. 'Friendship and Enstrangement: Margarete Schütte-Lihotzky and Otto Neurath'. In *Margarete Schütte-Lihotzky: Architecture, Politics, Gender; New Perspectives on Her Life and Work*, edited by Marcel Bois and Bernadette Reinhold, 186–95. Basel: Birkhäuser 2023.

–. *Otto Neurath: eine politische Biographie*. Vienna: Zsolnay, 2014.

–. 'Rudolf Modley and the Americanization of Isotype'. *Journal of Austrian-American History* 5 (2021): 32–61.

–. *Weltsprache ohne Worte: Rudolf Modley, Margaret Mead und das Glyphs-Projekt*. Vienna: Turia und Kant, 2022.

Stadler, Friedrich, *The Vienna Circle: Studies in the Origins, Development, and Influence of Logical Empiricism*. Vienna & New York: Springer, 2001.

Stadler, Friedrich (ed.), *Arbeiterbildung in der Zwischenkriegszeit: Otto Neurath – Gerd Arntz*. Vienna & Munich: Österreichische Gesellschafts- und Wirtschaftsmuseum / Löcker Verlag, 1982.

Twyman, Michael, 'Observations on Isotype symbols and Their Varied Applications'. In *Neurath Zeichen*, edited by J. Bernard and G. Withalm, 161–79. Vienna: Österreichische Gesellschaft für Semiotik und Institut für sozio-semiotische Studien, 1996.

–. 'The significance of Isotype'. In [University of Reading], *Graphic Communication Through Isotype*, 7–17.

[University of Reading], *Graphic Communication Through Isotype*. Exhibition catalogue. Department of Typography & Graphic Communication, University of Reading, 1975; 2nd edn, 1981.

Vossoughian, Nader, *Otto Neurath: The Language of the Global Polis*. Rotterdam: NAi, 2008.

–. 'The Language of the World Museum: Otto Neurath, Paul Otlet, Le Corbusier'. *Transnational Associations* 1–2 (2003): 82–93.

Waldner, Gernot (ed.), *Die Konturen der Welt: Geschichte und Gegenwart visueller Bildung nach Otto Neurath*. Vienna / Berlin: Mandelbaum, 2021.

Walker, Sue, 'Explaining History to Children: Otto and Marie Neurath's Work on the "Visual History of Mankind"'. *Journal of Design History* 24, no. 4 (2012): 345–62.

–. 'Graphic explanation for children, 1944–71'. In Burke, Kindel, Walker (ed.), *Isotype*, 390–437.

Wenzel, Heidrun-Ulrike, *Vergessen? Niemals! Die antifaschistische Ausstellung im Wiener Künstlerhaus 1946*. Vienna / Berlin: Mandelbaum, 2018.

Archive sources (Abbreviations)

AAK	Archiv der Arbeiterkammer Wien / Archives of the Chamber of Labour, Vienna.
IC	Otto and Marie Neurath Isotype Collection, University of Reading (UK).
IISH	International Institute of Social History / Netherlands Economic History Archive, Amsterdam.
INF	Ministry of Information Records, The National Archives, Kew, London.
LOC	Library of Congress, Washington DC.
MSI	Museum of Science and Industry (Archives), Chicago.
NARA	National Archives and Records Administration, Maryland (USA).
OeStA, AdR	Österreichisches Staatsarchiv, Archiv der Republik / Austrian State Archives, Archive of the Republic.
ÖGWM	Österreichischen Gesellschafts- und Wirtschaftsmuseum (Archiv) / Austrian Social and Economic Museum (Archives).
ÖNB	Österreichische Nationalbibliothek, Handschriftensammlung (Wien) / Austrian National Library, Department of Manuscripts and Rare Books (Vienna).
PAM	Private Archive Peter Modley.
RAC	Rockefeller Archive Center (Sleepy Hollow, New York).
SLA	Salzburger Landesarchiv / Salzburg Provincial Archives.
VGA	Verein für die Geschichte der Arbeiterbewegung / Association for the History of the Labour Movement, Vienna.
WStLA	Wiener Stadt- und Landesarchiv / Municipal and Provincial Archives of Vienna.

Image sources

All images are taken from the Otto and Marie Neurath Isotype Collection, courtesy of the University of Reading, except the following:

Österreichischen Gesellschafts- und Wirtschaftsmuseum:
2.9, 2.10, 3.3, 3.4, 5,6, 5.7

Private collections:
3.1, 3.2, 4.17, 5.4, 5.5, 6.13, 7.8, 7.9, 7.10

Burke and Jansen, *Soft Propaganda, Special Relationships, and a New Democracy*:
4.13, 4.14

The Vienna Circle Archive, Noord-Hollands Archief, Haarlem:
6.16

Index

Der Abend (newspaper) 107, 111
Action Group (Nigeria, Western Region) 141
Adprint 94, 97, 131, 132, 146
 'America and Britain' (book series) 94, *95*, 97
 Future Books and magazine 132, *133–4*
 Social Insurance 99
 Social Security 98–9, *98*
 'The Soviets and Ourselves' (book series) *96*, 97
Africa, Isotype in 135, 140–4
Aicher, Otl 162
Alma, Peter 23
 and Izostat 50
Amsterdam 44
 World Social Economic Congress 44, *45*, 109, 111
'Arbeiterbildung in der Zwischenkriegszeit' (exhibition) 114, 125
Arbeiter-Zeitung 34, 40, 57, 63
Arntz, Agnes 127
Arntz, Gerd 8, 9, 23, 69, 84, 120–1, 125, 130–1, 144
 as artist 50, 78, 129, 147
 comes to Vienna 22
 in The Hague 76, 87, 109
 and Izostat 47, 50, 52, 56–8
 Marie Neurath on 146–8
 Otto Neurath on 127
 during Second World War 128–9, 145
Austria 7, 9, 11, 39, 57, 58, 61, 75, 76, 109, 110, 114–15, 118, 119, 122
 Anschluss 63, 70–1
 civil war 37, 75
 magnetic map of 24
Austrian Institute for Pictorial Statistics 63–6, 105, 108
 Arbeitsschlacht 63–4, *64–5*
 Industrie und Wohlstand 66–9, *67–8*
Austrian People's Party 115
Austrian Settlement and Allotment Garden Association 11

Austrian Social and Economic Museum (1949–) 107–08, 114–15, 118–25
 exhibitions 114–15, 122, 124–5
 Österreich: Gesellschaft und Wirtschaft 118–19
Austrofascism 61, 63, 66, 70, 74, 105, 109, 111, 112
Awolowo, Obafemi 141

Basic by Isotype 79, 81, 141
Basic English 51, 76–7, 79–80
Baszel, Günter von 72, 108, 110
Bauermeister, Friedrich 50
Bavarian Revolution 21
Bayer, Herbert 130–1
BBC 45
Berlin 9, 25, 38, 40, 42, 47, 70, 72–3, 83, 84, 100, 111
 Gesundheitshaus (Health House) am Urban 26, 38–9
 Karl Marx School 26
 Kreuzberg 26, 39, 42
 School Board 26
Bernath, Erwin 52, 76, 128
Beveridge, William 97, 99, 100
Das Bild (journal) 14–23
Bildstatistik nach Wiener Methode in der Schule (book) 26–31
Bliss, Charles 165–6
Blissymbolics 165
Böß, Gustav 40
Borodajkewycz, Taras 112
Bournville (Birmingham) 101
Bracken, Brendan 93
Brenner, Ann 47
Brinton, Willard Coop, *Graphic Methods for Presenting Facts* 49
Brussels, Palais Mondial 42
Buchenwald (Concentration Camp) 111
Bühler, Charlotte 13
Bühler, Karl 13
Building Big Things 136, *138–9*
Bukharin, Nikolai 180
Die bunte Welt (book) 12, *13*

Cadbury, Paul 101
Calder-Marshall, Ara 93
Calder-Marshall, Arthur 90, 91
Caminada, Richard 62–3
Carnap, Rudolf 15, 87
Central Bureau voor de Statistiek (CBS) 128, 129
 see also Nederlandse Stichting voor Statistiek
Central Executive Committee (Soviet Union) 56
Chicago 83, 152
 Museum of Science and Industry 151, *152*, 153
children's books 135–9
Cologne 12, 50
Comenius, John Amos, *Orbis sensualium pictus* 43
Communist Party
 Austria 106
 Britain 97
 USSR 50, 56
Container Corporation of America 131
Contact (periodical) 132
Compton's Pictured Encyclopedia 83
Congress of the Third International in Moscow (1921) 50
constructivism 50
 see also figurative constructivism
Cooke, Morris Llewellyn 153–4
Council of People's Commissars (Soviet Union) 48
Czechoslovakia 47, 72, 75

Department of Pictorial Statistics (Soviet Union), series of postcards *48*, 49
Deutsch, Julius 11–12, 62
Disney, Walt 91
Docekal, Josef 122–5
Dollfuß, Engelbert 61
Drexel, Karl 62
Dreyfuss, Henry 162, 165
 Symbol Sourcebook 165
Düsseldorf 33, 38
 Imperial Museum for Social and Economic Studies 61

199

Dutch Foundation for Statistics *see* Nederlandse Stichting voor Statistiek
Education, Ministry of (Austria) 105
Einstein, Albert 127
Elton, Arthur 90, 92
Ernst Mach Association 38
Ettinger, Jan van 128

Federal Statistical Office (Austria) 62
A Few Ounces a Day (film) 89, 90
figurative constructivism 69
Firnberg, Hertha 122
First Scientific Films Conference (London, 1942) 90
First World War 7, 45
Fischer, Alois 66, 69, 70, 72, 108, 109–11, 115
  Historisch-statistisches Handbüchlein 69
  Quo vadis, Europa? 110
  Taschen-Atlas 69
Five-Year Plans 9, 48, 49, 52, 53–4, 57, 58–9, 173
Fleddérus, Mary 44, 45, 75–6, 88
Fleischmann, Trude 154
Florence, Lella Secor 97
Florence, Philip Sargant 97
Foges, Wolfgang 94, 99, 131
Food, Ministry of (UK) 93
Ford Foundation
  Fund for the Advancement of Education 162
Fortune magazine 132
Frank, Josef 34, 42
Frank, Lawrence K. 163, 167
Frisch, Otto 135
Futura typeface 63, 144
Future Books and magazine 132, 133–4

Games, Abram 132
Gauss, Adalbert Karl 120
gender-neutral pictogram 176
'GeSoLei' (exhibition) 33, 38, 61
Gesellschaft und Wirtschaft (atlas) 22, 22–3, 30, 35, 36, 42, 43, 50, 69, 109, 116, 117, 118, 174, 175

Gesellschafts- und Wirtschaftsmuseum, *see* Social and Economic Museum
Gestapo 111
Glöckel, Otto 12, 15, 23
Glyphs 161–66, 168, 169
Glyphs newsletter 164
Goebbels, Joseph 70
Gold Coast (Ghana) 141
Goldfinger, Ernő 101
Grimme, Adolf 41
guide-pictures 22, 23

The Hague 42, 78–9, 84, 86, 87, 146, 168, 172
  International Peace Palace 44
  move to 58, 75–6
  Otto Neurath in 83
  see also International Foundation for (the Promotion of) Visual Education; Mundaneum, in The Hague
Hartl, Karl 120
Hellwig, Rudolf 62
Henrion, F.H.K. 100–01, 132
Herz, Carl 38, 40, 42, 55
Hickmann, Leo 48
Hitler, Adolf 45, 66
Honay, Karl 106

Ichheiser, Gustav 37
ICOGRADA (International Council of Graphic Design Associations) 162
Idenburg, Philippus Jacobus 128, 129
If You Could See Inside 131, 132, 135
Information, Ministry of (UK) 89–90
Inside the Atom 135, 136
Institute for Exhibition Technique and Pictorial Statistics 69–71
  'Der ewige Jude' (The eternal Jew; exhibition) 70
  see also 'Das Sowjetparadies'
Institute for German Cultural and Economic Propaganda 70
Interglossa 141
International Commission on Travel Signs and Symbols (ICTSS) 162

International Committee for the Breaking of Language Barriers (ICBLB) 162
International Foundation for (the Promotion of) Visual Education (IFVE) 58, 75–6, 78, 83, 127–30, 171
  exhibition technique and museum plans 86–7
  'Het rollende rad' (exhibition) 85
  'Rondom Rembrandt' (exhibition) 84–5, 85
International Industrial Relations Institute (IRI) 44, 45, 47, 75
International Organization for Standardization (ISO) 162
International Picture Language 79–80, 80–1
Isle of Man, internment camp 87, 100
Isotype
  and Basic English 76–7, 79–81
  on film 88–94
  imitations and precursors 8, 9, 48, 78, 99–103, 131–2, 172
  leaflet introducing name and symbol 77
  legacy 171–76
  name created by Marie Reidemeister 76–7
Isotype Institute (UK) 17, 92, 94, 97, 99, 101, 102
Ivanitskii, Ivan Petrovich 49, 52
  filmstrip method 48, 49
  Pictorial statistics and the Vienna Method 49
Izostat (All-Union Institute of Pictorial Statistics of Soviet Construction and Economy)
  15 let Oktiabria 51–2, 51
  Kharkiv branch 50
  Reconstruction of the Soviet Union Under the Five-Year-Plan 53–4, 59
  The Second Five-Year Plan in Construction 58–9
  The Struggle for Five Years in Four 52

200 INDEX

Izvestia, Izostat charts in 52, 154

Jahn, Otto 70, 72
Jahnel, Friedrich (Fritz) 69, 151, 160, 168
Jahoda, Marie 37, 69
Jamlitz-Lieberose (Concentration Camp) 111
Jodlbauer, Josef 105
Junge, Richard 42

Kaempffert, Waldemar 47, 83, 132, 151–2
Kanter, Peter de 44, 128, 130
Kanter, Anneke de 44
Kato, Soichi 165–6
Katsumi, Masaru 163
Kaufmann, Günter 72
Keller, Hugo 73–4
   'Zur Psychologie des volkstümlichen Zahlenbildes' 73
Kharkiv 50
Kinross, Robin 56
Kleeck, Mary van 47
Klein, Viola 144
Kleinschmidt, Harry E. 83
Health education by Isotype (with Otto Neurath) 83
Knight, Eric 90–1
Knopf, Alfred (publisher) 83, 132
Konir, Fritz 115
Krampen, Martin 162
Kurganov, Nikolai 51

Labour Party (UK) 94
Lahr, Fritz 62–4
Lambert, Richard S. 45
Land of Promise (film) 90, 93
Lasswell, Harold 161, 163
Lauwerys, Joseph 136
Le Corbusier (Charles-Édouard Jeanneret) 42
Leichter, Käthe, *So leben wir ...* 144
Leichter, Otto 34
Leipzig, Museum of War Economy 11
Lendl, Egon 116, 120
Leningrad 49
Lepore, Jill 161
'Leprosy' (poster-leaflet) 142

Lissitzky, El 50, 97
Lissitzky-Küppers, Sophie 50
The Listener (magazine) 45
Litvinova, Ivy (née Low) 50
Living in the world 146, 147
Löbe, Paul 40
Logical Empiricism 27
see also Vienna Circle
London
   World Association of Adult Education 45
   US Embassy 97, 127
Look and Learn 140
Lowenstein, Dyno 111, 160
Lublin-Maydanek (Concentration Camp) 111

Malthus, Robert 46
Mannheim 26
Marxism 55
Matejka, Viktor 106, 108
Matzalik, Edith 50, 52, 105, 120
Mayer, Carl 89
McCarthy, Joseph 160
Mead, Margaret 162–3, 165–6
   Coming of Age in Samoa 162
   Growing Up in New Guinea 162
Mexico 83–4, 162
   National Council of Higher Education and Scientific Research 83
Meyer, Ernst 89
Modley, Rudolf 101, 151–67, 173
   and charts for Chicago museum 152, 152–3
   establishes Pictograph Corporation 153
   establishes Pictorial Statistics Inc. 153
   and Isotype 152, 153, 163, 166–9
   moves to USA 151
   on Otto Neurath 163, 167
   proposal for a dictionary of graphic symbols 161
   relationship with Otto Neurath 166
   work with Marie Neurath and Henry Dreyfuss 162

Handbook of Pictorial Symbols 164, 165
A History of the War 157
How to Use Pictorial Statistics 154, 155, 167
New York Primer 157
The United States: a Graphic History 156
see also Glyphs
MOI, see Information, Ministry of
Montessori, Maria 23
Montessori schools 23, 25
Moscow 47–51, 55, 56, 57, 58, 75
   Bolshoi Theatre 51
Moskauer Rundschau (newspaper) 51
Mundaneum 17
   established in Vienna 44
   in The Hague 78, 130
   Le Corbusier and 42
   London branch 45
   Otlet and 42–3
   Otto Neurath on 75
   plans for Czech branch 47
   and related organizations 45, 47
Munich 70, 72
   Olympics (1972) 162
   Central Economic Office 38
Museum of Settlement and Town Planning 11
Myrdal, Alva 144

National Socialist Party (NSDAP) 69, 72, 115
National Tuberculosis Association (USA) 83
Fighting Tuberculosis posters 82, 83, 166
Natural History (magazine) 165
Nederlandse Stichting voor Statistiek (NSS) 127–31, 145, 147, 148
Statistisch Zakboek 129
Netherlands 44, 58, 75–6, 79, 83, 86, 109, 145, 147, 171
   De Bijenkorf (department store) 84–5
   Nazi occupation 87, 127, 129
   see also The Hague
Neubacher, Hermann 40

Neue Freie Presse (newspaper) 63
Neurath, Marie (née Reidemeister) 100, 102, 106, 108, 109, 112, 114, 116, 118, 120–2, *149*
  and Adprint 131
  in Africa 135, 140–4, 175
  and Arntz 145–8
  centrality to Vienna Museum 7, 11
  and children's books 135–9
  creates the name Isotype 76–7, 171
  flees from The Hague 87
  internment on Isle of Man 87–8
  on Isotype 77, 131–2
  and Izostat (in Moscow) 50
  marriage to Otto 88, 127
  and Modley 162, 168
  on Otto Neurath 148, 168
  in Oxford 88
  on pictograms 131, 168
  and Rembrandt 84
  scientific background 11, 135
  as 'transformer' 7, 121, 172
  see also Reidemeister, Marie
Neurath, Otto 7, 9, 11, 13, 14, 19, 38, 40–1, 58, 61, 83–4, 94, 101, 110–11, 120, 122–3, 125, 130, 135, 148, *149*, 151, 153, 163, 166–7
  In America 47, 83–4
  and Arntz 127
  as director of Izostat Institute 56
  as director of Mundaneum Wien 44
  flees from The Hague 87
  and Social and Economic Museum (Vienna) 11–15
  in The Hague 58, 75–6
  ideas about Africa 140, 175
  and International Foundation for Visual Education 75
  internment on Isle of Man 87–8
  on Isotype 19, 79–80, 166
  on Izostat 55, 57
  marriage to Marie 88, 127
  on museums 12, 86–7
  Marie Neurath on 148, 168
  in Oxford 88
  on pictograms 21
  relationship with Modley 166
  and Rotha 88–94
  and Schütte-Lihotzky 57
  in Soviet Union 55–8
  on 'transformation' 8
  and Vienna Circle 8, 15, 27, 47
  Bildstatistik nach Wiener Methode in der Schule 11, 26–31, *27*
  Health Education by Isotype (with Kleinschmidt) 83
  International Picture Language 79–80, *80–1*
  Modern Man in the Making 83–4, 89, 97, 131
  'Museums of the Future' 86–7
  'Visual Education' 140
Neurath, Paul 168, 172
Neurath, Walter 94, 98, 120
New York 47, 83
  American Museum of Natural History 86
  Russell Sage Foundation 47
  World's Fair (1939) 84, 97
The New York Times 111, 153
News Chronicle 93
Niemals vergessen! (exhibition) 108, 110, 120,
Nigeria, Western Region 141–2

Ogden, Charles Kay 50–1, 76, 77, 79, 81
'Olympics Under Dictatorship' exhibition (Amsterdam) 129
Olympics
  Mexico (1968) 162
  Munich (1972) 162
  Tokyo (1964) 162, 163
Operation Greenup 111
Österreichisch-Deutscher Volksbund (Austro-German People's League) 39
Österreichische Volkspartei *see* Austrian People's Party
Organizing Committee for the Institute for Visual Education 46, 47, 153
Orlova, Maria 50
Orr, John Boyd 90, 100
OSS (Office of Strategic Services) 111, 160
Otlet, Paul 42–4
Oxford 88

Paramount Pictures 93
Parker, Ralph, *How do you do tovarish?* 96
Pfitzner, Walter 115–16, 120
physicalism 15
pictograms 8, 15, 16, 20, 23–5, 29, 34, 63, 66
  automobile 80
  design of 21–2, 49, 52, 57–8
  and flags 18
  fractions of 155
  hotel signs 80
  human figures 21, 147
  Marie Neurath on 131, 168
  Munich Olympics 162
  Otto Neurath on
  in signage 80, *81*
  telephone 163
  Tokyo Olympics 162
  transport and travel 162
Pictograph Corporation 153, 160, 161
  1000 Pictorial Symbols 161
Pictorial Statistics Inc. 153–4
Planek, Adolf 106
Pointer, Louis 37
poster-leaflets (Africa) 142, *143*
Porges, Alfred 106
Post, Helen 154, 160
Posthumus, Nicolaas 44
Prague 47
'Pressa' (International Press Exhibition, Cologne) 12, 50
Public Works Administration (USA), Mississippi Valley Committee 153

Die Quelle (journal) 14

Raab, Julius 106
Railways Under London 135
Rauscher, Franz 70, 106–08, 109, 110–15, 120–5

Darstellungsmethoden der Statistik 112, *113*
Reading, University of
  Isotype exhibition 114, *123*, 148
Reidemeister, Marie 7, 9, 11, 12, 14, 18, 19, 42, 50, 69, 75, 76, 79, 83, 84, 87, 88, 171, 175
  see also Neurath, Marie
Rembrandt van Rijn 84–5
Renner, Karl 35, 78
Rich Man, Poor Man 166, *167*
Rieger, Philipp 122
Rockefeller Center 83
Rockefeller Foundation 167
Rockets and Jets 136
Roosevelt, Curtis 163
Roosevelt, Franklin D.
  New Deal policy 153
Rotha, Paul 88–94, 100, 131
  The Film Till Now 89
Rural Electrification
  Administration (USA) 154

Salzburg, Institute for
  Geo-Graphics 115–6
Salzburg Atlas 116–8, *116–7*, 120
Salzburger Volksblatt 63
Scheer, Josef 50, 76, 109, 120, 128
Schmitz, Richard 61
Schütte-Lihotzky, Margarete 57
Schumann, Wolfgang 45
Second World War 9, 105, 157, 162, 172
Semantography 165
Shand, Philip Morton 45, 47
Sierra Leone 141
Slama, Victor 108, 115
Smollett, Peter (Hans Peter Smolka) 97
Sochi 56
Social and Economic
  Museum (Vienna, 1925–34) 11–14, *34, 35, 37*
  background and conception 11–12
  Berlin branch 9, 38–42
  dissolution 61–2, 69
  early films 35, 89
  exhibitions
    'Frau und Kind' 12
    'Germany's Economic situation' 42

'GeSoLei' 33, 38, 61
'Social hygiene and social insurance' 35
'Wien im Bild' 40–1
'Wien und die Wiener' 12
'World Economy' 35
links with schools and teachers 15–26
publications
  Entwicklung von Landwirtschaft und Gewerbe in Deutschland 20–1
'Zeitschau' branch 37
Social Democratic Party (Austria) 11, 33, 39, 48, 61, 62, 105, 106, 109, 110–11, 115
Social Insurance (White Paper booklet) 99
Socialist Realism 57, 58, 72
Social Security (Beveridge Plan) 97–9
Sociographics (Philadelphia) 153
Soviet Union (USSR) 9, 47–59, 72, 76, 97, 153, 172–3
'Das Sowjetparadies' (The Soviet Paradise; exhibition) 72–3, *73*, 108
Speeding into Space 136, *137*
Speiser, Paul 40, 61, 62, 105
Stadler, Friedrich 125
Stalin, Josef 9, 48, 50, 53, 55, 56
Survey Graphic 47

Tandler, Julius 62
Technik und Menschheit (atlas) 43–4
'Telefact' 154
Thames & Hudson 94
'They Lived Like This' (book series) 148
Tießler, Walter 72
The Times 94, 108
Tinbergen, Jan 128, 130
'transformation' 128, and Izostat 50
  Marie Neurath and 50, 121–2, 130
  Otto Neurath on 100, 168, 172
'transformer' 7, 8, 30, 50, 84, 121, 172

Trautenegg, Eduard 63, 64, 69–70, 72, 105–07, 108
Trotsky, Leon 55
Tschinkel, Augustin 23, 116
tuberculosis 82, 83, 166
Twyman, Michael 123, 148

Ukraine 50, 53, 56
Ulm, Hochschule für Gestaltung 162
Union for Democratic Action 161
United Nations 114, 122
  Conference on Food and Agriculture 93
  International Cooperation Year (ICY) 162
United States of America (USA) 9, 45, 83, 90, 97, 109, 111, 151–4, 157–9, 166–8, 171, 173
  see also Chicago; New York
USSR *see* Soviet Union
USSR (illustrated album) 97

Vienna
  Am Fuchsenfeld apartment block 35, 37, 43, 106
  Central Savings Bank 33
  Chamber of Labour 105, 106, 114, 115, 122, 125
  Municipality 11, 34, 75, 115
  Kaiser Pavilion, Hietzing 108, 115, 122
  Künstlerhaus 70, 108, 114
  Museum für Siedlung und Städtebau 11
  Neues Rathaus (New Town Hall) 12, 13, 34, 35
  Volkshalle (People's Hall) 33, 37, 39, 64, 106
  Österreichisches Institut für Bildstatistik 101
  'Red Vienna' 9, 11, 53, 106, 109, 115, 125
  School Board 12, 13, 23
  Soviet Embassy 47
  University 24
  Pedagogical Institute 13
  Wiener Arbeiterhochschule 110
  Wirtschaftspsychologische Forschungsstelle (Economic Psychology Research Centre) 69

Vienna Circle 8, 15, 38, 47
  physicalism 15
  Scientific World-Conception 15, 27
Vienna Method of Pictorial Statistics 11–19, 21–9, 31, 41–4, 66, 69, 73, 75, 98, 107, 109, 118, 151, 153, 154, 171, 174
  Arntz and 22–3
  and Izostat 47–9, 51, 52, 55–7, 72
  renamed Isotype 76–7
Vienna Museum *see* Social and Economic Museum
'Visual History of Mankind' (book series) 135
'Visual Science' (book series) 136
Die Volksschule (journal) 27
Vorwärts (newspaper) 42
Voysey, Brenda 45
Vredeshuis (Peace House, The Hague) 44

Weber, Anton 12
Weidenfeld, George 132
Weimar Republic 33, 38, 61
Wereldverkeer 79
Werkbund (Austrian) 62
White Paper (UK government) 99
Wilhelm, Wolfgang 89
Willvonseder, Kurt 116, 120
Wirlander, Stefan 106
'Wonders of the Modern World' (book series) 136, *137*
Worker and Warfront (documentary series) 89
World Geo-Graphic Atlas 131
Works Progress Administration (USA), Graphic Unit 154
World Social Economic Congress (Amsterdam, 1931) 44, *45*, 109, 111
The World is Rich (film) 90
World of Plenty (film) 90–3, *91*, 100

Zeitschrift für Geopolitik (journal) 110